EACH ONE TEACH ONE

EACH ONE TEACH ONE

Parental Involvement and Family Engagement in Jamaica's Education System

EDITED BY

Saran Stewart, Sharline Cole and Yewande Lewis-Fokum

The University of the West Indies Press
Jamaica • Barbados • Trinidad and Tobago

The University of the West Indies Press
7A Gibraltar Hall Road, Mona
Kingston 7, Jamaica
www.uwipress.com

© 2022 by Saran Stewart, Sharline Cole and Yewande Lewis-Fokum

All rights reserved. Published 2022

ISBN: 978-976-640-902-9 (print)
978-976-640-904-3 (ePub)

Cover image and design by Tashiya Young

A catalogue record of this book is available from the National Library of Jamaica.

The University of the West Indies Press has no responsibility for the persistence or accuracy of URLs for external or third-party internet websites referred to in this publication and does not guarantee that any content on such websites is, or will remain, accurate or appropriate.

Printed in the United States of America

Contents

List of Figures \ vii

List of Tables \ viii

Acknowledgements \ ix

Introduction \ 1
Sharline Cole, Saran Stewart and Yewande Lewis-Fokum

Section 1

1. Towards a Framework of Parental Involvement and Family Engagement in Jamaica: A Systematic Review \ 11
Yewande Lewis-Fokum and Kayon Morgan

2. Improving Parental Involvement for Students' Success: Outlining a Framework for a "Non-traditional" High School in Jamaica \ 33
Roncell Brooks and Carmel Roofe

3. A Conceptual Framework for Involving Parents in Improving Mathematics Learning Outcomes: Changing Mindsets, Conversations and Perceptions \ 56
Kadine Haynes and Lois George

Section 2

4. Parental Involvement and Academic Success at the Early Childhood Level \ 79
Danielle Campbell and Zoyah Kinkead-Clark

5. Exploring the Impact of Parental Involvement on the Education of Students: The Case of Students with Two Types of Disabilities \ 95
Susan Anderson and Sharline Cole

6   The Impact of Early Parental Involvement on Academic Outcome \ 116
Sharline Cole

Section 3

7   A Survey Design of the Rate of Parental Involvement and Reported Academic Performance of Grade 10 Students \ 143
Natalia Wright, Shenhaye Ferguson and Saran Stewart

8   An Investigation into the Scope and Prevalence of Parental Involvement at a Rural High School in Jamaica \ 169
Natrecia Whyte Lothian and Tashane Haynes-Brown

9   School Violence in Jamaica: The Impact of Parental Involvement \ 201
Claudine Mighty and Therese Ferguson

Conclusion \ 226
Saran Stewart, Yewande Lewis-Fokum, Shenhaye Ferguson and Sharline Cole

List of Contributors \ 233

Index \ 236

Figures

Figure 1.1 The framework of family engagement in postsecondary and workforce readiness / 24
Figure 2.1 COMVOL PI framework for non-traditional high schools / 49
Figure 3.1 Parental involvement conceptual framework Jam Dung Style / 67
Figure 6.1 Report of parental involvement and parent efficaciousness / 128
Figure 6.2 Parental involvement variables predicting students' outcome / 134
Figure 7.1 Is school/parent partnership important to students' academic success? / 154
Figure 7.2 My school provides a variety of ways for my parents/guardians to volunteer at my school / 156
Figure 7.3 School schedules events at different times during the day and evening so that all families can attend some throughout the year / 157
Figure 9.1 Pie chart showing responses to school-parent partnership / 216
Figure 9.2 Parents' responses about talking to their child about behaviour / 217
Figure 9.3 Percentage of fights over a two-year period / 218
Figure 9.4 Parents' responses to being notified by the school / 218

Tables

Table 1.1	A Sample of the Summary of Family Engagement (FE)/Parent Involvement (PI) Studies by Variable of Interest / 18
Table 3.1	Grade 4 Numeracy Performance Data of Jamaica from 2011 to 2018 / 58
Table 3.2	National Average Percentage Scores for GSAT Mathematics Examination from 2011 to 2018 / 59
Table 3.3	2019 PEP Mathematics Performance Data of Jamaica / 59
Table 3.4	CSEC Mathematics Examinations Pass Percentage of Public Schools from 2009 to 2019 / 60
Table 3.5	Translation of Jamaican Creole Terms to English / 67
Table 4.1	Demographic Data of Participants / 86
Table 6.1	C-Alpha for Variables Measuring Parental Involvement / 127
Table 6.2	Report on Invitation to Be Involved / 129
Table 6.3	Descriptive Results of Academic Outcome / 129
Table 6.4	Correlation between Parental Involvement and Academic Outcomes / 130
Table 7.1	Participants' Response Rate and Reliability Coefficient of Surveys / 150
Table 7.2	Defined Constructs for Parental Involvement Framework / 150
Table 7.3	Descriptive Statistics of Students' Demographic Background / 152
Table 7.4	Descriptive Statistics of Parents' Demographic Background / 153
Table 7.5	Model Summary for Parental Involvement / 159
Table 7.6	ANOVA for Parental Involvement / 159
Table 8.1	Participants' Response Rate and Reliability Coefficient of Parent Survey / 184
Table 8.2	Factors Affecting Parental Involvement in School-based Activities / 188
Table 9.1	Participants' Response Rate and Reliability Coefficient of Surveys / 213
Table 9.2	Participants' Response Rate and Reliability Coefficient of Survey / 213

Acknowledgements

"Never doubt that a small group of thoughtful, committed people can change the world".

– Margaret Mead

Throughout this edited book there has been a beautiful balance between leadership and collaboration among us as editors and co-authors. There has also been collaboration between the various authors of each chapter, some of whom were once our former graduate students asking the critical questions about parental involvement. For this, we would like to thank our former graduate students, most of them teachers, who year after year asked the question: How does parental involvement impact students' success? Shepherding a book from thought to manuscript requires meticulous attention to detail, and we would like to thank Nadine Valentine and Shenhaye Ferguson for their careful attention to detail. We cannot forget to mention Heather Munro who completed initial copy editing of the manuscript for us as well as Tashiya Young whose artistry and graphic design skills critically illustrate the background of this volume. No academic book would have rigour without the peer reviewers who took their time and expertise to read each chapter assigned and provide constructive feedback to the authors. We thank each reviewer for their input into making this book the quality publication that it is, with the caveat that all shortcomings are ours, the editors. We must also not forget to thank our colleagues, families and friends for their support and encouragement throughout the various stages of this book. And no book is worth 'its salt' without its readers. Our hope is that this book will be read by teachers, school principals, parents and various organizations interested in parental/family engagement and that by reading this book small but meaningful changes will be made that can make a difference in the lives of Jamaican students.

Introduction

SHARLINE COLE, SARAN STEWART AND YEWANDE LEWIS-FOKUM

Parents are the ultimate role models for children. Every word, movement and action has an effect. No other person or outside force influences a child more than the parent (Bob Keeshan, n.d.). It is evident that parents play a pivotal role in the academic achievement of their children (Hill & Taylor, 2004). While these models of parental involvement have a universal appeal, parenting is culture-specific (Gross-Loh, 2014). Yet, much of the research on parental involvement in education has been based on models from North America and the United Kingdom (Hoover-Dempsey & Sandler, 1997; Epstein, 2001). As such it is critical to have models that are culturally relevant and applicable to the Jamaican context.

With the significant closure of schools due to the Covid-19 pandemic, parents, guardians and the like have arguably had to grapple with redefining their relationship between parenting and schooling. In addition, many families have had to embrace the new normal of working from home, schooling online and maintaining social distance wherever and whenever necessary. The chapters in this book were written before the Covid-19 pandemic, which explains why there is no previous mention of the pandemic in the data collection procedures and its effects in the studies. However, the principles and undergirding frameworks illustrated and examined in the chapters remain applicable to the fundamentals of parental involvement and family engagement in Jamaica. Arguably, these chapters are even more necessary now as many families in Jamaica must rely heavily on increased parental involvement and family engagement for the success of their children.

Parental involvement and family engagement have been associated with students' overall outcomes and psycho-educational development. According to Haung and Mason (2008), parental involvement is a significant predictor of students' academic performance, school attendance, social skills and behaviour. Jamaica passed the National Parenting Commission Act of 2012, which seeks to "develop stronger and more sustainable partnerships between home and school" (p. 2). Anecdotal evidence from parents, school personnel, specialists and parenting associations converge on the impact of parental involvement and family engagement on students' academic outcome and behaviour. Desforges and Abouchaar (2003) stated that children of involved parents exhibit more resilience, self-control and are more self-directed. Conversely, children of uninvolved parents were more likely to exhibit behavioural problems and lower cognitive functioning.

Accordingly, parental involvement is critical at all levels and stages of development. Given the socio-economic situation and the prevalence of homes with single parents in Jamaica, the phenomena of "barrel-children" (Jokhan, 2017; The Gleaner, 2015), family engagement plays an important role when examining the extant roles of guardians and parental figures in a child's education. By interrogating this work, we hope to close the cultural and contextual gap in the literature and add to the canons of critical research in this field.

Educators are interested in knowing how to get parents and families involved and engaged in the education of their children. In Jamaica, the celebration of parent month every November highlights positive parenting and symbolizes its importance in the Jamaican context. Through its different programmes, the Ministry of Education endorses parents' active participation in their children's education. The introduction of the Coalition for Better Parenting (CBP) and the National Parenting Support Commission (CNPSC) are programmes that support parents' active involvement in their children's education. The different realities and contexts of parental involvement and family engagement in Jamaica are worthy of investigation and exploration. Understanding how parents and families are involved and why and in what ways they get involved should provide readers with a better sense of how their social circumstances, experiences within the family and makeup of families contribute to quality involvement and engagement. In addition, the type of school and level of education (early childhood, primary, secondary and special education) influence family involvement and engagement.

Schools with a vibrant parent teacher association (PTA) help shape school policies if parents and families embrace a shared vision of the direction in which the school is heading. Active parental involvement and family engagement minimize disruptive behaviours and allow for greater cohesive relationships between teachers and students, parents and teachers, and administrators and parents. Accordingly, this book aims to (1) discuss the conceptual underpinnings and frameworks for parental involvement and family engagement and (2) examine empirical data on the effects and impact of parental involvement across the early childhood, primary and secondary levels.

This edited book looks at parental involvement and family engagement across different academic disciplines: leadership, psychology, special education, early childhood, literacy studies, mathematics and teacher education. It provides empirical evidence on the status of parental involvement and family engagement in Jamaica. A team approach is used in completing the various chapters in which graduate researchers collaborate with lecturers in their areas of specialization. The different voices and data from the participants and relevant literature shape the dialogue on the importance of home and school collaboration in students' overall outcomes.

In the first section of the book, we begin by synthesizing the rich research already conducted by social scientists and educational researchers regarding parenting in Jamaica, with a specific focus on education. Chapters in this section describe and critically analyse the models of Epstein (2001) and Hoover-Dempsey and Sandler (1997) in light of parenting and education in Jamaica. The chapters look at factors that influence parental involvement and family engagement. These chapters extend global frameworks to create a more *Caribbeanized* model that better reflects the family structures, challenges and strengths of parents in postcolonial contexts like ours in the Anglophone Caribbean. The different forms of family engagement from the perspectives of parents and teachers – values, goals and aspirations, engagement at home, engagement at school, communication from home to school and from school to home – are equally important because the situations, experiences and realities of families are different.

In chapter 1, Yewande Lewis-Fokum and Kayon Morgan provide concept-based case studies which that how to build a model of parental involvement and family engagement that is suited to promote success for Jamaican students, the majority of whom attend non-traditional[1] schools. In this chapter, the constructs of parental involvement and family engagement are discussed and separate definitions are arrived at. Involvement is considered activity-based, and engagement includes partnerships and collaboration. As this chapter seeks to conceptualize parental involvement and family engagement in Jamaica, frameworks have been developed in light of the Jamaican reality. Additionally, they advanced an inclusive model of family engagement that explains how family engagement contributes to students' transitioning seamlessly to postsecondary education and then into the workforce. For this chapter, family engagement takes different forms from the perspectives of families and teachers. The different forms include

---

[1] Majority of government-built secondary schools constructed after independence in 1962 are commonly under-resourced and receive many students with lower grades from the grade 6 national assessments.

helping at home, volunteering and communicating as dominant features that contribute to active family engagement and parental involvement in improving the outcomes of Jamaican students.

In chapter 2, Roncell Brooks and Carmel Roofe adopted two tenets of Epstein's (2001) Overlapping Spheres of Influence Model: mainly *communicating* and *volunteering*, along with the cultural capital theory, were used to explore and explain parental involvement in students' success in non-traditional high schools. This chapter highlights how the cultural capital of parents has an impact on students' outcomes. Schools that uphold middle-class values negatively impact the involvement of parents whose children attend upgraded high schools. Class structure is considered a barrier to involvement when some parents want to volunteer. How information is communicated to parents by teachers can make all the difference.

For chapter 3, Kadine Haynes and Lois George present their own Jamaican-based conceptualized framework as a result of the survey of the literature on parental involvement and family engagement in Jamaica. The 'Jam Dung Style' model for improving mathematics was developed, which explains how teachers and parents communicate and how parents help children at home. The framework emphasizes the importance of parents encouraging and motivating their children. Communicating with parents in their mother tongue (Jamaican creole) helps parents regardless of their level of education to change their negative mindset surrounding involvement in their children's education. It is also important that there is equity and equality in how the education system responds to parents in supporting students' transition into postsecondary education and the workforce.

The second section of the book looks at parental involvement and family engagement in the Jamaican early childhood, primary and special education sectors. Rickets and Anderson (2009) reported that younger children or those in lower grades were more likely to receive help from their caregivers, while older children may not receive that much help because of the complexity of the assignments. In this section, the authors report on the influence of parental involvement on students' academic performance. Throughout this section, the authors sought to contextualize parental involvement, its scope, prevalence and its impact on students' outcomes. This section reports on research that highlights the importance of the partnership between teachers and parents. The researchers report on the influence of parental involvement in students' cognitive and social outcomes.

Chapter 4, by Danielle Campbell and Zoyah Kinkead-Clark, covers parental involvement and academic success at the early childhood level. This chapter points to the differences in how parental involvement is interpreted by parents and how schools can foster parental involvement through parenting education. For example, for some parents, parental involvement is helping their children with homework and visiting their school. Additionally, parents' efficacy beliefs determine the strategies that they utilize to assist them in helping their children to achieve. In addition, the inability of parents to provide the necessary resources due to financial constraints and uncertain employment status are barriers to effective parental involvement.

In chapter 5, Susan Anderson and Sharline Cole explored the impact of parental involvement among parents whose children attend special needs schools at grade 1 level. It highlights the fact that parents are actively involved in their children's education as they seek to learn from their children and their schools. Additionally, parental involvement is influenced by their sense of efficacy in helping their children, their active participation in their children's education and their beliefs and role in the construction of parental involvement. The level of involvement of parents in the lives of students with special needs is affected by their socio-economic status and their level of education. Lastly, the relationships that are built between the schools and parents facilitate greater involvement.

Chapter 6 by Sharline Cole presents the impact of early parental involvement on student outcomes as they transition from grade 1 through grades 4 and 6. This research investigated the extent to which parental involvement in grade 1 impacts students' outcomes in the national assessments done in grades 4 and 6. The chapter reinforces the fact that early parental involvement, namely involvement at home, parents' sense of efficacy and invitation to be involved contribute to students' outcomes throughout primary school. It is noteworthy that this study found that teachers are more likely to invite parents of boys than parents of girls to be involved; this has implications for gender differences in education.

The final section presents chapters that focus on parental involvement at the secondary level. Because of the decline in the number of males at the upper secondary level and tertiary level education, the authors decided to investigate the impact of parental involvement on the outcomes of males and its effect on male's access to higher education. The chapters present empirical research done in high schools located in rural and urban Jamaica. Research at the secondary level is important because as students matriculate to secondary education there is a reduction in the level of parental involvement. Within this section researchers investigate the impact of parental involvement on students' academic and behavioural outcomes. Assisting adolescence at home, parenting, communicating with school about the progress of their adolescents, volunteering and being a part of the decision-making process concerning their children are important features for involving parents whose children are at the secondary level.

Chapter 7, by Natalia Wright, Shenhaye Ferguson and Saran Stewart, examines the academic performance of grade 10 students, utilizing Epstein's theory in Jamaica. The chapter highlights the differences in parents and students reporting on parental involvement (parenting, communicating, volunteering, learning at home and decision making) and students' academic performance. Overall parental involvement predicts academic outcomes; however, there was no clear predictor of what aspects of parental involvement contribute to students' performance. As students advance to higher grades in high school, parental involvement declines; however, parents volunteering at school and communication with teachers may contribute to students' academic success.

In chapter 8, Natrecia Whyte Lothian and Tashane Haynes-Brown investigate the scope and prevalence of parental involvement in an upgraded rural high school. Guided by Epstein's (2001) and Hoover-Dempsey and Sandler's (1997) models of parental involvement, this chapter reinforces the importance of learning at home where parents are involved in home-based activities that contribute to students completing assignments. In addition, parents' understanding of their role as primary caregivers influences their desire to help at home. The monitoring of students at home helps students. However, the competing responsibilities of parents could serve as barriers to active parental involvement. The school plays a critical role in providing parents with information on how to effectively monitor their adolescent children.

Chapter 9, by Claudine Mighty and Therese Ferguson, highlights the importance of parents having a positive relationship with their children's school through volunteerism. Positive relationships between parents and schools are likely to contribute to positive students' behaviour and reduce school violence. In addition, when parents are involved there are fewer suspensions. Factors other than parental involvement influence students' participation in aggression and violence. It can be argued that the reduced influence and involvement of parents at the secondary level may influence students' negative behaviours. Schools should be more supportive of parental involvement at the secondary level.

Given the importance of parental involvement and family engagement, this compilation of research studies and chapters on the subject is a timely addition to the body of research available to decision makers, parents, researchers and students. The findings, implications and recommendations can guide policymakers in the formulation of strategic initiatives compatible with the needs of the schools, students and families. Additionally, the findings provide indispensable data for policymakers, school principals, teachers and parents on how to effectively work together to optimize students' success.

References

Desforges, C. & Abouchaar, A. (2003). *The impact of parental involvement, parental support and family education on pupil achievement and adjustment: A literature review.* https://www.nationalnumeracy.org.uk/sites/default/files/the_impact_of_parental_involvement.pdf

Epstein, J.L. (2001). *School, family, and community partnerships: Preparing educators and improving schools.* Westview.

Gross-Loh, C. (2014). *Parenting without borders: Surprising lessons parents around the world can teach us.* Penguin Group.

Hill, N. & Taylor, L. (2004). Parental school involvement and children's academic achievement. *American Psychological Society, 13*(4), 161–64.

Hoover-Dempsey, K.V. & Sandler, H.M. (1997). Why do parents become involved in their children's education? *Review of Educational Research, 67*(1), 3–42.

Huang, G.H.C. & Mason, K.L. (2008). Motivations of parental involvement in children's learning: Voices from urban African American families of preschoolers. *Multicultural Education, 15*(3), 20–27.

Jokhan, M. (2017). *Exploring the "barrel children" cycle: Parent-child separation due to migration.* Childhood Explorer: Childhood Education International. https://www.childhoodexplorer.org/exploring-the-barrel-children-cycle-parentchild-separation-due-to-migration

Keeshan, B. Quotes. (n.d.). *Brainy Quote.com.* https://www.brainyquote.com/quotes/bob_keeshan_620874

National Parenting Support Commission Act. (2012). https://japarliament.gov.jm/attachments/341_The%20National%20Parenting%20Support%20Commission%20Act,%202012.pdf

Rickett, H. & Anderson, P. (2009). *Parenting in Jamaica.* A study conducted on behalf of the Planning Institute of Jamaica. Planning Institute of Jamaica.

The Gleaner. (2015, September 23). *JTA president warns of barrel children syndrome.* http://jamaica-gleaner.com/article/news/20150925/jta-president-warns-barrel-children-syndrome

Section 1

Chapter 1

Towards a Framework of Parental Involvement and Family Engagement in Jamaica

A Systematic Review

YEWANDE LEWIS-FOKUM AND KAYON MORGAN

The Debate between Terminologies: Parent Involvement or Family Engagement?

The literature highlights that families have an important role in the academic achievement of their children, and that strong home-school relationships are critical (Englund et al., 2004; Froiland, Peterson & Davison, 2013; Simons-Morton & Chen, 2009; Weiss, Caspe & Lopez, 2006; Weiss et al., 2009). Many schools, however, struggle with how to cultivate positive relationships between school, community and families (Mapp & Hong, 2010).

In the Jamaican context, the literature does not address the term "family engagement", rather terms such as "parent involvement", "father engagement", "paternal and maternal engagement", "family functioning" and "home and school partnerships" are predominantly used. Because there are so many variations around the construct of *parent involvement* and *family engagement*, this study uses *family-school partnerships* to acknowledge and encompass all the terms that are used in the various studies. However, there is advocacy for the adoption of the term "family engagement" and the chapter concludes by utilizing only the term "family engagement".

Research continues to evolve around ideal terminologies for family-school partnerships, with the intention to increase understanding of who is involved in the educational process of children so as to encourage schools to have a more inclusive acknowledgement of the multicultural community in which they exist (Morgan, 2019). By constantly referring to just *parents*, the terminology becomes limiting and does not acknowledge other extended members of a family or community who might be engaged in the educational process of children (Kiyama et al., 2015). On the other hand, by using the word "family", schools will recognize and honour the multiple people who support and influence the education of children on a regular basis. It is an acknowledgement beyond the immediate relation of mother and father which further considers adoptive or foster parents, grandparents, aunts, uncles and siblings, who are often the ones who provide support (Bogenschneider et al., 2012; Constantino, 2003; Moles & Fege, 2011; Morgan, 2019). This acknowledgement is also important in Jamaica where the upbringing of children is fostered by extended family members within different types of family structures (Ricketts & Anderson, 2009).

Equally, the word "involvement", as opposed to *engagement*, bears its own challenge. Involvement tends to convey a more activity-based approach. Inherently, a focus on involvement becomes more prescriptive and tells families how they can contribute in the school environment (Ferlazzo, 2011). As such, schools focus on school-directed activities where the expectation is that families who are involved show up for parent-teacher meetings, volunteer at school and help with homework as is evident in the study conducted by Chunnu (2016) in Jamaica. Involvement tends to ignore the other ways families contribute and provide support to their children or the manner in which they interact with their children in other settings, for example, taking them on an outing, buying school supplies, preparing meals and teaching values; all of which contribute to the overall education of their children. Therefore, when schools strive for *involvement*, they have a more programmatic approach and expectations about how families should be involved (Morgan, 2019).

Engagement, on the other hand, suggests a partnership. It creates collaborative environments that listen to what parents think, aspire to and worry about, focusing on gaining families as partners rather than seeing them as clients (Ferlazzo, 2011). By virtue of the very definition itself, engagement encourages commitment from all parties in the existent relationship and recognizes that there may be different forms and levels of commitment. The term "engagement" also minimizes a school-centric approach, one which is gaining preference by scholars in the field (Edwards & Kutaka, 2015). Nevertheless, the literature (as reviewed in this study) uses the terms "involvement" and "engagement" interchangeably, with a focus on the participation of families at the school level. Considering the debate over the terms "parent" and "family", as well as "involvement" and "engagement", it provides context for understanding why the term "family engagement" is more inclusive and presents a participatory and collaborative relationship between school and home.

Academic Achievement in the Jamaican Context

At the centre of any education system is the goal for students to succeed and be productive citizens in their respective societies. Likewise, in the Jamaican context, education continues to be a mobilizing factor and a major tool for advancement (Chunnu, 2016; Dede Yildirim & Roopnarine, 2017). As a result, Jamaica has increased its focus on graduating all students and preparing them for postsecondary pursuits. The Ministry of Education and Youth and the schools are examining their practices in supporting how students are successfully prepared. One such practice that has gained more focussed attention is family engagement in the education of students. In 2012, the Jamaican government passed the National Parenting Support Commission Act, in keeping with the widely held view that parental support is key to the development of the child within and outside the setting of the school. A study on school effectiveness in Jamaica found that "effective schools were four times more likely to have high levels of parental involvement than ineffective schools" (Watson-Williams & Fox, 2013, p. 41). While Watson-Williams and Fox (2013) acknowledged that school effectiveness went beyond test scores, it was noteworthy that the effective schools did well on the national measures of assessment, from Grade 4 Literacy Test at the primary level to the Caribbean Secondary Examinations Council's exams at the secondary level.

Methodology

Why a Systematic Review?

We initially embarked on conducting a meta-analysis of existing research, but the literature lacked research that was statistically similar, as is the required criteria when conducting meta-analyses. On the other hand, qualitative publications and dissertation studies on the subject matter were more prominent. As a result, our research shifted to reviewing the relationship between family engagement and students' academic achievement in the literature published between 1994 and 2018 through the methodology of a systematic review. We selected a 24-year period to have sufficient articles for the review, which yielded a surplus of dissertation studies on family-school relationships and its impact on academic achievement. However, peer-reviewed articles were critically limited.

The goal, therefore, of this systematic review was (1) to make sense of the research that was already completed in the field and identify common threads; (2) to produce a knowledge synthesis of the existing literature;

(3) to identify the patterns of family engagement in the Jamaican context; and (4) to identify limitations in the evidence and propose an actionable framework which is more appropriate to the Jamaican context.

This is likely the first study of its kind, as there are no previous comprehensive reviews of the literature on parental involvement or family engagement in relation to children's academic achievement in Jamaica or even the wider Caribbean region. The literature is significantly sparse in this content area (George et al., 2015). It is the hope that this systematic review will contribute to the overall understanding of family engagement in education in Jamaica (especially as a post-colonial British nation) and provide a practical framework for schools to use in their local contexts. This chapter provides an overview of the literature and pays homage to the work that was done before. In doing so, we can find opportunities to shift deficit-based systems and mindsets to more strength-based approaches in education, which this edited book seeks to address.

Research Questions

Clearly formulated research questions informed the review process and helped to ascertain why and how the relationship between school and family occurs and in what circumstances (Denyer & Tranfield, 2009). Subsequently, this systematic review sought to answer the following research questions:

R.1. What is the existent research on family-school partnerships in education in Jamaica?
R.2. What is the relationship between family-school partnerships and student achievement as evident in the literature?
R.3. What are the recommendations for effective partnerships between families and schools?

Inclusion and Exclusion Criteria

To be eligible for inclusion in this systematic review, the studies had to be (1) focused on the Jamaican context; (2) focused on the Caribbean, with mention of the Jamaican context; (3) specific to education but include a specific focus on family-school partnerships in education; (4) contain variations of the term "family engagement" such as parent involvement, parent engagement, family-school partnerships and family-school connections; (5) published during the period 1994–2018 in a peer-reviewed journal (see Appendix for a complete list of articles included in this review).

We excluded studies from the natural sciences, for example, family engagement as it related to child health, and studies that investigated family engagement or parental involvement on maladaptive student behaviours such as student aggression, depression or bullying. Studies that addressed learning or developmental disorders as it related to the influence of parental involvement were also excluded.

Selection of Articles

We attempted to provide a summary of the state of the research related to family-school partnerships in education in Jamaica by carefully reviewing and evaluating previous studies. Studies included in the review were those conducted from 1994 to 2018 that were related to family or parental involvement in education in Jamaica as a post-colonial society.

Search Procedures

The authors used various procedures to locate articles included in this systematic review. Specifically, search procedures involved online library databases and physical searches at local libraries. From these procedures, a total of twenty-one studies were included in the review.

Online library Databases. Studies that investigated family engagement and parental involvement and their relationship to the academic achievement of children were identified through several databases such as Proquest Central and the SAGE Full-Text Collection. A combination of keywords was entered into the search engines to generate a list of relevant articles. Keywords included *Jamaica* and *family-school, family-school partnership, parent-school partnership, family-school relationship, parent-school relationship, family involvement, parent involvement or family engagement, academic achievement or academic attainment,* and *student outcome or student effect*. Abstracts of the articles were reviewed to assess relevance and appropriateness for inclusion based on selection criteria. If there were no abstracts available, the entire article was sourced and examined for inclusion or exclusion (Gough, Oliver & Thomas, 2017).

Physical presence at libraries. As the authorship of this study is a collaboration between one local researcher present in Jamaica and the other a Jamaican native living in the United States, we used the opportunity to physically visit local libraries in Jamaica to search for publications that were not available online. As is sometimes true in developing countries, books and other research publications are still reserved in hard copies.

Reference searches. Studies that were identified in the prior two procedures were reviewed closely to further identify additional studies of family engagement in Jamaica. In particular, the literature reviews and reference sections were examined to identify and locate additional relevant studies based on the title and/or description within the primary article. The authors considered the potential implications of reference list checking in that it could produce endless checking (Gough, Oliver & Thomas, 2017). Additionally, the reference list of dissertations was reviewed for relevant articles to the study. Any publications that appeared relevant were vetted according to the procedure outlined for inclusion or exclusion in this study.

Coding Procedures

The authors coded each article on variables identified as important to family-school partnerships and their effect on Jamaica's academic achievement. The first author coded all articles uncovered in the search, and the second author coded a random sample of 90 per cent of them. Articles were first coded based on whether or not the author(s) provided a definition or description of "parent involvement" for their study (i.e. yes/no). Each article was then examined as to whether or not the study was specific to Jamaica (i.e. yes/no). Due to the limitations in the number of studies available for the current research, the authors did not code specifically for rural or urban schools, for early childhood, primary, high school or even tertiary contexts, or across school types such as public and private.

The next step involved the assessment of research questions, and the purpose statements in each study (if one existed) were assessed to determine how they fit the context of family-school partnerships on academic achievement of students (i.e. yes/no). Lastly, the authors reviewed the design of each of the twenty-one studies. The research design for each study was classified as either qualitative (e.g., case study, ethnography) or quantitative (e.g., descriptive, single-group pre-/post-test, causal-comparative, correlational or quasi-experimental).

The authors further evaluated the family-school construct investigated in each study to gain a better understanding of how it was conceptualized. The construct under investigation for each study was classified into one or more of the following categories: parent/family involvement/engagement, family-school partnership, school-community partnership or child-rearing practices. Table 1.1 provides a sample of how the variables of interest for each study were examined according to the coding procedures outlined in this section. Using the review matrix in table 1.1 allowed the authors to create order and synthesize the literature (Garrard, 2016).

Findings and Discussion

In light of the research questions, "What is the existent research on family-school partnerships in education in Jamaica?" and "What is the relationship between family-school partnerships and student achievement as evident in the literature?" we identified twenty-one studies for the systematic review. Of the twenty-one studies identified, none used the term "family engagement". The closest study to use engagement was one in which the authors referenced the term "fathering engagement". In this study by Devonish and Anderson (2017), the authors examined the relationship between fathers and their children outside of the family home. In this article, fathering engagement was defined as "behaviours that reflect a commitment to the child including face-to-face communication [such as] phoning, caretaking, financial support" (p. 38). The authors continued by saying that the concept included engagement, accessibility and responsibility, and that they focused on engagement as "direct one-to-one interaction with the child" (p. 39). This is a narrower definition of the term "engagement" that exists within the literature on family engagement. In this study they also alternated between engagement and involvement.

Additionally, the terms related to family engagement that were included in the studies reviewed were varied, and no concrete definitions were given. "Parental involvement" was the most consistent term used in the studies reviewed and is used predominantly by graduate students when conducting research on family engagement in education in Jamaica. Other terms or phrases that were used included the following: home-school collaboration and home-school communication (Johnson & Carpenter, 2006), and parental interest, parental voice, family involvement and parenting responsibilities (Watson-Williams, 2011). Many of the terms included the word "parent" as opposed to family – in keeping, we surmise, with the utilization of the more frequently used term of parental involvement.

Nevertheless, there is the acknowledgement in these studies that parents also included guardians and other family members. Indeed, within research carried out in Jamaica, there has been a long tradition acknowledging the fact that both biological and non-biological persons play a parenting role as it relates to the raising of children. As such, Samms-Vaughan (2001) briefly describes the different types of family constructions in Jamaica and hence the parenting roles that can be played by different persons in these family structures: marriage (a monogamous relationship sanctioned by law), common-law union (a male and female partner living together in a stable union largely due to procreation) and visiting union (the female partner

Table 1.1 A Sample of the Summary of Family Engagement (FE)/Parent Involvement (PI) Studies by Variable of Interest

Author	Sample	Location	Definition of FE/PI	FE specific	Research questions specific to FE/PI	Design	Findings related to family engagement in education
Christopher Clarke (2007)	2 primary schools, 2 female teachers, 12 parents, 6 boys (8-10 yrs), 24 boys in Focus group	One rural and one urban primary school	None	No	No	Multi-case ethnographic study with criterion-based sampling over 10 or 15 weeks	Mothers especially "felt powerless to change the attitudes of boys towards school work" (p. 126); "The boys who have their fathers highly involved in their lives do well in school" (p. 147); only 2 of the X fathers blamed their lack of time on sons' underachievement; "Parents have high expectations of their sons. They want them to do well in school so that they can be independent as adults. Their socialization practices, however, are often not consistent with realizing their expectations" (p. 150).

Edilma Yearwood (2001)	16 participants aged 9 to 60+	Church, New York, USA	None	Note the focus on parents' views on education	Yes	Ethnographic study – emic, interpretive interactionism approach over 18 months	Education was a critical element in child-rearing. One female participant said, "Education is the key . . . that's the one thing that nobody can take away from you, a strong education" (pp. 13–14). Education is also a means to social mobility given Jamaica's complex social structure. Adults saw teachers as part of their family in reflecting about Jamaica but did not see teachers in the United States in the same light.
Julian Devonish & Patricia Anderson (2017)	252 urban fathers, Jamaica – middle class, blue collar and low income	Kingston Metropolitan Region		Yes	Yes	Survey	Difference between a "strong ideological commitment to fatherhood" and actual practice. Employment and social class identification impacted school mentoring of outside children. Fathers who self-identified as middle class and working class (versus lower income), and who completed secondary education more likely to engage in school mentoring behaviours regardless of area of residence.

lives at her family home and is visited by a male partner, p. 141). Particularly in the latter case, parenting assistance is usually given by another female relative such as a grandmother or aunt. As such, "children may be parented by biological parents, a single biological parent and a surrogate parent or two surrogate parents" (p. 142). Therefore, the move from speaking only about parental involvement to family engagement in education within the international literature already reflects Jamaican family dynamics and the reality of the parenting role being played by multiple adults within the life of many children locally.

Of interest is also the noticeable absence of a concrete definition of the term "parental involvement". Instead, there is an assumption that the term is understood. However, the authors contend that this is inadequate and that the terms "parental involvement" and "family engagement" need to be explored, discussed, described and defined from a local epistemological context, especially given the shift in the international literature from parental involvement to family engagement (Morgan, 2019).

Many, if not all, of the studies reviewed referred to the work of Epstein (1995), but little reference was made about more current works nor was there cross-referencing of local work conducted on parental involvement/family engagement. This indeed is a twofold gap in the local literature. First, it points to the need to publish local work that has been done on parental involvement in education, which this book addresses. Second, it points to the need to update the current local literature to include newer research that expands on the work of Epstein (1995). Although more recent local research on parental involvement includes the work of Hoover-Dempsey (1997) and Hoover-Dempsey, Whitaker and Ice (2010), which build on Epstein's work, there is still need to contextualize these theoretical models to take account of the particularities of the family structures and family involvement in schools in Jamaica (Cole, 2013).

Parental involvement was more a by-product within many of the studies, yet the authors eventually came around to parenting in education and the relationship between parental involvement and academic achievement. We contend that this eventual refocus on parental involvement is due to the appreciation backed by a substantial body of international research, which indicates that student achievement is impacted by the support given to students by a parenting figure.

Three Sample Articles

Of the twenty-one studies that were reviewed, the following three will be described in more detail as these focused most centrally on parental involvement/family engagement in Jamaica: Cook and Jennings (2016), a quantitative survey study of parents' views on absenteeism; Johnson and Carpenter (2006), a comparison of two qualitative case studies regarding home-school partnerships; and Watson-Williams (2011), a conceptual paper that examines parental involvement through the social construct of power relations and how this impacts children of the poor in Jamaica.

Watson-Williams (2011) uses Jamaica as a case study to discuss the challenges poor Jamaican parents face in helping their children to achieve the education necessary for intergenerational transformation out of poverty and what schools can do to change this. The article is divided into four sections. A brief overview of Jamaica's educational history is given, taking into consideration its historical beginnings in post-emancipation Jamaica and the "two-tiered nature of the secondary system" (p. 64), which the nation inherited and still exists today. Citing international research, Watson-Williams (2011) then goes into the importance of parental involvement in the education outcomes of children and frames this discussion within the context of "social power relations". She continues in the third section by giving a description of the barriers that "poor and vulnerable parents face" citing some examples from interview data. The article ends with the author suggesting approaches that schools can undertake to give parents of the poor a "voice" to ensure that their children can take advantage of the benefits of a good education.

The strength of this article is that it captures some of the real struggles of parents who are considered underprivileged in relation to their involvement in the education of their children. As such, Watson-Williams (2011) does not shy away from discussing parental involvement within the framework of power. For example, she examines barriers that undermine the agency of poorer parents and discusses how the "voices" of these parents are often sidelined by middle-class parents with monetary and cultural capital who dominate the home-school leadership groups in schools. Another insight that Watson-Williams offers is her examination of parenting behaviours that either do not challenge the status quo or that are overly "suspicious" of schools and therefore hostile. In both cases she contends that parents do not feel as if the school values their worth as parents or that the school has their children's interests at heart.

Indeed, the concept of the transformative power of education is a common concept within all the articles surveyed. For example, in the ethnographic study of Jamaican parents in the United States, one mother shared: "Education is the key ... that's the one thing that nobody can take away from you, a strong education" (pp. 13–14). Given Jamaica's complex social structure, many Jamaican parents at home and abroad see education as a means to social mobility (Chunnu, 2016; Dede Yildirim & Roopnarine, 2017). Indeed, the role of education as a transformative system that enables the poor to move out of poverty is a central belief within the psyche and experiences of many post-Emancipation Jamaicans and is echoed in the second article which will be discussed now.

Cook and Jennings (2016) is a quantitative survey study that focused on parents' views regarding the causes of absenteeism of secondary school children. The study had a sample of 221 participants (parents and adult relatives) who responded to a questionnaire about student absenteeism. While on the surface, this may not seem to relate to parental engagement, it is linked because student absenteeism has a direct link to students' school performance. Moreover, in the home-school partnership, it is the expectation that parents are responsible for sending their children to school. The three main reasons parents gave for student absenteeism were "little value for education", "lack of resources at the personal and community levels" and "school environment".

For the purposes of this chapter, we shall only discuss the first finding, that is, "little value for education". On face value, this finding seems to contradict the prevailing ethos that Jamaican parents believe in the importance of education. In fact, the authors say as much: "education in Jamaican society is the route to social mobility and the poorest of the poor wish their children to have a better education than they did so that they can rise up the social ladder" (p. 108). So, this finding on face value seems to go against even their own interpretation. However, the authors further state that "perhaps then it is not that the parents do not value education, but rather that meeting basic needs has to take precedence over the child's attendance at school" (p. 108). In other words, the lack of financial resources greatly constrains parents' ability to send their children to school regularly, especially in the rural areas. Friday was the most problematic day in terms of attendance, as both students and parents do not place value on what was being taught on this day. Moreover, "many respondents felt powerless in decreasing truancy among their children due to the lack of respect demonstrated by children for parents and teachers" (p. 104). Indeed, what is evident from this article are the economic constraints that hinder parents' ability to fully engage with schools, even at the basic level of ensuring that their children attend school regularly and the powerlessness that parents feel in impacting their children's behaviour.

The third and final article is the qualitative study by Johnson and Carpenter (2006). This article compared two case studies at the elementary level looking at the experiences of school children in grade 5 at a public elementary/primary school and a grade 1 classroom at a private/preparatory school. Whereas the grade 5 study focused on the teacher's classroom management approach and the ways in which she engaged the parents, the grade 1 study specifically examined the experiences of three children and how a lack of communication between parents and the teacher undermined home-school collaboration. Central to both studies was the idea that the teacher should play a major role in initiating communication within the home-school collaboration dynamic. In closing, the authors also discuss the four parent-school myths (e.g., some parents cannot help their children to be successful in school) by Coleman (1998) and contend that when these myths exist "withdrawal, power struggle, and tensions" exist between the parent/family and the school.

This article was highlighted because of its focus on elementary education and because it squarely focused on the home-school relationship within this context. The other article that also examined issues of parental involvement in education at the primary level was Cook and Ezenne's (2010), which addressed parents' perception of student absenteeism. There is a need to conduct research on parental involvement/family engagement at the different levels of the education system – early childhood, primary, secondary and even tertiary. Other strengths of the article include its investigation of parental involvement across school types (public versus private); its focus on the teacher as a central player within the home-school collaboration dynamic; and the foregrounding of communication as a significant component of building trust between families and the school.

Recommendations

While the findings in this systematic review highlight several benefits of family engagement on students' academic success, there are also deficit-based perspectives that need to be addressed – especially related to Jamaica as a post-colonial society. The issue of family engagement is complex and multifaceted; there is no step-by-step, prescriptive method to address it. Instead, the task of engaging families will require significant time, resources, effort, mutual understanding and fundamentally different visions of schools and families (Mapp & Hong, 2010). As such, the recommendations of this chapter suggest a recursive and collaborative approach through the Framework of Family Engagement in Postsecondary and Workforce Readiness as depicted in figure 1.1 (Morgan, 2019):

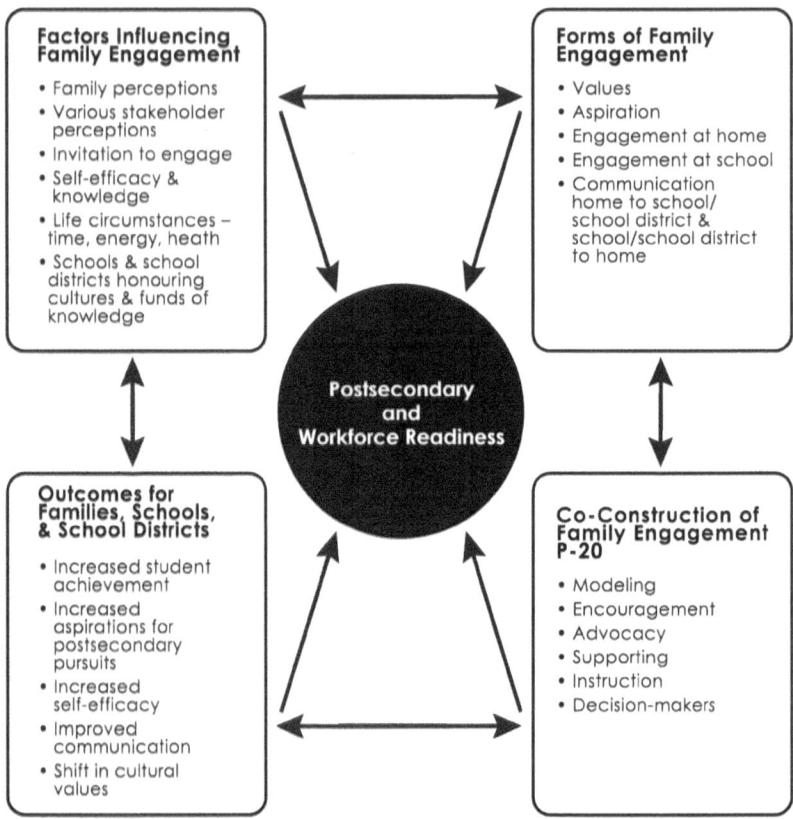

Figure 1.1 The framework of family engagement in postsecondary and workforce readiness.

> The FEPWR framework is the basic recognition that family engagement intersects between students' external and internal environments at school and outside the school context. It seeks to identify the influence of culture, values, and families' aspirations. These characteristics, however, are not in the vacuum of the family environment and separate from that of the school environment. (p. 154)

Figure 1.1 is a diagrammatic representation of the framework.

The first quadrant encourages schools to examine the factors influencing family engagement. As reviewed in the literature, there are several factors that influence family engagement in schools. Some of these factors are perceptions held by families about what family engagement is (e.g. Hoover-Dempsey, Whitaker & Ice, 2010; Hornby & Lafaele, 2011; Kim, 2009; Koonce & Harper, 2005; Leiber-Miller, 2012), perceptions held by educators about what they perceive as family engagement (e.g. Hornby & Lafaele, 2011; Knopf & Swick, 2007; Lawson, 2003; McWayne et al., 2016) and the invitation to be engaged (Hoover-Dempsey, Whitaker & Ice, 2010) among others. Schools and families need to be authentic and open about biased perspectives they may hold about what is considered engagement. Families must expand their definition of family engagement – viewing themselves as assets, leaders and active participants (Mapp & Hong, 2010). Schools and educators likewise must expand and acknowledge the multiple caregivers who are involved in the education of children and consider them as family. In Jamaica, other adults outside of biological parents are five times more likely to engage in "parenting" activities (Samms-Vaughan, 2001). Other factors such as time, energy, self-efficacy of families and educators and cultural backgrounds all influence the partnership created between school to home and home to school.

Forms of Family Engagement

The second quadrant acknowledges that family engagement takes different forms – both from the perspectives of the families and the perspectives of educators (including teachers, principals and Ministry of Education and Youth personnel). From a more inclusive definition, family engagement recognizes values, goals and aspirations, engagement at home, engagement at school and communication from home to school and from school to home. The varied forms of family engagement in this quadrant minimize the tendency for educators to privilege particular forms of engagement over others. Helping with homework is not necessarily more important than walking a child to the bus stop or preparing a meal. Each form of engagement brings value to different aspects of the educational process. The study by Cook and Jennings (2016) emphasizes that placing value on the educational process is similar between children and parents. As a result, it is imperative that schools examine what is considered as valued forms of engagement, both from the children's and family members' perspectives.

Co-construction of Family Engagement

The third quadrant places emphasis on family engagement as a co-constructed process and diminishes the power dynamics often present where the voices of some parents are dismissed by those with monetary and cultural capital who control the home-school decision-making groups (Watson-Williams, 2011). Mapp and Kuttner (2013) refer to this co-construction as a shared partnership. This quadrant recognizes that families and educators can be engaged in preparing students for the future (what is referred to in this framework as postsecondary and workforce readiness) through modelling, encouragement, advocacy, instruction, decision-making and other supportive roles. The relationship is not solely dependent on any single environment, such as the academic setting, the home construction and the social setting. The relationship is also not just between teachers and families but includes principals and other school personnel, health-care providers and places of employment. As such, it is imperative that various entities such as the Ministry of Education and Youth and other sectors collaborate to open up spaces and conversations and create opportunities for families to be more engaged in the education of their children (Cook & Jennings, 2016).

Outcomes for Families and Schools

The last quadrant observes the outcomes not just for schools but identifies that there are also outcomes for other entities, such as the Ministry of Education and Youth, and for families. The outcomes demonstrate a sustained system that brings value to all the stakeholders engaged in the education of children (Morgan, 2019). By explicitly stating that the outcomes relate to families, schools and other external stakeholders, the language of the framework immediately becomes more inclusive and considers not only teachers (as mentioned in previous models). Schools must begin to recognize that family engagement influences academic achievement, which has a ripple effect in the society at large. We have been conditioned to think that academic achievement mainly benefits schools through the evidence of test scores and other related outcomes. However, the FEPWR framework is a paradigm shift that advocates for asset-based and visionary thinking.

Postsecondary and Workforce Readiness

All four quadrants point to PWR because they essentially shape and support how students pursue postsecondary options, whether in college or the workforce. It also highlights that family engagement is not a concept relegated to preschool or early childhood, as is common in the wider literature. Rather, family engagement should be seen as having value beyond tertiary education.

The FEPWR framework asserts that family engagement is purposefully aligned with the core factors of educational goals and is not merely programmatic. Integrated family engagement continues this strand by being embedded into structures and processes and considers the social and cultural wealth that families have to offer. Lastly, sustained family engagement builds partnerships to impact student learning for the long term that essentially prepares students for the demands of a global society (Weiss, Lopez & Rosenberg, 2010).

Conclusion

The international literature points to positive ways in which family engagement impacts students' achievement and prepares them beyond high school for college and work (Bornstein, 2006; Dearing & Tang, 2010; Englund et al., 2004; Hill & Tyson, 2009; Jeynes, 2005, 2010). Jamaican literature also indicates that family support is a key component of school effectiveness (Chunnu, 2016; Watson-Williams & Fox, 2013). Based on this systematic review, more local research is needed to address the gaps in the literature. Different types of research studies need to be conducted to address the various questions that still need to be answered. For example, what are the various types of family engagement by school types or levels? What do the students themselves think about how their families support them in their educational journey? What are the types of family activities that help to produce greater academic achievement? How can schools value the different ways in which families support their children?

These distinctive questions also suggest different methodologies. More quantitative research needs to be conducted, as well as longitudinal ethnographic studies which trace students and families over time at different educational levels.

Given the nation's post-colonial history, this systematic review points to the need for a contextualized understanding of family engagement in Jamaica. Family engagement needs to be defined and described in the Jamaican context based on new research studies as suggested. And finally, the theoretical and actionable framework presented offers a renewed perspective from which to investigate family engagement with various empowerment mechanisms in mind. Having reviewed what currently exists and having identified various disparities, it is imperative to also include recommendations based on actionable studies for the improvement of the family-school collaborative dynamic, so that education for all children can be truly transformative.

References

Bogenschneider, K., Little, O., Ooms, T., Benning, S., Cadigan, K., & Corbett, T. (2012). The family impact lens: A family-focused, evidence-informed approach to policy and practice. *Family Relations, 61*(3), 514–31.

Bornstein, M.H. (2006). Parenting science and practice. In W. Damon & R.M. Lerner (series Eds.) & I.E. Sigel & K.A. Renninger (Vol. Eds.), *Handbook of child psychology, Vol. 4. Child psychology and practice* (6th ed., pp. 893–949). Wiley.

Chunnu, W. (2016). Negotiating worlds (yards, shantytowns, ghettos, garrisons): Inequality maintained and the epistemologies of social factors influencing stratification and education in Jamaica. *International Journal of Educational Research, 78*, 32–40.

Clarke, C. (2007). Boys' gender identity, school work, and teachers' and parents' gender beliefs. *Caribbean Journal of Education, 29*(1), 126–60.

Cole, S. (2013). *An investigation into the impact of parental involvement on the cognitive and social skills of grade one students in Jamaica*. Doctoral dissertation. The University of the West Indies.

Coleman, P. (1998). *Parent, student and teacher collaboration: The power of three*. Sage Publications.

Constantino, S.M. (2003). *Engaging all families: Creating a positive school culture by putting research into practice*. Scarecrow Education.

Cook, L.D. & Ezenne, A. (2010). Factors influencing students' absenteeism in primary schools in Jamaica: Perspectives of community members. *Caribbean Curriculum, 17*, 33–57.

Cook, L.D. & Jennings, Z. (2016). Perspectives of Jamaican parents and their secondary school children on the value of education: Effects of selected variables on parents' perspectives. *International Journal of Educational Development, 50*, 90–99.

Dearing, E. & Tang, S. (2010). The home learning environment and achievement during childhood. In S. Christenson & A.L. Reschly (Eds.), *Handbook of school-family partnerships*. Routledge.

Dede Yildirim, E. & Roopnarine, J.L. (2017). Paternal and maternal engagement across six Caribbean countries and childhood outcomes. *Journal of Applied Developmental Psychology, 53*, 64–73.

Denyer, D. & Tranfield, D. (2009). Producing a systematic review. In D.A. Buchanan & A. Bryman (Eds.), *The Sage handbook of organizational research methods* (pp. 671–89). Sage Publications.

Devonish, J. & Anderson, P. (2017). Fathering the "outside" child: Differences and shortfalls among urban Jamaican fathers. *Social and Economic Studies, 66*(1), 33–77, 276–77, 283–84.

Edwards, C.P. & Kutka, T.S. (2015). Diverse perspectives of parents, diverse concepts of parent involvement and participation: What can they suggest to researchers. In S. Sheridan & E. Kim (Eds.), *Foundational aspects of family-school partnership research* (Vol. 1). Springer International Publishing.

Englund, M., Luckner, A., Whaley, G., Egeland, B., & Harris, K.R. (2004). Children's achievement in early elementary school: Longitudinal effects of parental involvement, expectations, and quality of assistance. *Journal of Educational Psychology, 96*(4), 723–30.

Epstein, J.L. (1995). School/family/community partnerships: Caring for the children we share. *Phi Delta Kappan, 76*(9), 701–12.

Ferlazzo, L. (2011). Involvement or engagement? *Educational Leadership, 68*(8), 10–14.

Froiland, J.M., Peterson, A., & Davison, M.L. (2013). The long-term effects of early parent involvement and parent expectation in the USA. *School Psychology International, 34*(1), 33–50.

Garrard, J. (2016). *Health sciences literature review made easy.* Jones & Bartlett Learning.

George, J., Pierre, P., Alexander, J., & Taylor-Ryan, M. (2015). Can the "gown" act as a bridge between the "town" and the school? An analysis of the operations of the PEEPS Project in Trinidad. *Caribbean Curriculum, 23,* 167–91.

Gough, D., Oliver, S., & Thomas, J. (Eds.). (2017). *An introduction to systematic reviews.* Sage Publications.

Hill, N.E. & Tyson, D.F. (2009). Parental involvement in middle school: A meta-analytic assessment of the strategies that promote achievement. *Developmental Psychology, 45*(3), 740–63.

Hoover-Dempsey, K. & Sandler, H. (1997). Why do parents become involved in their children's education? *Review of Educational Research, 67*(1), 3–42.

Hoover-Dempsey, K.V., Whitaker, M.C., & Ice, C.L. (2010). Motivation and commitment to family-school partnerships. In S. Christenson & A.L. Reschly (Eds.), *Handbook of school-family partnerships.* Routledge.

Hornby, G. & Lafaele, R. (2011). Barriers to parental involvement in education: An explanatory model. *Educational Review, 63*(1), 37–52.

Jeynes, W. (2010). *Parental involvement and academic success.* Taylor & Francis.

Jeynes, W.H. (2005). A meta-analysis of the relation of parental involvement to urban elementary school student academic achievement. *Urban Education, 40*(3), 237–69.

Johnson, J. & Carpenter, K. (2006). Home-school relationships: Bridging educational gaps. *Caribbean Journal of Education, 28*(2), 163–86.

Kim, Y. (2009). Minority parental involvement and school barriers: Moving the focus away from deficiencies of parents. *Educational Research Review, 4*(2), 80–102.

Kiyama, J., Harper, C., Ramos, D., Aguayo, D., Page, L., & Riester, K. (2015). Parent and family engagement in higher education. *ASHE Higher Education Report, 41*(6), 1–94.

Knopf, H.T. & Swick, K.J. (2007). How parents feel about their child's teacher/school: Implications for early childhood professionals. *Early Childhood Education Journal, 34*(4), 291–96.

Koonce, D. & Harper, Jr., W. (2005). Engaging African American parents in the schools: A community-based consultation model. *Journal of Educational and Psychological Consultation, 16*(1–2), 55–74.

Lawson, M.A. (2003). School-family relations in context: Parent and teacher perceptions of parent involvement. *Urban Education, 38*(1), 77–133.

Leiber-Miller, R. (2012). Families as partners: Making the connection. *Principal Leadership*, 12(5), 12–16.

Mapp, K.L. & Hong, S. (2010). Debunking the myth of the hard-to-reach parent. In S. Christenson & A.L. Reschly (Eds.), *Handbook of school-family partnerships* (pp. 345–61). Routledge.

Mapp, K.L. & Kuttner, P.J. (2013). *Partners in education: A dual capacity-building framework for family–school partnerships*. Southwest Educational Development Lab.

McWayne, C.M., Melzi, G., Limlingan, M.C., & Schick, A. (2016). Ecocultural patterns of family engagement among low-income Latino families of preschool children. *Developmental psychology*, 52(7), 1088–102.

Moles, O.C. & Fege, A.F. (2011). New directions for Title I family engagement: Lessons from the past. In S. Redding, M. Murphy, P. Sheley & Academic Development Institute (Eds.), *Handbook on family and community engagement*. Academic Development Institute/Center on Innovation and Improvement.

Morgan, K.K. (2019). Preparing students for the twenty-first century through family engagement in postsecondary and workforce readiness. In S. Blackman, D. Conrad & L. Brown (Eds.), *Achieving inclusive education in the Caribbean and beyond* (pp. 145–70). Springer International Publishing.

Ricketts, H. & Anderson, P. (2009). *Parenting in Jamaica*. Policy Research Unit, Planning Institute of Jamaica. https://www.pioj.gov.jm/product/parenting-in-jamaica/

Samms-Vaughan, M. (2001). *Cognition, educational attainment and behaviour in a cohort of Jamaican children*. Planning Institute of Jamaica.

Simons-Morton, B. & Chen, R. (2009). Peer and parent influences on school engagement among early adolescent. *Youth & Society*, 41(1), 3–25.

Watson-Williams, C. (2011). Challenges to achieving generational transformation in Jamaica through parental involvement in children's education: The role of schools. *Caribbean Journal of Education*, 33(1), 61–78.

Watson-Williams, C. & Fox, K. (2013). School effectiveness in Jamaica: What do successful schools look like. *Report submitted to the Inter-American Development Bank*.

Weiss, H., Caspe, M., & Lopez, M.E. (2006). *Family involvement in early childhood education*. Harvard Family Research Project.

Weiss, H.B., Bouffard, S.M., Bridglall, B.L., & Gordon, E.W. (2009). Reframing family involvement in education: Supporting families to support educational equity. *Equity Matters: Research Review No. 5*.

Weiss, H.B., Lopez, M.E., & Rosenberg, H. (2010). *Beyond random acts: Family, school, and community engagement as an integral part of education reform*. National Policy Forum for Family, School & Community Engagement. Harvard Family Research Project.

Appendix

List of Articles Included in Systematic Review

1. Brown, J. (1994). *Men and their families: Contributions of Caribbean men to family life. A discussion guide for use by groups in church, school, community and other settings.* Caribbean Child Development Center School of Continuing Studies, University of the West Indies. https://files.eric.ed.gov/fulltext/ED392514.pdf.
2. Chunnu, W. (2016). Negotiating worlds (yards, shantytowns, ghettos, garrisons): Inequality maintained and the epistemologies of social factors influencing stratification and education in Jamaica. *International Journal of Educational Research, 78*, 32–40.
3. Clarke, C. (2007). Boys' gender identity, school work, and teachers' and parents' gender beliefs. *Caribbean Journal of Education, 29*(1), 126–60.
4. Cook, L.D. & Ezenne, A. (2010). Factors influencing students' absenteeism in primary schools in Jamaica: Perspectives of Community members. *Caribbean Curriculum, 17*, 33–57.
5. Cook, L.D. & Jennings, Z. (2016). Perspectives of Jamaican parents and their secondary school children on the value of education: Effects of selected variables on parents' perspectives. *International Journal of Educational Development, 50*, 90–99.
6. Dede Yildirim, E. & Roopnarine, J.L. (2017). Paternal and maternal engagement across six Caribbean countries and childhood outcomes. *Journal of Applied Developmental Psychology, 53*, 64–73.
7. Devonish, J. & Anderson, P. (2017). Fathering the "outside" child: Differences and shortfalls among urban Jamaican fathers. *Social and Economic Studies, 66*(1/2), 33–284.
8. Fearon, D., Copeland, D., & Saxon, T. (2013). The Relationship between Parenting Styles and Creativity in a Sample of Jamaican Children. *Creativity Research Journal, 25*(1), 119–28.
9. Harris, M. & Kahn, M. (2005). Parenting, education, and well-being: The case of Jamaican men and women. *Wadabagei: A Journal of the Caribbean and Its Diaspora, 8*(3), 34–53.
10. Johnson, J. & Carpenter, K. (2006). Home-school relationships: Bridging educational gaps. *Caribbean Journal of Education, 28*(2), 163–86.
11. Kinkead-Clark, Z. (2017a). Bridging the gap between home and school – Perceptions of classroom teachers and principals: Case

studies of two Jamaican inner-city schools. *Education and Urban Society*, 49(8), 762–77.

12. ———. (2017b). Early childhood care and education in Jamaica. Stakeholders' perceptions of global influences on a local space. *Early Child Development and Care*, 187(10), 1484–95.

13. Lambert, M.C., Puig, M., Lyubansky, M., Rowan, G.T., Hill, M., Milburn, B., & Hannah, S.D. (2001). Child behavior and emotional problems in Jamaican classrooms: a multimethod study using direct observations and teacher reports for ages 6–11. *International Journal of Intercultural Relations*, 25(5), 545–62.

14. Martin, T., Evans, A., Liem, P., Chong, G., & Chong, W. (2017). Student engagement in the Caribbean region: Exploring its role in the motivation and achievement of Jamaican middle school students. *School Psychology International*, 38(2), 184–200.

15. Morrison, J., Ispa, J., & Milner, V. (1998). Ideas about child rearing among Jamaican mothers and early childhood education teachers. *Journal of Research in Childhood Education*, 12(2), 166–75.

16. Munroe, G. (2009). *Parental involvement in education in Jamaica* (Working Paper No. 11). Planning Institute of Jamaica.

17. Smith, D. & Ashiabi, G. (2007). Poverty and child outcomes: A focus on Jamaican youth. *Adolescence*, 42(168), 837–58.

18. Stubbs, N. & Maynard, S. (2017). Academic self-efficacy, school engagement and family functioning among postsecondary students in the Caribbean. *Journal of Child and Family Studies*, 26(3), 792–99.

19. Watson-Williams, C. (2011). Challenges to achieving generational transformation in Jamaica through parental involvement in children's education: The role of schools. *Caribbean Journal of Education*, 33(1), 61–78.

20. Watson-Williams, C. & Fox, K. (2013). School effectiveness in Jamaica: What do successful schools look like. *Report submitted to the Inter-American Development Bank. Kingston, Jamaica.*

21. Yearwood, E. (2001). "Growing up" children: Current child-rearing practices among immigrant Jamaican families. *Journal of Child and Adolescent Psychiatric Nursing*, 14(1), 7–16, 40.

Chapter 2

Improving Parental Involvement for Students' Success

Outlining a Framework for a "Non-traditional" High School in Jamaica

RONCELL BROOKS AND CARMEL ROOFE

Introduction

Parental involvement in education has long been a concern of many teachers and school administrators in Jamaica. Many high school teachers perceive parental involvement as the number one priority for school improvement and student achievement (Langdon & Vesper, 2000). Hill and Taylor (2004) note that parental involvement remains an important predictor of school outcomes through to adolescence, but few parents monitor the academic progress of their children of high school age. The idea that parental involvement engenders students' academic achievement is intuitively appealing – such that society in general and educators in particular have considered it an important ingredient for the remedy of many ills in education (Shute et al., 2011). Parental involvement is usually measured in one of three ways: (1) from students' report, (2) from parents' report and (3) from teachers' report (Fan, 2001).

According to Park and Palardy (2004), parental involvement is a form of social capital in which the relationship between the parent and the child, school administrators and even other parents is a means to assist the academic achievement of the child. This involves parents working with schools and with their children to benefit their children's educational outcomes and future success (Hill & Taylor, 2004). However, parental involvement within particular types of schools in Jamaica is of concern. At the high school level, schools are stratified and various disparities exist, creating clear distinctions (National Education Inspectorate, 2015). The two main types of stratification are traditional high schools and non-traditional high schools. Traditional high schools are secondary schools built prior to Jamaica's independence in 1962, while non-traditional high schools are those built after Jamaica gained independence (Miller, n.d.). In the traditional high schools, parent-school engagement is usually stronger because it tends to have a greater mix of parents from middle to high socio-economic status (CAPRI, 2017; Murphy, 2002). These are schools which Ho Sui-Chu and Willms (1996) refer to as high socio-economic status (SES) schools because parents in these schools are usually from middle to wealthy backgrounds. SES is a composite of a number of variables, including family income and parents' educational and occupational levels (Ho Sui-Chu & Willms, 1996; Stacer & Perrucci, 2013). On the other hand, within non-traditional high schools, parents are usually from low socio-economic backgrounds. This influences student's ability to acquire learning resources, the relationship between their parents and the school, and student's absenteeism (Jennings & Cook, 2015). As a result, principals in these schools usually complain about the challenges of getting parents involved in school activities and students' school life.

Consequently, the Parent Teachers' Associations of non-traditional high schools in Jamaica struggle to get parents involved. The struggle manifests itself through parental tardiness in engaging teachers in consultations and other forms of home-school communication. There is also a challenge to get parents to give their time in a spirit of volunteerism, whether it is through cash or kind. According to the Jamaica Partners for Educational Progress (2011), the main avenues for parent-school engagement are orientation meetings at the beginning of the school year, rushed five-minute conferences to discuss the child's performance, Parent Teachers Associations and consultations with teachers resulting from children's behaviour. The report pointed out that these avenues were considered to be inadequate for producing good parent-school engagement. For the Jamaica Partners for Educational Progress (2011, p. 5), meaningful parent-school engagement requires parents to be involved in the following ways:

- Creating a school climate in which parents can volunteer, drop in and observe, and help children with their work.
- Teachers and principals engaging parents in goal-setting and improvement plans for individual children as well as sharing methods for assisting children with homework.
- Increasing teachers' accessibility to parents by having regular conference spaces and schedules when teachers are available.

- Capacity building for PTAs to become true monitors of all aspects of school life, holding all stakeholders accountable (not functioning solely as a fundraising mechanism for the school).
- Schools and parents goal-setting together (for children and schools) and developing strategies to achieve their goals.

Anecdotal experience from principals of some non-traditional high schools participating in the association for principals suggests that parental involvement is not at an ideal level for many school administrators in non-traditional Jamaican high schools. According to the Jamaica Partners for Educational Progress (2011), the low level of parental involvement and its impact on the quality of education in Jamaica has led to attempts by many school administrators (especially those who operate in the non-traditional high school contexts) to improve the level of parental involvement. To this end, the National Parent Teachers' Association (NPTA) (which was one recommendation of the 2004 National Taskforce on Education) was launched (The Jamaica Information Service [JIS], 2006). The role of the NPTA was to develop and disseminate a handbook for PTAs in schools focused on best practices to encourage parental involvement, establish parent-teachers' organizations and revitalize and promote November as parent month. While some of these initiatives have been implemented, they do not seem to have curbed the issue of a lack of parental involvement in some schools.

There is also a significant problem with volunteering, and attendance at PTA meetings and related activities are very low. Parents do not find it important to visit the school and participate in devotional exercises or even to accompany teachers on a school outing with students. Parents also do not see monetary donations as important because they believe that the government provides free education. The reality of many parents in the non-traditional high school context is that they earn meagre wages and work long hours to get the money to buy uniforms, books and other necessities for school (Munroe, 2009). Additionally, students and parents view non-traditional high schools as schools with low status, as traditional high schools are the preferred choice of most parents and students in Jamaica (Roofe, 2015). The perception is that parents and students do not want to be in non-traditional high schools because of this perceived status. These are some of the reasons parents find it difficult to participate in their adolescent students' education.

This chapter explores the literature to determine the reasons for the lack of parental involvement. The literature explored related to the ways in which parents are involved in their adolescents' academic success, challenges parents face, particularly those relating to their SES, which would prevent them from getting involved, and ways in which parents can overcome these challenges in order to be actively involved in their adolescents' school life and ultimately their success. Several research journals, books and published dissertations were searched, using key concepts relating to the objectives of the study. Based on findings from the exploration of the literature, a parental involvement framework is proposed which we believe is applicable to the context of non-traditional high schools in Jamaica. This is expected to aid school administrators and teachers in understanding some of the barriers faced by parents and highlight strategies that can help address and minimize some of these barriers.

Theoretical Framework

According to Epstein (2005), parental involvement is a component of school and classroom organization and therefore requires multi-level leadership. Through his theory of overlapping spheres, Epstein (2001) posits that students learn more and better when the home, school and community share responsibilities for their success. The theory states that students succeed at higher levels when the internal and external models of influence intersect and work together to promote student learning and development. The internal model includes the intersections of interpersonal relations and patterns of influence that occur between individuals at home, at school and in the community (Epstein et al., 2002). The external model posits that students learn and achieve more when the external contexts in which they live work together to support and enhance their academic learning and success. Six types of parental involvement within the theory of overlapping spheres act as a framework for organizing behaviours, roles and actions performed by school personnel and family and community members working together to increase involvement and student achievement (Epstein et al., 2002). Griffin and Steen (2010) state that the theory outlines and defines the six types of involvement in the following ways:

(i) Parenting: helping families (e.g., parents and extended family members) to become aware and knowledgeable about child development and providing resources that enable them to establish home environments that can enhance student learning.
(ii) Communicating: effective, appropriate, relevant, two-way contact about school events (e.g., open houses, conferences, testing

workshops), student academic or personal development and progress, and insight (e.g., success or challenges) within the home environment.

(iii) Volunteering: organizing and participating in activities initiated by school personnel (e.g., parent-teacher associations) or generated by community members aimed at supporting students and school programmes, such as service-learning projects, Big Brothers Big Sisters programmes or violence-reduction assemblies.

(iv) Learning at home: providing information to parents and families about school procedures (e.g., homework expectations, grading scales) in order to help them augment their children's academic activities.

(v) Decision making: including parents and family members from all backgrounds as representatives and leaders on school committees.

(vi) Collaborating with the community: identifying and integrating resources, services and other assets from the community to help meet the needs of school personnel, students and their families.

These six types of parental involvement address a wide range of ways that parents can get involved in their children's success. Given the socio-economic status of most parents whose children attend non-traditional high schools in Jamaica, these six types of involvement provide an opportunity for parents to be involved regardless of their situation. However, for the purposes of this chapter, we draw on only two types of parental involvement by Epstein: communicating and volunteering.

Additionally, Lareau (1987) proposed three major conceptual approaches to understanding variations in levels of parental involvement. These are the culture of poverty, the institutional approach and the cultural-capital approach. According to the culture of poverty approach, parental involvement varies because parents are from different social classes and working parents place less emphasis on the importance of schooling – distinguishing more between their roles as parents and those of school staff than middle-class parents (Ho Sui-Chu & Willms, 1996).

In the institutional approach, Lightfoot (1978), as cited by Lareau (1987), states that some schools discriminate and make middle-class families feel more welcome than working-class families, and this prevents parental involvement. The cultural capital (which is the third approach) maintains that schools are largely middle-class institutions with middle-class values, organizational patterns and forms of communication (Ho Sui-Chu & Willms, 1996). It was further pointed out by Ho Sui-Chu and Willms

(1996) that this approach is not inconsistent with the first two approaches and, in some respects, integrates them in that it emphasizes the role of both schools and parents. They conclude that the cultural-capital approach emphasizes "the class structure embedded in school and home life and the process by which parents with different dispositions realize success in the school system" (p. 127). For the purposes of this chapter, we emphasize the use of the cultural-capital approach particularly because it focuses on both home and school conditions and that any parent regardless of SES can help their children to realize success (Hayes, 2011; Ho Sui-Chu & Willms, 1996).

Review of Literature

According to Cole (2017), the responsibility for socializing and educating children is a shared obligation between home and school. Therefore, in order for a child to achieve their fullest potential in school, parents must participate. We now turn to a further exploration of the literature by focusing on themes such as effective parent-school communication, parental volunteering and students' success, and socio-economic status and parental involvement to determine reasons for the decline in parental involvement, especially at the high school level.

Effective Parent-School Communication

According to Epstein et al. (2002), effectively communicating activities includes school-to-home and home-to-school communications about school and classroom programmes and children's progress. Burke (2010) points out that parental involvement includes regular communication with teachers for feedback on the child's progress. Epstein et al. (2002) posit that two-way communications between teachers and parents increase understanding and cooperation between school and home. Thoughtful two-way communications also show students that their teachers and parents are working together to help them succeed in school (Epstein et al., 2002).

Epstein et al. (2002) believe that a number of activities can be used to increase two-way communication between school and home. These include parent-teacher conferences, phone calls, homework hotlines, newsletters with reaction sheets, report card pickups, emails, websites and other creative strategies. According to Epstein et al. (2002), these kinds of two-way communications encourage parents to provide reactions, ideas and preferences and to ask questions about school programmes and students' progress. Furthermore, two-way communication ensures that parents understand what it means to be involved and the school understands what interpretations or misunderstandings parents hold (Grady, 2016).

Dubis and Bernadowski (2015, p. 170) cited the work of Zafar et al. (1989), which found that most principals and vice-principals believe that a number of things lead to the failure of school meetings to communicate effectively with parents, which are as follows:

- parents have little understanding of the importance of school meetings;
- parents tend to ignore invitations to school meetings;
- parents have other responsibilities that, in their opinion, are more important than their children's school progress;
- parents believe that the school is fully responsible for their children's education;
- meetings are usually held during school time, which requires parents to have their employers' consent to take time off work to visit the school.

Dubis and Bernadowski (2015) posit, however, that regardless of what exists to hinder communication, schools must put things in place to overcome these challenges that prevent effective communication between school and home. Dubis and Bernadowski (2015) also cited the work of Al-anqoodi (2012), who proposed some mechanisms to enhance effective communication:

- sending hardcopy invitations to parents,
- sending a short message service (SMS) to parents' mobile phones two days before the meeting,
- updating the information on the school's website and
- arranging for transportation to take parents to and from the meeting (pp. 170–1).

The authors believe that these extensive attempts to involve parents in school meetings help define the importance of those meetings.

In the study by Dubis and Bernadowski (2015), it was found that using email may help to close the communication gap between home and school and improve parental involvement in a child's education at school. They further found that parents believed their child's education was a priority and that their own educational level would not be an obstacle to their involvement in decisions related to their child's academic and behavioural performance. Dubis and Bernadowski concluded that educators must find ways to actively engage parents to improve the partnership between home and school. They concluded that implementing an effective and efficient email protocol for communication between parents and teachers could improve parental involvement and, potentially, student achievement. This argument was supported by Stacer and Perrucci (2013), who noted that parents who reported more contact from the school were more involved there than parents who reported less contact.

According to Olmstead (2013), existing and emerging electronic communication technologies may provide the capability for schools to increase parental involvement in their children's academic lives. Thus, schools should be seeking ways to maximize emerging technological tools to promote better communication between teachers and parents. Many schools, however, are not using electronic communication technologies as widely as they should, perhaps because many teachers may lack the requisite training in using these technologies to improve communication, or there may not be adequate research in this area as use of these new technologies is relatively new in education (Olmstead, 2013). Olmstead found that the preferred means of communication between school and home were email, phone messages and flyers.

Other means of technological communication, as highlighted by Olmstead (2013) and Sad et al. (2016), include text messaging, instant messaging and the use of social networks, such as Twitter and Facebook. Olmstead concluded that a majority of parents were interested in receiving communication about their children by text messaging, but most teachers were not willing to use this method since they would have to use their personal phones as they were not provided with phones by their schools. Olmstead (2013) believed that these are good communication methods that provide quick and direct access to teachers.

Conversely, Ho Sui-Chu and Willms (1996) suggest that relatively few schools have strong influences on the learning climate in the home. They believe that through effective communication, big gains in achievement could be realized through programmes that give parents concrete information about parenting styles, teaching methods and school curricula. Hayes (2011) also found that greater parental educational aspirations for adolescents were related to increased parents engaging in communication about school and learning with their adolescents in both lower and higher SES. Where parental involvement relating to communication was good, Hayes (2011) found that there was greater teacher support, regardless of SES. The findings as posited by Hayes (2011) suggest that where the aspiration for students' educational success was high, parents will do what is necessary to ensure that this success is realized. It is important to note that in the study by Hayes (2011), teachers were willing to go above and beyond to give the necessary support to students whose parents are involved. This then positively impacted students' success.

Parental Volunteering and Students' Success

According to Epstein et al. (2002), volunteering in the parental involvement process is where opportunities are provided for parents to share their time and talents to support the school, teachers and students. They posit that volunteer activities may be done at school, in the classroom or even at home or in the community. Some of these activities include helping individual teachers; assisting in the library, the computer room, the lunchroom, the playground, after school programmes; attending students' performances, sporting activities, assemblies and school celebrations (Epstein et al., 2002). It is further suggested by Epstein et al. (2002) that various strategies may be used to recruit and train volunteers, and that it is the role of the school to schedule opportunities so that parents can volunteer even if they work during the school day. Volunteering may involve soliciting the services of parents who have access to resources such as supplies, transportation, equipment or technology (Smar, 2002). Parental volunteering is essentially being actively involved in school activities and attending school functions and meetings.

Ho Sui-Chu and Willms (1996) emphasize the importance of schools getting parents to volunteer, as this may not only improve the quality of schooling but also reduce inequality between social class groups. Parental involvement can therefore affect students' success independently of children's family backgrounds (Ho Sui-Chu & Willms, 1996). Ho Sui-Chu and Willms (1996) also note that parental involvement made a significantly unique contribution towards explaining the variation in children's academic success, over and above the effects associated with parental background. Smar (2002) notes, however, that it was very important for the school to ensure that all parent volunteers knew that their efforts were welcome and that schools express the importance of parental volunteering and how it can impact the general success of students. According to Fan (2001), volunteering has a positive effect on students' academic growth. However, some parents are not aware of how to offer their services to schools. In a study of parental involvement in selected Jamaican schools, Murphy (2002) reported that 50 per cent of the parents in the study indicated that the schools did not do well at asking them to be involved.

In a study by Ng and Lee (2015) on the attitudes of ninety-three parents towards their involvement at various levels of school education in a special school in Hong Kong, they found that while many parents were not against parental involvement, many were more inclined to be involved in activities outside the school (including two-way communication and supervision of children at home) than to be involved in the school with activities such as volunteering, providing advice on school policies and decision making, and membership on school committees – at the expense of looking after their children at home. This was similar to findings shared by Murphy (2002) in her study on Jamaican parental involvement. In contrast, Stacer and Perrucci (2013) found that parents who reported higher levels of school outreach also had greater parental involvement at the school. Walsh (2010) reported that the larger the size of the school, the lower the level of volunteering, due to the notion of "free-riding" (benefitting from the collective effort but not being actively involved) in large schools.

Socio-Economic Status and Parental Involvement

One factor contributing to a lack of parental involvement is SES. SES is a composite of a number of variables, including family income and parents' education and occupation (Ho Sui-Chu & Willms, 1996; Stacer & Perrucci, 2013). Yoder and Lopez (2013) addressed the issue of tangible barriers in their study, defining them as any external task, activity or responsibility that makes involvement difficult, such as time restrictions, lack of finances or lack of access to technology, lack of access to transportation and language or cultural barriers. These barriers were considered by parents to be practical challenges that often stood in the way of involvement. Not having enough time, lacking finances, transportation or access to technology were all concrete obstacles facing parents (Yoder & Lopez, 2013).

According to Lareau (1987), parental involvement is linked to parents' class position and the social and cultural resources that social class yields. Lareau (1987) revealed that working-class parents had poorer educational skills and relatively low occupational prestige compared to teachers, and limited time and disposable income to supplement and intervene in their children's schooling. Highlighting that middle-class parents, on the other hand, had educational skills and occupational prestige that matched or surpassed that of the teacher, Lareau also noted that they had the necessary economic resources to manage the child care, transportation and time required to meet with teachers, hire tutors and become intensely involved in their children's schooling. Finally, Lareau (1987) found that economic differences between middle- and working-class parents are evident in their different responses to requests to attend school events. This, Lareau (1987) stated, was because attendance at school events (especially those in the afternoon) required transportation and childcare arrangements as well as flexibility at the workplace – which is more likely to be available to the middle class.

Mayo and Siraj (2015) believe that children need practical help with school and learning. They suggested that parents need to set certain basic conditions in order for children to be able to engage in school-related work and activities in the family environment. Mayo and Siraj (2015) posited that such conditions include providing a computer for school work, regulating activities in the home environment and interacting with teachers. Similar findings were also reported by Orr (2003). According to Mayo and Siraj (2015), some of these conditions may pose financial challenges that could make it difficult for parents of low SES, and this may impact their level of parental involvement.

Although parents had a variety of tangible barriers or lack of resources, they found ways to overcome these barriers on their own as they were able to draw on personal resources and external support (Berryhill & Vennum, 2015). As suggested by Berryhill and Vennum (2015), these barriers were not as difficult for families to circumvent because they could rely on their communities, agencies, family members or other loved ones for support. As such, resources and supports act as mitigating factors that allow parents to be involved in education despite the barriers. The theme "resources and supports", as proposed by Berryhill and Vennum (2015), was defined as anybody or anything that can help their child achieve an educational goal by helping the parent – especially those with challenging SES. In addition to resources and support, Burke (2010) points out that parents should never let insecurities about their abilities, level of education, level of income and employment status prevent them from getting involved in their children's educational success. These points raised in Burke's (2010) article are relevant to many parents in the non-traditional high school context in Jamaica.

Ho Sui-Chu and Willms (1996) found that the SES of a school had an effect on achievement that was comparable to the effects associated with the SES of a family. They also found that, irrespective of their own SES, parents were more likely to volunteer or attend PTA meetings if their children attended high SES schools rather than low SES schools. Ho Sui-Chu and Willms (1996), however, pointed out that parents in two-parent families were more likely to participate in the school and to provide higher levels of home supervision than were single parents; but the extent to which parents discussed school programmes and activities or communicated with school staff was not related to family structure.

It is likely that when there is a strong concentration of high SES parents in a school community, an ethos of greater school participation is more easily established (Ho Sui-Chu & Willms, 1996). They further posit that parental involvement made a significantly unique contribution towards explaining the variation in children's academic achievement, over and above the effects associated with parental background. Hayes (2011) found that on average, parents from higher SES had higher levels of parental education, employment status, marital status, family income, educational aspirations for their adolescents and more positive perceptions of teacher support for their adolescents than parents from lower SES families. Hayes (2011) indicates that parents from lower SES show a greater likelihood to engage in school involvement when they are more educated. However, Hayes (2011) and Ho Sui-Chu and Willms's (1996) findings do not support the notion that parents from working-class backgrounds place less emphasis on the importance of schooling or that they view education as the sole purview of the school.

Discussion

As mentioned by Dubis and Bernadowski (2015), teachers often say that parents are unwilling to participate in school at any level. If so, schools will have to work overtime to surmount this hurdle, as parents are important stakeholders in the education process. To encourage parental involvement, Jamaica Partners for Educational Progress (2011) pointed out that schools can organize parenting courses, ensure that pre-service and in-service teachers undergo intensive parent engagement courses, conduct parenting seminars, host parent and child workshops, and host parent and child competitions.

Parental involvement is a crucial aspect of students' learning. This is a serious challenge in non-traditional high schools, where parents are not as involved as they ought to be due to many challenging factors, particularly their socio-economic status. Parents must be encouraged to get involved in their children's learning regardless of their socio-economic background (Munroe, 2009). Given the context of the non-traditional high schools in this section of the chapter, we focus on two of the six types of parental involvement outlined by Epstein (2002): improved communication and volunteering. It is our belief that these two will help with the provision of both human and non-human resources for non-traditional high schools and better understanding of the importance of providing human and non-human resources to schools, especially in a context of limited resources.

Improving Communication between Home and School

For improved communication to occur, a one-way channel where the school dictates to parents will not be effective. A two-way process that includes school-to-home and home-to-school communications about school and classroom programmes and children's progress and success should be employed (Epstein et al., 2002). This suggests that schools must find ways to inform parents about school activities and their child's performance, while parents should also contact the school about these issues.

Communicating involves both the school and the home working together and must be a two-way process which demonstrates to students that school and home are working together for their success (Epstein et al., 2002). The school often has to take the lead role in parental involvement (PI) engagement by being innovative. The Jamaica Partners for Educational Progress (2011) suggests that schools can organize parenting courses/seminars/workshops, engage parents and children in competitions and ensure that in-service teachers undergo parent engagement sessions – initiatives which will no doubt aid in the home-school relationship and boost parental involvement.

Printed circulars along with text messages sent to parents' cellular phones – methods identified by Olmstead (2013) as those usually preferred most by parents – seem not to work well with parents in non-traditional high school settings. While Olmstead (2013) and Sad and Gurbuzturk (2013) suggest text messaging as a means by which schools can communicate with parents, this technological method alone is limited and must be incorporated with other forms of communications.

Most parents in contemporary Jamaica have access to smartphones, and so we believe that the methods of communicating with parents can be broadened. This can be done through a modern SMS which can facilitate direct communication with parents using email. This could be an opportunity where the school through its Information and Technology Department can help parents set up email accounts so that this form of communication can be facilitated. This could very well help in reducing the problem of parents not being able to do face-to-face visits to pick up students' reports.

We also believe that other forms of technological communications could be used to communicate with parents. As suggested by Olmstead (2013) and Sad et al. (2016), these include instant messaging (such as WhatsApp) and social networks (such as Twitter and Facebook). These applications are free once parents have internet access. Though the low

SES of parents may pose an access barrier for some, many would be willing to use the mobile plans being offered by telecommunication companies since most parents have access to a smartphone and could be kept up to date by the school. These methods could complement the preferred methods of circulars/flyers or phone messages. Schools should not just send information about a school event to parents once but devise a strategy for giving parents frequent advance notice of events while at the same time not bombarding them with the information. Schools that have challenges communicating with parents and getting them involved in their children's learning should adopt an approach similar to that used by promoters when they are hosting events. Promoters ensure that the information about their event is ever-present in the traditional and online media and within the view and hearing of their target group. Schools could use a similar approach in communicating with parents, taking advantage of the popularly used technological communication platforms.

One of the approaches used by a school known to one of the authors to improve communication between school and parents is community visitation. Given the population of the school, the principal theorized that they would normally gather in their communities, and so the principal visited places such as churches and the "hang out" spots (popular places) of parents to host the PTA meeting in the community. After having the meetings with these parents in popular places, a snowballing approach was used to encourage other parents to attend school meetings. Snowballing included parents contacting other parents.

Many parents want their children to succeed regardless of SES, so once communication (i.e., information about teaching methods, school curricula and parenting styles) between school and home is strong and effective, Ho Sui-Chu and Willms (1996) point out that big gains in learning and achievement can be realized. It is very important that parents seek to find out what is happening at school so that they can plan and implement strategies to support their children. Many teachers make their cellular phone numbers and email addresses available to parents, so parents should take advantage of these opportunities to show interest in their children's education and aspirations. Hayes (2011) notes that greater parental educational aspirations for adolescents were related to increased parents' engagement in communication about school and learning with their adolescents in both lower and higher SES. Where parental involvement relating to communication was good, Hayes (2011) found that there was greater teacher support regardless of SES. For the success of the child, PI should be about regular communication with teachers for feedback on the child's progress (Burke, 2010).

Parental Volunteering and the Success of Students Attending Non-traditional High Schools

Volunteering is one of the six types of parental involvement purported by Epstein et al. (2002), where parents are expected to give freely of their time to help with school activities by working with other parents and school officials for the overall benefit of the school and their children. Attendance at PTA meetings and other PTA fundraising events is considered to be part of parents' volunteering. This type of parental involvement can also involve working with community groups.

Volunteering is one of the weakest forms of parental involvement in Jamaica's non-traditional high school context. For example, in a known school of approximately 1,800 students whenever a PTA meeting is held, approximately 100 parents usually attend, and teachers' attendance is equally poor. The need exists for research to discern the challenges for the target audience. It may also be difficult for parents from low SES to volunteer as many of them have to go to work and may have difficulty accessing transportation to attend meetings and other activities. Dubis and Bernadowski (2015) cited Al-anqoodi (2012), who argued that where transportation may be an issue for parents, school administrators could arrange transportation for them to get to meetings. Smar (2002) highlights that other parents can be volunteers by providing transportation to the school. This provision of transportation could assist other parents in travelling to school activities or taking students to school events. It could also involve the covering of the costs associated with transporting other parents or students to and from meetings or school events. Volunteering calls for parents to be actively involved in school activities such as attending school functions and meetings (Burke, 2010). It is about organizing and participating in activities initiated by school personnel, such as parent-teacher association meetings or those facilitated by community members aimed at supporting students and school programmes (Griffin & Steen, 2010).

Davies (2000) noted that parents who volunteer at school tend to have a better relationship with school administrators and teachers. When there is an excellent relationship between family and school the child tends to be more focused in the school environment, perhaps because when parents are known to teachers the child may feel that if they do something out of the norm, their parents will be informed. As a result, schools need to place focus on the processes by which they build relationships with families to support children's learning.

Volunteering promotes a social bond between home and school. Through volunteering some parents also receive employment at the school, as once there is a job vacancy these parents (if they possess the requisite skills) become the first avenue for recruiting. This social bond also extends to the children of these parents, as upon leaving, they often express the desire to give back to the school. Wigfield and Eccles (2002) reported that adolescents who believe that there is strong social and emotional support from parents often demonstrate positive academic competence, a sense of relatedness to peers and academic effort and interest in school. Volunteering is a good indicator for students' learning. Fan (2001) concurred that volunteering has a positive effect on students' academic growth.

Not all parents believe in volunteering, however. Some think that it is a waste of time and will negatively impact their children's learning as the time spent volunteering at school could be better spent at home helping their children with homework and other parenting duties. This type of thinking is evident in research done by Ng and Lee (2015). The authors, however, further pointed out that parents have a part to play in the PI process, including participation in PTA meetings as this provides opportunities for parents to consolidate ties to the school and show support for their goals (the success of their children). Teachers are also very important stakeholders in this process – they are encouraged to listen to parents' views of their children and to conduct home visits, which will show parents that teachers are interested in their child's welfare (Jamaica Partners for Educational Progress, 2011).

All stakeholders should seek to overcome the barriers to parental involvement. In a *Gleaner* article, Burke (2010) pointed out that parental involvement is one of the core indicators of children's later success. In addition, she highlighted that PI inspires and motivates parents to continue the advancement of their children and helps them to understand that they are one of the most important keys to their children's academic success. Burke's (2010) *Gleaner* article notes that students with involved parents are more motivated to succeed, are less disruptive and have a greater chance of being enrolled in post-secondary institutions.

Developing a Parental Involvement Framework for the Jamaican Context

Having gleaned information on communicating and volunteering, two key characteristics of parental involvement outlined in Epstein's (2002) theory provide guidance for a framework specific to the Jamaican context and one that the authors believe could be useful for non-traditional high schools (see figure 2.1). Based on the literature reviewed, effective communication between home and school must be two-way. Parental volunteerism will not thrive if communication is poor and does not utilize all the available communication platforms to which the parents and school have access. Molnar et al. (2008) noted that day-to-day language usage causes difficulties and discomfort between educators and parents. Furthermore, Evans (2001) in her research on classroom interaction in schools in Jamaica noted that student's language skills were linked to their socio-economic status. The onus therefore would be on schools to find different ways to communicate with parents of different socio-economic status. The language utilized could therefore be the difference in how school and home communicate.

Lareau's (1987) research – which indicates that working-class parents have poor educational skills, relatively low occupational prestige compared to teachers and limited time and disposable income to supplement and intervene in their children's schooling – provides a necessary starting point for schools to think through how parental communication and involvement can be improved. Since a majority of the parents in non-traditional high

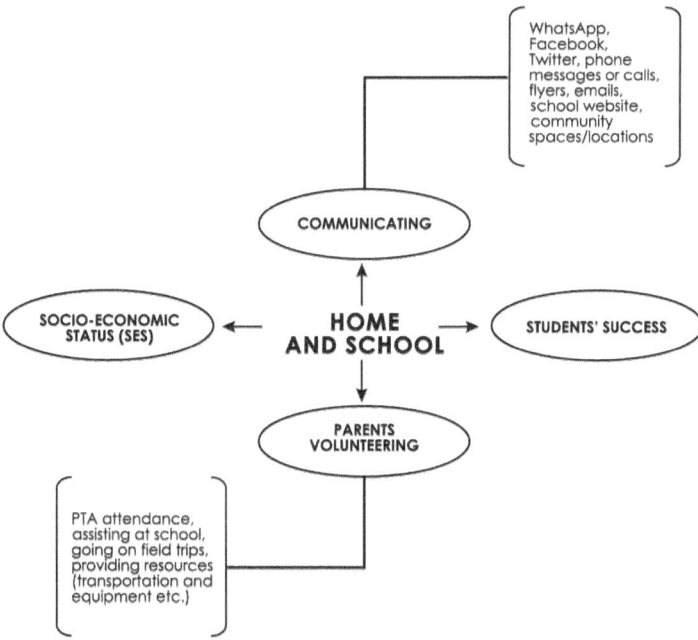

Figure 2.1 COMVOL PI framework for non-traditional high schools.

schools are in a low to middle socio-economic grouping, strategies that include increased cost and time away from earning will likely yield minimal success (Ho Sui-Chu & Willms, 1996).

For school-to-home communication to be effective, schools must see technological communication as an investment and not a mere cost (Olmstead, 2013; Sad et al., 2016). Although most of the technological methods suggested here utilize free platforms, some parents (as a result of their SES) may still have difficulty accessing them. It is therefore the remit of schools to help parents use what they have to enable communication between home and school. Methods such as WhatsApp and other instant messaging services, Facebook, Twitter and the SMS, can complement traditional forms of communication such as using flyers, hosting meetings at common community spaces and phone messaging (Olmstead, 2013).

Effective communication is the best tool to create a partnership between school and home, and once there is good communication between school and home, more parents will become involved. Davies (2000) highlights that when partnership/relationship attributes exist, educators and families act in ways that show engagement and support for children's success. This communication partnership will undoubtedly positively affect students' success (Fan, 2001). The volunteering activities that can improve students' success include helping individual teachers; assisting in the library, the computer room, the lunchroom, the playground and after school programmes; attending students' performances, sporting activities, assemblies and school celebrations; and providing resources such as supplies, transportation, equipment or technology (Smar, 2002). Ho Sui-Chu and Willms (1996) and Griffin and Steen (2010) pointed out that volunteering also includes attending PTA meetings.

Figure 2.1 shows that SES has some impact on parental involvement. Yoder and Lopez (2013) opine that not having enough time and lacking finances, transportation or access to technology were all concrete obstacles facing many parents which may affect their involvement. This seemed to be supported by Lareau (1987), who noted that parental involvement is linked to the class position of the parents and to the social and cultural resources that social class yields. Lareau in her research further made the comparison between middle-class parents and parents from a lower class, reporting that middle-class parents had educational skills and occupational prestige that matched or surpassed that of the teacher; they also have the necessary economic resources to manage the child care, transportation and time required to meet with teachers, hire tutors and become intensely involved in their children's schooling success. Therefore, parental involvement in non-traditional schools is compounded by SES (Ho Sui-Chu & Willms, 1996).

Ho Sui-Chu and Willms (1996) argued that the SES of a school has an effect on success comparable to the effects associated with the SES of a family and that parental involvement made a significantly unique contribution towards explaining the variation in children's success, beyond the effects associated with parental SES. Non-traditional high schools therefore need to help parents understand that their SES is not a prerequisite for involvement in their child's schooling, and that the school can assist them in identifying opportunities for involvement that align with their circumstances. Parents need to understand that parental involvement is a form of social capital in which the relationship between the parent and the child, school administrators, and even other parents is a means to assist in the success of the child (Park & Palardy, 2004).

Implications for Practice in Jamaica's Non-Traditional High Schools

There are a number of ways in which non-traditional high schools can improve their communication practices. The most dominant, outlined in the literature, is the increased use of technological communications. Schools do not need to give up their traditional ways of communicating with parents but can use technology to complement what already exists. Hayes (2011) purports that a parents' SES level does not matter and that greater parental educational aspirations for adolescents increase when parents engage in communication with the school and with their adolescents. Hayes's (2011) findings also show that where good communication exists between school and home, there is greater teacher support. Hence, teachers in non-traditional high schools should be oriented to their responsibility to help parents understand the importance of their involvement to the success of their children. Additionally, teachers will need to form relationships with parents that build trust, so that parents can be receptive to their suggestions. Such trust can be built through ongoing dialogue where the students and parents see a demonstrated interest in the success of the student.

It can be reasonably assumed that good communication impacts parent volunteers. Volunteering does not necessarily mean being at the school and participating in activities; one could provide a service or resource that can benefit the general school community (Smar, 2002). Burke (2010) highlighted a number of the benefits of parental involvement, including inspiring and motivating parents to continue the advancement or success of their children, helping parents to understand that they are one of the key aspects of their children's academic success and improving interaction between parents and teachers/administrators. Burke also revealed that students with involved parents are more motivated to succeed and have a greater chance of enrolling in post-secondary institutions.

It would be good to conduct an empirical study in schools to find out from parents which of the communication and volunteering methods from those the literature suggest are best for them to become more involved in the school and to affect their children's success. An empirical study could also focus on the issue of schools being considered high or low SES schools (Ho Sui-Chu & Willms, 1996). Such a study could use an ethical approach, looking at how students are placed in secondary schools by the Ministry of Education Youth and Information after sitting their primary school exit examinations. During placement after the primary exit examinations it seems more students with lower performances and who are from low SES homes seem to be placed in non-traditional high schools. Could it then be that such schools may not be able to have strong parental involvement regardless of their efforts knowing some of the challenges that low SES families present? Policymakers may therefore need to consider how increased resources can be allocated to such schools to support the efforts of their administration to ensure effective parental involvement which will ultimately improve students' success.

Conclusion

Active parental involvement through effective communication and volunteering will positively impact students' success. SES can affect the level of involvement; however, the findings of Hayes (2011) and Ho Sui-Chu and Willms (1996) do not support the notion that parents from working-class backgrounds place less emphasis on the importance of schooling, or that they view education as the sole purview of the school. Their findings show that all parents can participate in parental involvement regardless of SES. Volunteering can reduce the inequalities between high SES and low SES families and also improve the quality of schooling (Ho Sui-Chu & Willms, 1996). Sad et al. (2016) believe that schools should enable parents with feedback through effective communication channels. According to Sad and Gurbuzturk (2013), parents need to be informed and encouraged about parental involvement tasks, especially school-based activities. Kuperminc, Darnell and Alvarez-Jimenez (2008) conclude that parental involvement can support and maintain students' sense of belonging to school, which will no doubt affect their success. Finally, Burke (2010) stated that parental involvement is one of the core indicators of children's success, and that it is through this involvement that children understand and appreciate the importance of a solid education.

References

Al-anqoodi, Y. (2012). Communication between home and school to where? *Journal of Educational Development, 10*(69), 25–31.

Berryhill, M. & Vennum, A. (2015). Joining forces: Bringing parents and schools together. *Contemporary Family Therapy: An International Journal, 37*(4), 351–63. doi:10.1007/s10591-015-9357-3

Burke, T. (2010, October 4). Benefits of parental involvement in education. *The Gleaner.* http://jamaica-gleaner.com/gleaner/20101004/news/news7.html

Cole, S.A. (2017). *The impact of parental involvement on academic achievement* (Order No. 10602196) [Doctoral dissertation, Northcentral University]. ProQuest Dissertations & Theses Global. (1931045774).

Davies, D. (2000). How to build partnerships that work. *Principal, 80*(1), 32–34.

Dubis, S. & Bernadowski, C. (2015). Communicating with parents of children with special needs in Saudi Arabia: Parents' and teachers' perceptions of using email for regular and ongoing communication. *British Journal of Special Education, 42*(2), 166–82. doi:10.1111/1467-8578.12061

Epstein, J.L. (2001). *School, family, and community partnerships: Preparing educators and improving schools.* Westview Press.

———. (2005). Attainable goals? The spirit and letter of the no child left behind act on parental involvement. *Sociology of Education, 78*(2), 179–82.

Epstein, J.L., Sanders, M.G., Simon, B.S., Salinas, K.C., Jansorn, N.R., & Van Voorhis, F.L. (2002). *School, family, and community partnerships: Your handbook for action* (2nd ed.). Corwin Press.

Evans, H. (2001). *Inside Jamaican schools.* The University of the West Indies Press.

Fan, X. (2001). Parental involvement and students' academic achievement: A growth modeling analysis. *Journal of Experimental Education, 70*(1), 27–61.

Grady, C.E. (2016). *Educational stakeholders' perceptions of parental involvement in an urban school setting* (Order No. 10196553) [Doctoral dissertation, Walden University]. ProQuest Dissertations & Theses Global. (1834109283).

Griffin, D. & Steen, S. (2010). School-family-community partnerships: Applying Epstein's theory of the six types of involvement to school counselor practice. *Professional School Counseling, 13*(4), 218–26.

Hayes, D. (2011). Predicting parental home and school involvement in high school African American adolescents. *High School Journal, 94*(4), 154–66.

Hill, N.E. & Taylor, L.C. (2004). Parental school involvement and children's academic achievement. *Current Directions in Psychological Science (Wiley-Blackwell), 13*(4), 161–64. doi:10.1111/j.0963-7214.2004.00298.x

Ho Sui-Chu, E. & Willms, J. (1996). Effects of parental involvement on eighth-grade achievement. *Sociology of Education, 69*(2), 126.

Jamaica Information Service. (2006, July 24). *National group to promote greater parental involvement in education process.* http://jis.gov.jm/national-group-to-promote-greater-parent-involvement-in-education-process/

Jamaica Observer. (2017, May, 12). Principal lauds gov't for removing auxiliary fees, increase PATH allocation. http://www.jamaicaobserver.com/latestnews/Principal_lauds_govt_for_removing_auxiliary_fees,_increasing_PATH_allocation?profile=1228

Jamaica Partners for Educational Progress. (2011, June). Parental involvement in education: Do schools and teachers have a role? *CoP Edu Exchange E-Discussion Summary.* https://www.mona.uwi.edu/cop/sites/default/files/consolidated_reply_files/EduExchange%204_Summary%20_Final_0_0.pdf

Jennings, Z. & Cook, L. (2015). Causes of absenteeism at the secondary level in Jamaica: Parents' perspectives. *Development in Practice,* 25(1), 99–112.

Kuperminc, G.P., Darnell, A.J., & Alvarez-Jimenez, A. (2008). Parent involvement in the academic adjustment of Latino middle and high school youth: Teacher expectations and school belonging as mediators. *Journal of Adolescence,* 31(4), 469–83.

Langdon, C. & Vesper, N. (2000). The Sixth Phi Delta Kappa poll of teachers' attitudes toward the public schools. *Phi Delta Kappan,* 81(8), 607–11.

Lareau, A. (1987). Social class differences in family-school relationships: The importance of cultural capital. *Sociology of Education,* 60, 73–85.

Mayo, A. & Siraj, I. (2015). Parenting practices and children's academic success in low-SES families. *Oxford Review of Education,* 41(1), 47–63. doi:10.1080/03054985.2014.995160

Miller, E. (n.d.). Educational reform in independent Jamaica. http://www.educoas.org/Portal/bdigital/contenido/interamer/BkIACD/Interamer/Interamerhtml/Millerhtml/mil_mil.htm

Molnar, B.E., Cerda, M., Roberts, A.L., & Buka, S.L. (2008). Effects of neighborhood resources on aggressive and delinquent behaviors among urban youths. *American Journal of Public Health,* 98, 1086–93. doi:10.2105/AJPH.2006.098913

Munroe, G. (2009). *Parental involvement in education in Jamaica-book.* Caribbean Partners for Educational Progress. https://www.mona.uwi.edu/cop/library/parental-involvement-education-jamaica-book

Murphy, S. (2002). *The attitudes of Jamaican parents towards parent involvement in high school education.* http://www2.uwstout.edu/content/lib/thesis/2002/2002murphys.pdf

National Education Inspectorate Report. (2015). Chief inspector's baseline report 2015. http://www.nei.org.jm/Portals/0/Content/Documents/Chief%20Inspector's%20Baseline%20Report%202015.pdfer=2016-06-23-130247-730

Ng, S. & Lee, T. (2015). How parents were involved in a special school in Hong Kong. *International Journal of Educational Management,* 29(4), 420–30.

Olmstead, C. (2013). Using technology to increase parent involvement in schools. *Techtrends: Linking Research & Practice To Improve Learning,* 57(6), 28–37. doi:10.1007/s11528-013-0699-0

Orr, A.J. (2003). Black-White differences in achievement: The importance of wealth. *Sociology of Education, 76*, 281–304.

Park, E. & Palardy, G.J. (2004). Impact of parental involvement and authoritativeness on academic achievement: A cross ethnic comparison. In S.J. Paik & H. Walberg (Eds.), *Advancing educational productivity: Policy implications for national databases: Research in educational productivity* (pp. 95–122). Information Age Publishers.

Roofe, C. (2015). The urban teacher: Towards a context-responsive teacher preparation curriculum. *International Studies of Education Administration, 43*(1), 5–15.

Sad, S. & Gurbuzturk, O. (2013). Primary school students' parents' level of involvement into their children's education. *Educational Sciences: Theory and Practice, 13*(2), 1006–11.

Sad, S., Konca, A., Özer, N., & Acar, F. (2016). Parental e-nvolvement: A phenomenological research on electronic parental involvement. *International Journal of Pedagogies & Learning, 11*(2), 163–86.

Shute, V., Hansen, E., Underwood, J., & Razzouk, R. (2011). A review of the relationship between parental involvement and secondary school students' academic achievement. *Education Research International, 2011*, 1–10.

Smar, B. (2002). 6 Ways to partner with parents and community. *Teaching Music, 10*(2), 48–53.

Stacer, M.J. & Perrucci, R. (2013). Parental involvement with children at school, home, and community. *Journal of Family and Economic Issues, 34*(3), 340–54. http://dx.doi.org.rproxy.uwimona.edu.jm/10.1007/s10834-012-9335-y

Walsh, P. (2010). Is parental involvement lower at larger schools? *Economics of Education Review, 29*(6), 959–70.

Wigfield, A. & Eccles, J.S. (2002). *Development of achievement motivation.* Academic Press.

Yoder, J. & Lopez, A. (2013). Parent's perceptions of involvement in children's education: Findings from a qualitative study of public housing residents. *Child & Adolescent Social Work Journal, 30*(5), 415–33. doi:10.1007/s10560-013-0298-0

Zafar, A.R., Shami, M., & Al-Hussein, Z. (1989). *Parent–teachers' meeting from the school officials' perspective: A field study* (first edition, vol. 7). Mecca, KSA: Umm Al Qura University. Institute of Scientific Research andIslamic Heritage Revival. Psychological & Fostering Research Center.

Chapter 3

A Conceptual Framework for Involving Parents in Improving Mathematics Learning Outcomes

Changing Mindsets, Conversations and Perceptions

KADINE HAYNES AND LOIS GEORGE

Background

In Jamaica, unsatisfactory mathematics achievement is a long-standing problem at all educational levels (Ministry of Education, 2013). Data from the national assessments done in primary schools, such as the Grade 4 Numeracy Test (GFNT), the Grade 6 Achievement Test (GSAT) and the Primary Exit Profile (PEP), show a general trend of poor performance in mathematics.

The GFNT is completed by all grade 4 students and was created to capture student performance data after four years in primary school. It also provides a profile of individual students for targeted interventions, if needed (Ministry of Education, 2016). This test is comprised of five mathematical strands (Number–Representation and Operation, Measurement, Geometry, Algebra and Statistics) and overall mastery is obtained based on attainment in three combined strands: Number–Representation and Operation, Measurement and Geometry, Algebra and Statistics.

Performance on the test is reported using three levels:

- **Mastery**: The child has mastered the three combinations by obtaining at least 50 per cent in each strand combination and is considered to have successfully attained the requisite mathematical knowledge, skills and competencies.
- **Almost Mastery**: The child has mastered one or two of the three combinations.
- **Non-Mastery**: The child has not mastered any of the three combinations.

The GSAT was a national placement examination sat by all Jamaican Grade 6 students. High school placement was decided either by student choice or by the Ministry of Education, depending on their scores. Mathematics was one of five subject areas assessed by the GSAT. In 2019, the PEP replaced the GSAT. It includes several assessments administered at different points from grades 4 to 6 that assess students' knowledge and twenty-first-century skills such as critical thinking and communication (Ministry of Education Student Assessment Unit, 2017). PEP provides an academic profile of students, their proficient and weak areas, as well as readiness for grade 7, which is the start of high school in Jamaica.

Tables 3.1 and 3.2 present, respectively, Grade 4 Numeracy Test performance data and national average percentage scores for the mathematics component of the GSAT from 2011 to 2018. Table 3.3 presents the 2019 national PEP mathematics performance data of Jamaica.

From table 3.1, over the eight-year period (2011–18), approximately 59.4 per cent of the students who sat the GFNT achieved mastery in mathematics by grade 4. This suggests that slightly over 40 per cent of students were not proficient in either two or three mathematical strands. This has negative implications for subsequent knowledge acquisition and performance in mathematics since students build upon prior knowledge of mathematical concepts and skills as they learn new topics in mathematics (Sidney & Alibali, 2015). If one assumes that generally the 2011 grade 4 cohort would complete the 2013 mathematics GSAT two years later; the 2012 GFNT cohort would sit the 2014 mathematics GSAT, it is not wholly surprising that on average over the eight-year period (2011–18), students' mean GSAT mathematics score is approximately 60 per cent. This average GSAT mathematics score suggests that at the end of grade 6, similar to grade 4, many students still have substantial deficiencies in mathematics. The data in table 3.3 also shows that a large percentage of grade 6 students (59 per cent) are not working at the proficient achievement level in mathematics. These deficiencies at the primary school level may account for the consistently dismal performance at the end of secondary school in the Caribbean Secondary Education Certificate (CSEC) mathematics examinations, administered by the Caribbean Examinations Council (CXC). Table 3.4 shows the percentage of Jamaican students passing the CSEC mathematics examinations from 2009 to 2019 (Ministry of Education Youth & Information – Policy Analysis Research & Statistics Unit, 2020) with an average pass rate of 48.5 per cent over the eleven-year period.

The aforementioned data, as well as concerns expressed by key educational stakeholders in policy documents and newspaper articles (e.g., Benjamin, 2012; Buddo, 2017; Ministry of Education, 2013), suggest that

Table 3.1 Grade 4 Numeracy Performance Data of Jamaica from 2011 to 2018

Year	Sitting	N			%		
		Mastery	Almost Mastery	Non-Mastery	Mastery	Almost Mastery	Non-Mastery
2011	45,741	22,511	13,444	9,786	49.2	29.4	21.4
2012	43,447	23,623	12,872	6,952	54.4	29.6	16.0
2013	42,436	24,760	12,626	5,050	58.3	29.8	11.9
2014	40,981	23,591	11,255	6,135	57.6	27.5	15.0
2015	39,501	25,133	13,004	1,364	63.6	32.9	3.5
2016	37,207	22,263	9,563	5,381	59.8	25.7	14.5
2017	38,017	25,441	9,555	3,021	66.9	25.1	7.9
2018	38,346	25,162	10,340	2,844	65.6	27.0	7.4

Table 3.2 National Average Percentage Scores for GSAT Mathematics Examination from 2011 to 2018

Year	National Average Percentage Score (%)
2011	62.0
2012	63.0
2013	61.0
2014	60.0
2015	56.0
2016	58.0
2017	62.4
2018	61.2

Table 3.3 2019 PEP Mathematics Performance Data of Jamaica

Achievement Levels	Students (%)
Highly Proficient	6
Proficient	35
Developing	52
Beginning	7

strategies to improve mathematics achievement are urgently needed to address the issue of poor mathematics achievement in Jamaica.

Mathematics Improvement Strategies

Several strategies have been recommended by stakeholders in education and adopted by the Ministry of Education to tackle the issue of underachievement in mathematics. These focus mainly on six core areas:

- The teaching and learning experiences within the classroom;
- Equity, which is ensuring that all students have access to high-quality mathematics teaching and learning;
- A standardized curriculum;
- Adequate tools and technology;
- Assessment, which is making sure students receive feedback;
- Professionalism, whereby teachers take responsibility for their own development (Hunter, May 2017, p. 1).

Some of the specific strategies that have been implemented to date include providing "job-embedded professional development for teachers, training of principals and heads of departments to improve the leadership

Table 3.4 CSEC Mathematics Examinations Pass Percentage of Public Schools from 2009 to 2019

Year	No. of Candidates Writing Exam	No. of Candidates Passing Exam	Total Pass Percentage (%)
2009	19,990	8,185	40.9
2010	20,742	9,271	44.7
2011	20,850	8,318	39.9
2012	23,729	8,890	37.5
2013	22,870	9,659	42.2
2014	23,351	12,963	55.5
2015	23,639	14,657	62.0
2016	23,993	11,456	47.7
2017	23,567	11,838	50.2
2018	22,214	12,845	57.8
2019	21,320	11,645	54.6
Average	–	–	48.5

of Mathematics in primary and secondary schools"; funding individuals enrolled in degrees related to mathematics education; implementing an ongoing public education campaign; deploying mathematics coaches across primary and secondary schools; and using mathematics specialist teachers in primary schools (Hunter, May 2017, p. 2).

A close inspection of the core areas and individual strategies for improving mathematics performance across all educational levels reveals that a key factor that considerably affects students' achievement (parents/guardians) is missing from the national discourse to improve mathematics achievement in Jamaican schools. The authors of this chapter recognize that parental involvement in children's general schooling is emphasized in Jamaica's national policy documents on education (e.g., Ministry of Education, 2012). However, because of the long-standing problem relating to poor performance that exists in mathematics, there is a need to focus specifically on parental involvement in children's mathematics education. This chapter aims to fill this gap by presenting a conceptual framework for how parents can be or become involved in their child's mathematics education.

The Link between Mathematics Achievement and Parental Involvement

Parental involvement includes "actions taken by parents on behalf of their children both at school and at home, for example, helping with homework, structuring children's time at home for school-work, communicating with teachers and, volunteering at school" (Flores de Apodaca et al., 2015, p. 36). Following Henderson and Berla (1994, p. x) although the term "parental involvement" is used throughout this chapter, the authors embrace a wider view of involvement beyond parents, since, consistent with the Jamaican context, "In many communities, children are raised by adults who are not their parents, or by older siblings. For many, this provides an extended support system, and those who are responsible for the children and who function effectively as their family deserve recognition" (Henderson & Berla, 1994, p. x).

A parent's involvement in their child's mathematics education takes various forms. Bourne (2019), based on empirical research, reports that in Jamaica, parental involvement in mathematics may typically include paying for extra lessons/tutoring, assisting with homework, providing school supplies and attending meetings or school consultations. These roles are consistent with Nyabuto and Njoroge (2014), who conducted research in Kenya, and Cai et al. (1999) whose research in the United States involved 220 grades 6–8 students who attended a public school in a large urban district and their primary guardians. In Cai et al.'s (1999) research, parental involvement in students' education was categorized as "parent participation in a range of school activities aimed at strengthening the overall school program, and assistance of one's own child at home in informal and in school-directed learning tasks" (p. 3). They further list five parental roles related to the learning of mathematics at home: motivator, resource provider, monitor, mathematics content adviser and mathematics learning counsellor. The mathematics learning counsellor role entails "parents understanding their children's current situation, learning difficulties, potential, needs and demands, and providing appropriate support to help their children overcome learning difficulties" (p. 4).

There is a general consensus that when parents are involved in their child's schooling, academic performance and behaviour are positively influenced (Bourne, 2019; Ministry of Education, 2012; Munroe & Brown, 2011, April; Park & Holloway, 2018). As it relates to mathematics in particular, the findings are mixed as to the impact of parental involvement on children's achievement. In Jamaica and the wider Caribbean, there is a dearth of literature relating to parental involvement and mathematics achievement, and this is reflected in the examination of literature. Bourne et al. (2015) found in a study involving 130 grade 6 students from one primary and one preparatory schools in St. Andrew, Jamaica, that parental involvement was a statistically significant factor which influenced students' academic performance in mathematics component of the 2013 GSAT. In this study, parental involvement was consistent with the five parental roles related to learning mathematics at home put forward by Cai et al. (1999). Conversely, Patall et al. (2008) in a meta-analysis involving twenty-two samples from twenty studies found a negative association between the mathematics achievement of primary school students and parental involvement. The types of involvement were not explicitly outlined, but Patall and her associates concluded that "different types of parent involvement in homework have different relationships to achievement" (p. 1039).

Based on empirical research in Jamaica, Munroe (2009) asserts that although parents want to participate in their children's education, factors such as "strong parental role construction; weak perceived sense of parent efficacy; and moderate perception of invitation from others, which is attributed to frequent general invitation from the school and infrequent specific invitation from the teacher" (p. 12) hinder them from doing so at home and at school. Munroe (2009) further opines that the findings revealed that "an invitation from others, especially teachers, can positively influence parental involvement, provided that the invitation and opportunities for involvement are mindful of the life context of the parent and the learning needs of the child" (p. 13). While this is applicable to all subject areas, it is particularly true for mathematics. Poor performance in mathematics at the school level has resulted in a large percentage of the adult population being unable to engage with basic primary school mathematics, and this may explain why so many parents are reluctant to get closely involved in their children's mathematics learning (Bourne et al., 2015). This stems from their low self-efficacy in being able to assist in any significant way. Other barriers to parental involvement in their children's mathematics learning in Jamaica may be due to past negative school experiences of learning mathematics and work obligations (Munroe & Brown, 2011).

The authors' experiences and anecdotal encounters have revealed that many parents have a fear of mathematics, consider mathematics to be a difficult subject or feel that only a chosen few have the ability to perform well in mathematics. These findings are consistent with international research, which suggests that many parents find it challenging to help their children with mathematics because of their own attitudes, anxieties and underachievement in the subject. In addition, differences between how mathematics is currently taught in schools and parents' mathematical knowledge impact the outcome of their involvement (Peters et al., 2008).

Parental attitudes, beliefs, verbalizations and practices serve as the first and foremost agents through which a child's behaviours, values and attitudes related to school are shaped through a process of academic socialization (Taylor et al., 2004). This suggests that it is plausible that parents who have had negative experiences in learning mathematics (or who hold negative views of mathematics) may transmit these schemas to their children. Taking into account the considerable influence that parents exert on their children, schools should endeavour to assist "those who are not aware of the significance of this influence by training in ways in which such influence can be fostered such as by offering vicarious experiences of educational success" (Cook & Jennings, 2016, p. 98). Hoover-Dempsey and Sandler (1995) also suggest additional approaches that parents can use, including giving "verbal persuasion intended to develop attitudes, behaviours, and efforts consistent with school success" (p. 329).

The authors therefore propose a conceptual framework that seeks to transform negative parental perceptions, conversations and mindsets about learning mathematics and to suggest feasible ways in which positive academic socialization towards mathematics can be fostered. In this regard, the conceptual framework proposed in this chapter is significant because it aims to add another dimension to the limited literature on parental involvement in Jamaica (e.g., Bourne et al., 2015; Cook & Jennings, 2016; Lawson, 2011; Munroe, 2009). Additionally, this chapter seeks to provide a parental involvement model which has several research-based characteristics that align with Jamaica's context and needs (e.g., Carter, 2002). In addition to considering international parental frameworks, the authors sought to base the proposed framework on key aspects of parental involvement highlighted in a report commissioned by the Jamaican Ministry of Education on school effectiveness (Watson Williams, & Hobbs, 2012). In this regard, the proposed model "adopts a philosophy of partnership: shared power and responsibility for children's education" and aims to "build trustful, collaborative relationships and two-way communication with families" (Watson Williams & Hobbs, 2012, p. 36).

In the next section, the authors situate the proposed conceptual framework within an international, well-established framework for parental involvement. The literature review related to parental involvement and children's mathematics learning revealed that there were commonalities internationally and in Jamaica in the roles parents played in relation to parental involvement in mathematics (e.g., Bourne et al., 2015; Cai, Moyer, & Wang, 1999) and parents' general reluctance and challenges in providing content-related assistance in mathematics to their children (e.g., Bourne et al., 2015; Peters et al., 2008). The authors therefore do not feel compelled to "reinvent the wheel" as it relates to parental involvement models but to extend and elaborate on what already exists. In so doing, this chapter is linked to existing literature, yet at the same time extends the scholarly work on which it is based.

The Epstein Model of Parental Involvement

Epstein's model of parental involvement (1985) provides the theoretical underpinning for the conceptual framework for parental involvement put forward later in this chapter. This model was created and extended through extensive empirical research (Epstein, 1985, 2018; Epstein et al., 2002, 2011; Sheldon & Epstein, 2005) by Joyce Epstein, a professor of education at Johns Hopkins University, and associates. It posits that parental involvement focuses on how schools assist *all* families by helping them create home environments that will allow them to support children as students (Epstein, 1987; Epstein & Sanders, 2000; Epstein et al., 2018).

The child is placed at the centre of this model since they are the "main actors in their education, development, and success in school" (Epstein et al., 2002, p. 8). The spheres in the model (see Epstein et al., 2002) represent the main settings in which students learn and grow. On the one hand, the spheres may be conceptualized as pulled tightly together if there is an engagement or activity that occurs cooperatively to impact their knowledge acquisition and development. On the other hand, the spheres may be pushed apart if the family, school and community operate separately (Epstein et al., 2002). The intersecting nature of the spheres underscores the need for individuals within these contexts to work together so that a child can achieve scholastic success. These social interactions may occur at "the institutional level (e.g., when a school invites all families to an event or sends the same communication to all families) and at an individual level (e.g., when a parent and a teacher meet in conference or talk by phone)" (Epstein et al., 2002, p. 8).

The parent involvement model also shows that there are six types of parental involvement, later described by Sheldon and Epstein (2005, p. 197):

1. **Parenting:** Providing family support to foster a better understanding of the child as a student.
2. **Communicating:** Establishing an effective communication system between home and school.
3. **Volunteering:** Recruiting family members to assist with school activities.

4. **Learning at Home**: Creating the avenue for parents to become involved in students' learning while at home through homework, projects and extracurricular activities.
5. **Decision Making**: Including families in school governance, advocacy and decision making through activities such as Parent Teachers Association (PTA).
6. **Collaborating with the Community**: Integrating services from the community to assist with school demands.

The model posits that the school, family and community influence students' learning outcomes and that these elements must work together to do so positively. This has been used in practice and research to improve parental participation (Epstein, 2010) and to create programmes to improve students' learning outcomes (Smith et al., 2011).

As stated earlier, the Jamaican model of parental involvement proposed in this chapter is based on the Epstein model. This model was chosen because it provided several of the components that are applicable to Jamaican societal and educational settings. For example, the home, school and community elements that constitute the three overlapping spheres are key recognizable features of every community in Jamaica. Additionally, the six categories or types of parental involvement are aspects which could be used by schools and parents. It also specified general activities and avenues through which schools could engage parents within the learning community. This provides learning institutions with a starting point from which to organize and structure their plans for fostering parental involvement. In this regard, the model is conveniently flexible and user-friendly. Many Jamaican parents would already be familiar with some of the categories, such as learning at home, whether they have engaged in doing them or not. Another consideration is that the model and its diagrammatic representation make explicit the links between the home, school and community and so may be easier for parents to understand. Finally, the language used in presenting the model makes it accessible to parents from a wide range of backgrounds.

An Alternative Model of Parental Involvement – "Jam Dung Style"

While the Joyce Epstein model of parental involvement can be applied to the Jamaican context in some respects, we suggest two adaptations. Adapting or revisiting a model to suit a current context more closely is standard practice in education. For example, Walker et al. (2005) revised the Hoover-Dempsey and Sandler (1995) model of parental involvement to explore parents' motivation for participating in their child's learning. Based on evaluations undertaken on intervention programmes, Mattingly et al. (2002) suggested the addition of another category, labelled "parent academic education" to Epstein and Dauber's (1995) existing framework.

The authors of this chapter suggest that simplification of the model to focus first on aspects most directly associated with the parent, child and home is in order. From experience, we have found that it is better to suggest to a parent one or two things that are manageable or doable than to bombard them with many things that may be unattainable for several reasons (such as time and financial constraints). Two areas of the model that were deemed by the authors to be appropriate for adapting to align to the Jamaican context more closely are "communication" and "learning at home".

Findings from previous empirical studies relating to parental involvement and students' performance agree that communication and learning at home are important to realizing positive student learning outcomes. Bak-Srednicka (2018) explored parents as partners in the educational process. The sample for this study included a group of eleven pre-service teachers who had direct contact with parents through an eight-week parent-child-teacher enquiry-based assessment. The pre-service teachers individually interviewed parents. Bak-Srednicka (2018) found that there was a marked positive influence on student learning at home, stemming from parental support when parents communicated with their children's teachers. This indicates that there is a positive relationship between these two areas of Epstein's model of parental involvement.

In addition, Wright (2015) stated, based on empirical research conducted in Jamaica, "I realize from the parents' data that there are some statistically significant relationships between two of the five subscales (communicating and learning at home) and students' perceived academic performance" (p. 58). Amatea, Smith-Adcock and Villares (2006) also recognized the relationship between communication and learning at home when they suggested that teachers should communicate information to parents about what they can do at home to encourage and facilitate children's academic development. They added that this may be done by presenting ideas about how to assist students in the successful completion of homework. If appropriately structured, these school-to-home communications could impart information to help parents become more knowledgeable about children's learning activities, their positive qualities and progress, and how parents might help their children learn.

While focusing on two types of parental involvement instead of six, the authors of this chapter suggest a relabeling and redefinition of these categories. The official language of Jamaica is English; however, on a daily basis a Jamaican Creole or Patois is used for communication. To make the model more culturally relevant, therefore, the "communication" label was changed to *"taak tu di tiicha"* (talk to the teacher) and "learning at home" was converted to *"elp di pikni a yaad"* (help the child at home). These categories were used to create the parental involvement in mathematics framework – "Jam Dung Style" depicted in figure 3.1. "Jam Dung Style" (Jamaican Style) is Jamaican Creole "based on the Jamaican context". Table 3.5 presents a translation of the Jamaican Creole words used in the labels into English.

Using the Jamaican dialect allows all parents (regardless of their educational level) to easily understand and relate to this model. Jamaican Creole or dialect is not regarded as prestigious in formal circles (Frank, 2010). The dialect, however, generates interest and adds entertainment to conversations. The findings of a survey conducted on users of "the Dr. Bird Reader", a Jamaican school reader which is based on culturally relevant material for Jamaican school children, supports this view. The results revealed that the users found the text approachable and motivating as students were engaging with material to which they were able to relate. A similar finding was revealed from users of the poetry book, titled *Mi C-YaaN believe iT*, which reported that students who had little interest in poetry began to enjoy the same as they were able to relate to the use of

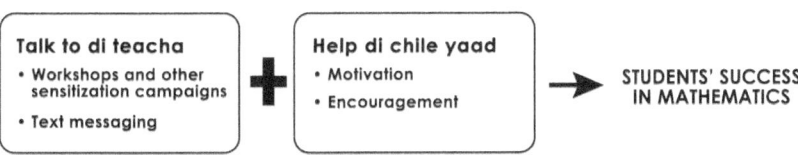

Figure 3.1 Parental involvement conceptual framework Jam Dung Style.

Table 3.5 Translation of Jamaican Creole Terms to English

Jamaican Creole Term	English Translation
Di	The
Teacha	Teacher
Chile	Child
A	At
Yaad	Home

the Jamaican dialect in writing (Frank, 2010). Based on these findings, the authors posit that the use of the Jamaican Creole in the framework will allow parents to see their dialect in written form which will make the material more understandable and relatable. It will also aid in bolstering cultural pride and acceptance of self and nativity as well as broadening educational scope (Devonish & Carpenter, 2007). It is hoped that it will also motivate teachers and other stakeholders to implement and organize programmes around this (uniquely Jamaican) framework. The next two sub-sections discuss the "taak tu di tiicha" (talk to the teacher) and "elp di pikni a yaad" (help the child at yard, i.e., home) categories in more detail. For each category, an application of the category that is appropriate to the Jamaican context is presented, as well as potential limitations.

The "Taak tu di Tiicha" Category

Establishing effective communication between home and school, along with appropriate and accessible mediums of communication, is essential. Communication may be in the form of one-way or two-way exchanges (Graham-Clay, 2005). Typical exchanges between teachers and parents involve a teacher providing information to parents about school activities or student performance/behaviour or engaging in a two-way dialogue about a given child.

"Taak tu di tiicha" is synonymous with communicating with the teacher. The *Miriam Webster* dictionary defines communication in the broad sense as a process by which information is exchanged between individuals through a common system of symbols, signs or behaviour. In this chapter, we go beyond the typical foci of parent-teacher communication to suggest that conversations surrounding student mathematics learning and achievement should be expanded to consider parental attitudes and perceptions and their potential impact on children's mathematics learning. This is in light of the historically poor mathematics performance of scores of Jamaicans and the negative mindsets, as well as attitudes held by many within the population. In support of this focus, Dowker, Sarkar and Looi (2016) state that "it is important to understand children's and adults' attitudes and emotions with regard to Mathematics if we are to remove important barriers to learning and progress in this subject" (p. 1).

Many Jamaican parents are not able to provide effective supplementary mathematics tuition at home and do not have the time to physically visit their children's school on a regular basis. However, they can be instrumental in helping their children to develop a positive perception of and liking for mathematics. For the many parents with negative mindsets towards mathematics, this will require a reshaping of negative views which will help parents to engage in positive discourse with their children about the subject, "model positive attitudes to Mathematics and avoid expressing negative ones to children" (Dowker, Sarkar and Looi, 2016, p. 10).

To accomplish this, we suggest a termly parental workshop on mathematics. This workshop will focus specifically on beginning a conversation with parents relating to their existing attitudes to and perceptions of mathematics and how this may be affecting their children's performance and attitudes. The aim would be to strengthen the perceptions of parents with positive mindsets and begin reshaping negative perceptions towards mathematics into positive ones. In keeping with Amatea, Smith-Adcock and Villares (2006), the workshops could specifically provide sensitization on the benefits of providing support, resources, encouragement and motivation to students in completing their mathematics activities. It would also offer tips for parents on how to provide daily affirmative statements to their children verbally and by having the students write down and repeat these positive statements. Existing literature has confirmed that self-affirmation positively impacts students' attitudes and academic performance (Sherman et al., 2013). The workshop would include speakers who would address the issue of parental perceptions about mathematics.

In one of his famous quotes, Marcus Garvey states, "liberate the minds of men and ultimately you will liberate the bodies of men". It is therefore essential that parents understand that there are several issues which may have led to their poor performance in mathematics; however, this does not prevent them from assisting their child with the subject as there is power in motivation and support (Dowker, Sarkar and Looi, 2016). The workshop would therefore seek to empower parents and the community to change their conversation with children about the subject to a more positive one. Another aspect of the "Taak tu di tiicha" category involves an alternative for face-to-face communication using technology such as the WhatsApp app. This is a free, widely used messaging app which is compatible with all smartphones. It is an efficient mode of communication since it allows the teacher to transmit information quickly and easily to a large number of people.

WhatsApp can be used for communicating in several ways. The mathematics teacher would first have to create a WhatsApp group for communicating with parents. All homework and school activities could be posted within this group. Teachers could send reminders and motivational thoughts to parents, which would assist them in having positive conversations with their children about the subject. Results of quizzes and monthly/unit tests in mathematics could also be communicated to parents, to allow them to track students' performance throughout the term. This would facilitate not only parent-teacher communication but also parent-child discussions about their progress in mathematics. Marshall, Browne and Fongkong-Mungal (2014) suggest that proximal results are beneficial to students' overall achievement. This indicates that progress reports may be used to support and improve students' performance.

The use of cellular telephones as a means of communication is ubiquitous in Jamaica. As of January 2020, there were 3.28 million cellular phone connections, which represented 111 per cent of the total population of the island (Kemp, 2020). In Jamaica, WhatsApp is overwhelmingly the most popular mode for individual mobile communication (Wade, 2020). This app could therefore be used to send motivational thoughts and reminders to parents to encourage and remind their children that mathematics, like any other subject, is manageable through hard work and dedication. Parents are likely to be able to fully take advantage of this approach, since in most homes in Jamaica, children typically leave for school with parents or before parents. Therefore, verbal motivation as previously detailed can be provided and the self-affirmation process can be monitored.

The "Elp di Pikni a Yaad" Category

Gonida and Cortina (2014) assert that homework involvement includes "both quantitative and qualitative aspects ranging from concrete support to more complex guidance (e.g., providing space and materials for doing the homework, developing rules to avoid distractions, tutoring, and doing the homework with the child)" (p. 376). While this definition provides a starting point for our conceptualization of "Elp di pikni a yaad", we further add that it also involves taking the time out to view students' class work, homework and projects while providing the motivation, encouragement and emotional support that children need to excel in mathematics. Parents may or may not be able to assist their children with their class work, homework or projects; however, looking at the work done and making positive comments about this work will indicate to the children that their parents take keen interest in their development. It also highlights the importance of them doing their best in the subject. Homework should be checked to ensure that students complete the task given by their teachers; parents may also ask students to explain to them how they arrived at a particular answer. In doing so, they inspire their children to work at their optimum through positive conversations in relation to the subject, as this will develop their children's confidence in their ability to do mathematics.

Despite the benefits of the approaches mentioned, there are also limitations. One such limitation is the unavailability of the internet in some localities in Jamaica – which may serve as a deterrent for some parents to engage in the WhatsApp group. In January 2020, Jamaica recorded a total of 1.63 million internet users, which represented an internet penetration rate of 55 per cent (Kemp, 2020). Presently, the government of Jamaica is vigorously undertaking a national broadband initiative that aims "to get national broadband throughout the entire Jamaica" (Morris, 2020).

Conclusion

As discussed earlier, mathematics is a subject that many adults and children find challenging. Consequently, parents may find it harder to offer support and help with children's mathematics homework, compared to the subjects like reading and writing, because of their achievement levels in mathematics, and their own attitudes towards the subject (Peters et al., 2008). Also, as children progress across grade levels, parent's efficacy in assisting their children at home in mathematics decreases (Sheldon & Epstein, 2005). Notwithstanding the aforementioned, parents exert considerable influence over their children. Regardless of parents' ability to solve mathematical equations or engage in mathematics-related activities, they all possess the will and skill to motivate and inspire their children to give their best.

Consequently, the authors of this chapter suggested that a key first step in involving parents in children's mathematics education that has not been previously explored in the Jamaican context relates to changing negative parental mindsets, conversations and perceptions about mathematics to the positive. In order to achieve this, we proposed that parents "taak tu di tiicha" and "elp di pikni a yaad" not to just engage in the typical exchanges related to student performance and behaviour but to learn and examine their own faulty beliefs about mathematics and how this may have impacted their children. It is also hoped that from "taakin tu di tiicha", parents would then be able to "elp di pikni a yaad" in relation to improving attitudes towards mathematics. Challenging and advocating for changing any deeply entrenched mindsets is unquestionably difficult. However, considering the immense impact that perceptions, beliefs and attitudes of parents can have on children's learning, motivation and performance, this critical aspect cannot be ignored. Therefore, this chapter aims to bring these to the fore.

Undoubtedly, the suggestions proposed in this conceptual chapter would need to be empirically validated to recommend adoption of the approaches in schools. However, it is hoped that this chapter would instigate the notion that a wider view of parental involvement in general, and in mathematics in particular, can be adopted. Beyond empirical validation, future research could focus on expanding this framework to include other critical components beyond the two presented in this chapter.

References

Amatea, E.S., Smith-Adcock, S., & Villares, E. (2006). From family deficit to family strength: Viewing families' contributions to children's learning from a family resilience perspective. *Professional School Counseling*, 177–89. https://doi.org/10.5330/prsc.9.3.43751461038m4m68

Bak-Srednicka, A. (2018). Foreign language teacher education: School placements as a source of knowledge about parents as partners in the educational process. *International Journal of Progressive Education*, 14(6), 51–60. https://doi.org/10.29329/ijpe.2018.179.4

Benjamin, T. (2012, February 12). Math's BIG problem. *The Gleaner*. http://jamaica-gleaner.com/gleaner/20120212/focus/focus4.html.

Bourne, P.A. (2019). Mathematics performance in Jamaica. *International Journal of History and Scientific Studies*, 1(4), 8–31. https://bit.ly/3d7tqWM

Bourne, P.A., Baxter, D., Pryce, C.S., Francis, C., Davis, A.H., Solan, I., Coleman, O.W., R, I., Brown, O.E., Nelson, S., & Quarrie, V. (2015). The psychology of the Grade Six Achievement Test (GSAT) in Jamaica. *Journal of Psychiatry*, 18(2), 1–12. https://doi.org/10.4172/2378-5756.1000255

Buddo, C. (2017, February 20). Mathematics education: A case for problem-solving. *Jamaica Observer*. http://m.jamaicaobserver.com/columns/Mathematics-education--A-case-for-problem-solving_90150

Cai, J., Moyer, J.C., & Wang, N. (1999). Parental roles in students' learning of mathematics: An exploratory study. *Research in Middle Level Education Quarterly*, 22(3), 1–18.

Carter, S. (2002). *The impact of parent/family involvement of student outcomes: An annotated bibliography of research from the past decade*. Consortium for Appropriate Dispute Resolution in Special Education (CADRE).

Cook, L.D. & Jennings, Z. (2016). Perspectives of Jamaican parents and their secondary school children on the value of education: Effects of selected variables on parents' perspectives. *International Journal of Educational Development*, 50, 90–99. https://doi.org/10.1016/j.ijedudev.2016.05.005

Devonish, H. & Carpenter, K. (2007). Towards full bilingualism in education: The Jamaican bilingual primary education project. *Social and Economic Studies*, 56 (1 & 2), 277–83.

Dowker, A., Sarkar, A., & Looi, C.Y. (2016). Mathematics anxiety: What have we learned in 60 years? *Frontiers in Psychology, 7*(508), 1–16. https://doi.org/10.3389/fpsyg.2016.00508

Epstein, J.L. (1985). Home and school connections in schools of the future: Implications of research on parent involvement. *Peabody Journal of Education, 62*(2), 18–41. https://doi.org/10.1080/01619568509538471

———. (1987). Toward a theory of family-school connections: Teacher practices and parental involvement. In K. Hurrelman, F. Kaufmann, & F. Losel (Eds.), *Social intervention: Potential and constraints* (pp. 121–36). DeGruyter.

———. (2010). School/family/community partnerships: Caring for the children we share. *Phi Delta Kappan, 92*(3), 81–96. https://doi.org/10.1177/003172171009200326

———. (2018). School, family, and community partnerships in teachers' professional work. *Journal of Education for Teaching, 44*(3), 397–406.

Epstein, J.L. & Dauber, S.L. (1995). Effects on students of an interdisciplinary program linking social studies, art, and family volunteers in the middle grades. *The Journal of Early Adolescence, 15*(1), 114–44. https://doi.org/10.1177/0272431695015001007

Epstein, J.L., Galindo, C.L., & Sheldon, S.B. (2011). Levels of leadership: Effects of district and school leaders on the quality of school programs of family and community involvement. *Educational Administration Quarterly, 47*(3), 462–95.

Epstein, J.L. & Sanders, M.G. (2000). Connecting home, school, and community: New directions for social research. In M. Hallinan (Ed.), *Handbook of Sociology of Education* (pp. 285–306). Plenum Press.

Epstein, J.L., Sanders, M.G., Sheldon, S.B., Simon, B.S., Salinas, K.C., Jansorn, N.R., Van Voorhis, F.L., Martin, C.S., Thomas, B.G., Greenfeld, M.D., Hutchins, D.J., & Williams, K.J. (2018). *School, family, and community partnerships: Your handbook for action* (4th ed.). Corwin Press.

Epstein, J.L., Sanders, M.G., Simon, B.S., Salinas, K.C., Jansorn, N.R., & Van Voorhis, F.L. (2002). *School, family, and community partnerships: Your handbook for action* (2nd ed.). Corwin Press.

Flores de Apodaca, R., Gentling, D.G., Steinhaus, J.K., & Rosenberg, E.A. (2015). Parental involvement as a mediator of academic performance among special education middle school students. *School Community Journal, 25*(2), 35–54.

Frank, M. (2010). Introducing Jamaican Creole into the Jamaican educational curriculum. *The English Languages: History, Diaspora, Culture, 1*, 1–12.

Full Mobile Penetration by 2016. (2014, June). *Jamaica Observer*. https://bit.ly/2WLsIKl

Gonida, E.N. & Cortina, K.S. (2014). Parental involvement in homework: Relations with parent and student achievement-related motivational beliefs and achievement. *British Journal of Educational Psychology, 84*(3), 376–96. https://doi.org/10.1111/bjep.12039

Graham-Clay, S. (2005). Communicating with parents: Strategies for teachers. *School Community Journal, 15*(1), 117–29.

Henderson, A.T. & Berla, N. (1994). *A new generation of evidence: The family is critical to student achievement.* ERIC.

Hoover-Dempsey, K.V. & Sandler, H.M. (1995). Parental involvement in children's education: Why does it make a difference? *Teachers College Record*, 97(2), 310–31.

Hunter, J.A. (May 2017). *Ministry continues measures to improve student performance in maths.* Jamaica Information Service. https://jis.gov.jm/ministry-continues-measures-improve-student-performance-maths/

Kemp, S. (2020, February 18). *Digital 2020: Jamaica.* https://bit.ly/3796MMH

Lawson, D.S. (2011, October 2). Many primary-level students lack parental support at school. *Jamaica Observer.* http://www.jamaicaobserver.com/magazines/career/Many-primary-level-students-lack-parental--support-at-school_9813152

Marshall, I.A., Browne, D., & Fongkong-Mungal, C. (2014). Investigating the relationship between parental involvement and student academic achievement in Barbados. *Psychology*, 45(3), 740–63. https://doi.org/10.1037/a0015362

Mattingly, D.J., Prislin, R., McKenzie, T.L., Rodriguez, J.L., & Kayzar, B. (2002). Evaluating evaluations: The case of parent involvement programs. *Review of Educational Research*, 72(4), 549–76. https://doi.org/10.3102/00346543072004549

Ministry of Education. (2012). *National education strategic plan: 2011-2020.* Ministry of Education. https://www.mona.uwi.edu/cop/sites/default/files/Jamaica_NESP_2011-2020.pdf

———. (2013). *National mathematics policy guidelines.* http://bit.ly/2yi7PrI

———. (2016). *2016 general achievement in numeracy (Grade Four Numeracy Test) results by school.* https://moey.gov.jm/grade-four-numeracy-test-results-school

Ministry of Education Student Assessment Unit. (2017). *Primary exit profile- frequently asked questions.* https://moey.gov.jm/sites/default/files/FAQs%20Updated.pdf

Ministry of Education Youth & Information – Policy Analysis Research & Statistics Unit. (2020). *Jamaica Public School Caribbean Secondary Education Certificate Mathematics Examinations Results [Unpublished raw data].*

Morris, A. (2020, October 23). *Gov't working on COVID response technology plan.* https://jis.gov.jm/govt-working-on-covid-response-technology-plan/

Munroe, G.-C. (2009). *Parental involvement in education in Jamaica.* Caribbean CoP. https://www.mona.uwi.edu/cop/library/parental-involvement-education-jamaica-book

Munroe, G.-C. & Brown, J. (2011, April). *Parental involvement in education: Do schools and teachers have a role?* https://urlzs.com/H23Ln

Nyabuto, A.N. & Njoroge, P.M. (2014). Parental involvement on pupils' performance in mathematics in public primary schools in Kenya. *Journal of Educational and Social Research*, 4(1), 19. https://doi.org/10.5901/jesr.2014.v4n1p19

Park, S. & Holloway, S. (2018). Parental involvement in adolescents' education: An examination of the interplay among school factors, parental role construction, and family income. *School Community Journal*, 28(1), 9–36.

Patall, E.A., Cooper, H., & Robinson, J.C. (2008). Parent involvement in homework: A research synthesis. *Review of Educational Research, 78*(4), 1039–101. https://doi.org/10.3102/0034654308325185

Peters, M., Seeds, K., Goldstein, A., & Coleman, N. (2008). *Parental involvement in children's education 2007 (Research Report DCSF-RR034)*. London, England: Department for Children, Schools and Families. https://dera.ioe.ac.uk/8605/1/DCSF-RR034.pdf

Sheldon, S.B. & Epstein, J.L. (2005). Involvement counts: Family and community partnerships and mathematics achievement. *The Journal of Educational Research, 98*(4), 196–207.

Sherman, D.K., Hartson, K.A., Binning, K.R., Purdie-Vaughns, V., Garcia, J., Taborsky-Barba, S., Tomassetti, S., Nussbaum, A.D., & Cohen, G.L. (2013). Deflecting the trajectory and changing the narrative: How self-affirmation affects academic performance and motivation under identity threat. *Journal of Personality and Social Psychology, 104*(4), 591. https://doi.org/10.1037/a0031495

Sidney, P.G. & Alibali, M.W. (2015). Making connections in math: Activating a prior knowledge analogue matters for learning. *Journal of Cognition and Development, 16*(1), 160–85. https://doi.org/10.1080/15248372.2013.792091

Smith, J., Wohlstetter, P., Kuzin, C.A., & De Pedro, K. (2011). Parent involvement in urban charter schools: New strategies for increasing participation. *School Community Journal, 21*(1), 71–94.

Taylor, L.C., Clayton, J.D., & Rowley, S.J. (2004). Academic socialization: Understanding parental influences on children's school-related development in the early years. *Review of General Psychology, 8*(3), 163–78. https://doi.org/10.1037/1089-2680.8.3.163

Wade, F. (2020, January 26). WhatsApp may yet become a big disrupter. *The Gleaner, Jamaica*. https://bit.ly/3m3jPWd

Walker, J.M., Wilkins, A.S., Dallaire, J.R., Sandler, H.M., & Hoover-Dempsey, K.V. (2005). Parental involvement: Model revision through scale development. *The Elementary School Journal, 106*(2), 85–104. https://doi.org/10.1086/499193

Watson Williams, C. & Hobbs, C. (2012). *School effectiveness toolkit*. https://ncel.gov.jm/sites/default/files/school_effectiveness_tool_kit.pdf

Wright, N.K. (2015). *The extent to which parental involvement impacts the academic performance of tenth grade students* [Master's thesis]. The University of the West Indies, School of Education.

Section 2

Chapter 4

Parental Involvement and Academic Success at the Early Childhood Level

DANIELLE CAMPBELL AND ZOYAH KINKEAD-CLARK

Introduction

Data suggest that over 90 per cent of Jamaican children are raised in single-parent households (PIOJ & STATIN, 2014). This is particularly significant because research also notes that this demographic feature places children at an increased risk of being unable to achieve their full developmental outcomes owing to many of the implicit challenges which often come with single parenting (Samms-Vaughan, 2004). Morsy and Rothstein (2015) noted that of all the demographic and socioeconomic indicators of children's childhoods (which are reliable predictors of their developmental outcomes), none are more impactful than the potential effects of single parenting. Because of the challenges faced by many single parents, including reduced financial capabilities, irregular work schedules and increased levels of mental stress, many of them are unable to provide the necessary support needed to help their children strive and thrive in the crucial early years of their lives (Jayakody & Stauffer, 2000; Department for Children, Schools and Families, 2008; Morsy & Rothstein, 2015).

For children (especially those of lower socio-economic backgrounds), the ecological systems surrounding them contribute to the layers of factors that put them at risk of social and academic failure (Smith & Ashiabi, 2007). Similar to their parents, many of these children present with poor cognitive, socio-emotional and psychosocial development, especially when compared to their more affluent counterparts (Smith & Ashiabi, 2007). According to Tucker-Drob and Harden (2012) and Hackman et al. (2014), parents' cognitive functioning is inextricably linked with their children's cognitive development. Stemming from this, parent education levels and parent involvement in their children's schooling are all directly related to their children's academic achievement. It is for these reasons that a number of researchers have sought to understand the other factors which impact parents' involvement in their children's schooling.

The Purpose of This Study

While there have been a number of studies, including that of Shen et al. (2008) and Harris and Goodall (2007) that examined parental involvement and its impact on children's academic performance, few have been conducted in early childhood institutions. Likewise, none have sought to elicit from the parents, their perceptions of how their involvement in their young child's education has implications for their child's academic performance.

With this in mind, the purpose of this study was to explore how parents of basic school children view the importance of their involvement in their children's academic achievement. This research is therefore guided by the research question: How do parents describe the importance of parental involvement in the academic achievement of children at the early childhood level?

Scoping Review of the Literature

In this section we present a brief review of the literature that focuses on the factors which shape parental involvement in schools. We situate this review in Vygotsky's (1978) Sociocultural Theory and Bronfenbrenner's (1979) Ecological Systems Theory that explicate how and why parents and their practices are informed by the systems which exist in the community and wider social space. It must be noted that while reference is made to foundational literature relevant to parental involvement, specific effort was also made to draw on locally derived literature.

Cultural Learning

Lev Vygotsky's (1978) Sociocultural Theory highlights the importance of interaction between a child and an adult on cognitive development and, subsequently, the academic development of children. This interaction is the basis for the development of holistic learning (Puckett & Black, 2005). Vygotsky's (1978) Zone of Proximal Development (ZPD) is rooted in the importance of parental involvement in a child's cognitive and academic development. The ZPD can be defined as the level of concept development that is too difficult for the child to accomplish alone but can be achieved with the help of adults through scaffolding (Puckett & Black, 2005). Scaffolding is the guiding of children as they explore their abilities, provided through the involvement of parents or family members to enhance the implementation of the official and hidden curriculum (any other lessons, values or ideas that have been learnt by a child while enrolled in the formal school setting). With the guidance of an adult and the introduction of dialogue within the first 1,000 days of life and continuously throughout the early years, as well as the scaffolding received at early childhood institutions, children can improve and develop skills that they lack.

Epstein and Daubner's (1989) study conducted in eight inner-city elementary and middle schools in Baltimore, Maryland, found that parents' attitude to parental involvement with children academically or developmentally was related to the school's practice of involving parents. The authors looked at the various elements involved in parental or family involvement and were able to narrow it down to six sub-concepts that were evaluated in their research: parenting, communicating, volunteering, learning in the home, decision making and collaborating with the community. These take into consideration the level of involvement at home and school, with homework and reading assistance. According to Epstein and Daubner (1989), most parents want the school to advise them on how to help their children, essentially, guiding the parental involvement in the child's academic progression, and those parents were also more likely to spend more time with their children. It was also found that parents who had higher education provided more involvement and support in the child's academic development. The overall results of the study indicated that there was a positive relationship between parental involvement and a child's academic success or development. This particular research is of relevance to this study because it lays the foundation for exploring the concepts of parental involvement and academic success, providing the groundwork for identifying the various elements attached to parental involvement and the depth with which it can and ought to be investigated.

Family/Community Involvement

Bronfenbrenner's (1979) Ecological Systems Theory explicates the diverse factors and agencies that shape the developmental outcomes of children. According to Bronfenbrenner, the multiplicity of factors or systems informs the child and provides a basis for what he is expected to do. Bronfenbrenner noted the role of families and communities as cultural institutions which set the foundation for children. For instance, research has been very clear on the link between family/community involvement and children's academic performance.

Communities are often seen as extensions of many Jamaican families. The physical space of home and "yard", especially in multiple family structures, are often not bound by walls: many homes physically and socially extend into the open space of the community. It is certainly for this reason that in Jamaica, communities are powerful players in shaping children's lives (Chamberlain, 2003). Moreover, within the Jamaican society, there are inextricable interlinkages among communities, schools (especially basic schools, which are ultimately community owned and operated institutions) and the persons who oversee these institutions.

Watson Williams (2011), in her examination of family learning in Jamaican families, noted that communities were also powerful transmitters of how parents "parented". In this, she averred, parents (as social beings) transmitted the lessons they learnt from the community to their children. It is important to note that Watson Williams (2011) suggested that much of what parents transmitted was not only inane facts but also an understanding of systems and structures and the dispositions required to navigate them. With regard to schools as one of these social systems, Watson Williams (2011) illuminated the constructs which had implications for how and why parents' involvement in schools benefitted children, and those factors which served as barriers.

Watson Williams (2011), for example, noted that schools often varied in their interpretations of parental involvement, and these differences impacted on how schools sought to facilitate the relationship between home and school. In order to minimize the dissonance between home and school, Watson Williams (2011) noted that initiatives such as supporting communication between teacher and school, the development of programmes to enhance parental involvement, and perhaps more importantly, initiatives to eliminate barriers to parental involvement, were crucial for schools to employ.

The navigation of the structures and systems of the school also emerged from Cole's (2020) mixed study in Jamaica among parents and teachers of children in a grade 1 cohort. Similar to Watson Williams (2011), Cole (2020) also identified variables within the Jamaican culture that affected parental involvement. The parents' level of efficaciousness was found to be a variant of their educational and financial background and whether they could provide the resources for the children to succeed (Cole, 2020).

Cole (2020) found that 50 per cent of parents in the sample said that they were involved in their children's school experience at a moderate level, while others reported it to a lesser extent. However, the parents contradicted the teachers in saying that they were infrequently invited to participate or asked to be involved in daily activities. Younger parents were likely to spend more time with their children and were approached more by teachers to be involved, possibly due to their eagerness to see their child succeed as early as grade 1. According to the teachers' report, parents are involved in their child's academic development and education, which coincided with the parents' report. The study reiterates that parents' involvements improves the interaction between the teacher and the student in a positive way, which aids in the promotion of improvements in the child's educational outcome (p. 8).

Family structure had little impact on the active involvement of parents as reports from teachers and principals showed that there was no visible difference in the level of involvement, whether the child was from a single-parent family or a nuclear family (Cole, 2020). This indicated that they were cognizant of the fact that spending time with the child is important. This importance may not be embedded in academic purposes but is significant for socialization, attachment and other developmental milestones. It is this desire for high-quality interactions with the child and the understanding of its importance that drives the involvement of parents.

Culturally, parents begin to place importance on the value and importance of education from a very early stage. As a result, the high cognitive skills determined in Cole's (2007) study came as a result of the emphasis placed by the parents on academic achievement. Parents want their children to do well at an early stage, with the hope that this success will carry through to further academic achievements. This was consistent with the parent's report that the teachers invited them to be involved and their receptiveness to the invitation, which indicated that both parties were aware of the value placed on parental involvement.

Barriers to Parental Involvement

Cole (2020) in her examination of some of the factors affecting parental involvement revealed that there were several barriers to parental involvement in Jamaica. These included (1) personal barriers, (2) educational barriers, (3) financial barriers and (4) school barriers. Personal barriers include parents' perception of not being able to help their child and thus being more involved in helping their child to succeed. Parents who have convinced themselves that they are unable to help their children may not want to get involved or be as involved as they should to help their child succeed at school. Their low self-efficacy creates a feeling of intimidation to meet or talk with teachers about their child. Cole's findings were also supported by Harris and Goodall (2007) and Epstein and Daubner (1989). In their 2007 study, Harris and Goodall confirmed that the notion of parental involvement is linked to raised academic achievement. They corroborated the fact that the parent's own personal achievement and academic level is a factor in their level of engagement with the child.

Englund et al. (2004) conducted a study using low-income mothers in Minneapolis, Minnesota, on children's early achievement in early elementary school and the longitudinal effects of parental involvement and quality of assistance. They had five hypotheses: (1) parents were involved in their children's school, (2) parents' educational level relates to both their actual behaviour and their expectation of their children, (3) parents quality of instruction prior to school entry has direct effects on children's IQ and achievement in early school, (4) parental expectations have direct effects on parental involvement and (5) parental involvement with the school has direct effects on children's academic achievement.

As it relates to children's IQ and academic performance, Englund et al. (2004) highlighted how the developmental outcome of the first-born child in the family was impacted by involvement of the mother in their schooling. Their study also notes that the extent of the mothers' involvement is contingent on the mother's education, the mother's level of instruction prior to entry to formal schooling, the child's IQ and parental expectations. Englund et al. (2004) looked for indicators of high-quality parental involvement including how much input the parent has given for the desired product (academic achievement) and whether or not the mother provided consistent and developmentally appropriate stimulation for the child from birth through to the age of enrolment, which would then translate into parental involvement with formal education.

The results of Englund et al.'s 2004 study indicate that there is a relationship between the aforementioned variables and children's academic performance in grade 3. In addition, early intervention in the forms of parent interaction and scaffolding for problem solving showed higher educational attainment for children in grades 1 and 3, and these mothers were more involved in their children's school (Englund et al., 2004). Parents who had higher educational expectations tended to have children who performed higher, and those parents were more involved than those who had lower educational expectations, or were nonchalant about their child's academic performance. This corroborates the results determined from the meta-analysis by Fan and Chen (1999). This research was limited to the parent-child interactions based on school activities and did not include interactions with the child at home, which is a key element based on Epstein and Daubner's (1989) indicators.

Methodology

This study employed a qualitative research design, more specifically, a generic approach, where the authors sought to understand the central concept of the attitude towards parental or family involvement and its influence on a young child's academic success. According to Denzin and Lincoln (2005), qualitative methodology is used when the researcher's aim is to capture powerful, thick and vivid descriptions of their co-constructors' beliefs, ideologies and experiences.

Data Collection

Ten parents, two from five basic schools in St. Andrew, Jamaica, were interviewed individually for this study. Questions asked throughout the interviews sought to glean information about the value they placed on parental/family engagement and involvement in their child's academic success. The interview sessions were audio recorded for ease of review and for analysis. The questions for the interview were derived from having read the various studies on parental/family involvement and academic success.

The data was collected over a six-week time frame based on access to the schools and the parents. Principals were briefed on the need to use their schools as part of the research, and how the research, when completed, could benefit them and their output as a school. Upon receipt of a grant of access, permission was sought from parents to participate in the semi-structured interviews. In total, each interview lasted one hour, using twenty-seven open-ended questions.

Recruitment of co-constructors. Using convenience sampling, ten parents, two from each school, volunteered to be interviewed. The parents were selected based on those who were present at the schools during the time it was visited. Parents were approached and asked if they would like to or would be able to participate in the study.

Co-constructors' demographic details. The participants' age ranged from twenty-five to forty-five years old, and both male and female parents were interviewed. Their employment status varied from unemployed to student to educator and accountant. Table 4.1 highlights the demographic data of participants who were quoted in the text. The names, going forward, are pseudonyms chosen by the participants of the research.

Data Analysis Procedures

After the data was collected through audio recordings and field notes, the information was transcribed verbatim and the relevant annotations about attitudes and body language were made. Having transcribed the notes and reading them through, the literature was segmented and coded broadly. Codes were then collapsed to create the themes from the data. During the interview, the concepts being researched were defined so that parents had a better understanding of what they were being asked, and their permission to

Table 4.1 Demographic Data of Participants

Name of Participants (Pseudonym)	Employment Status	Age Range (Years)
Kim	Self-Employed	30–40
Kay	Student	20–30
Ann	Unemployed/Volunteer	20–30
Max	Teacher	35–45
Pat	Unemployed	20–30
Jane	Accountant	35–45
Andy	Property Manager/IT	35–45

be audio recorded was sought. Pseudonyms were given for all interviewees and for the names of the schools.

Findings

The research question that framed the study was the following: How do parents describe the importance of parental involvement in the academic achievement of children at the early childhood level? Guided by this research question, three dominant themes were extricated from the data:

- Academic support (extending school into the home);
- Communication and parent/teacher interaction; and
- Resources (income, knowledge and education).

Academic Support-Extending School into the Home

The findings indicate that parents predominantly assumed parental involvement revolved on academic support. This was particularly noted in the interviews where eight out of ten parents noted that they specifically fulfilled their role of support by being involved in the child's completion of homework. Likewise, parents also saw their role as supporting teachers by extending the learning which takes place in the classroom, in the home. When asked what they believed parental involvement meant, one parent explained:

> Well I understand it means you are involved in your child's school-work and basically everything that has to do with school. (Kim, March 2018)

Interestingly, while most parents understood their role in extending the formal learning of the classroom into the home, three parents did not see the value of the converse, that is, "bringing the home into the classroom". In this regard, three of the parents vocalized their reluctance to participate at school as they did not see it as an important aspect of their child's development. The parents instead waited on the teacher to give directives which they would then act upon. One parent explained her experience with this. She shared that once the teacher explained to her what could be done at home to help her child, she followed the advice. The parent explained:

> "I decided to do something and once I did, I noticed a change". "I have seen extreme improvement and if I was doing it much more, I would be seeing tremendous improvement". (Kay, March 2018)

The findings indicate that parents leaned heavily on their children and on technology to help plan for learning. All but one parent said that she engaged in learning in the home in various ways, ranging from revising the work done during the day to reading to the child, to non-curricula content (e.g., watching developmentally appropriate engaging episodes on YouTube). "I create a classroom for myself and recreate what is done at school" was one parent's explanation of learning in the home (Kay, March 2018).

Another parent explained,

> I use the environment, for example the bus ride to and from school, I see words and ask him about them, or I see things and try to reference it to what he is doing at school. (Ann, March 2018)

Max also explained:

> I use his cues, sometimes he sees things and it triggers a memory and he starts singing a song and I go with it from there. (Max, April 2018)

One parent, Pat, expressed her frustration when her child rebuffed attempts to extend "formal learning in the home". As she explained:

> "taak likl mor sofli to her, I'm too rough at times", (speak to the child in a softer tone because she gets harsh at times) "when I'm helping with her work and I show her one or two times, shi fiil laik shi get it, yu nuh fi aks har agen; so dat get mi likl upset an wen yu aks har agen an shi tel mi fuulishnes, dat get mi mor upset an shi nuo it". ("when I'm helping her with her work and I've shown her once or twice and she thinks she understands it so I shouldn't ask her about it again, and when I ask her later on she responds incorrectly, that gets me upset and she knows that"). (Pat, March 2018)

Revision before an assessment or test administered at the end of the term was limited. However, Pat voiced that she only got the child's book on a

Friday and as such she was unable to review with the child when it was time for an assessment or a test. Three parents spoke specifically of studying words and learning vocabulary when they were referring to revision with their children.

Communication and Parent-Teacher Interaction

Throughout the interviews, the importance of communicating with teachers emerged as a key factor that shaped parents' involvement in the school. In this regard, the parents explained that through frequent and ongoing communication with the teacher, they had a better sense of what was happening in the classroom and what was expected of them. Aligned with this as well is the belief that lack of communication with teachers will also negatively impact on the parents' ability to understand the classroom space and the diverse activities which take place in it. All the parents stated that there was good communication between themselves and their child's teacher; there was open communication between both parties. Parents said they were able to communicate both face-to-face and via technological means, such as texting and instant messaging. One parent mentioned that her child's school was going paperless and would use technology to communicate, thus, forcing parents to stay in touch more so that they are aware of what is happening at school and in their child's academic development. This level of communication between parents and teachers lends to the availability of the teachers to the parents. Parents viewed the teachers of their respective children to be readily available and accessible to them, and as such parents had a good rapport with the teacher, even if they did not visit as often as they ought to.

The parents noted that while they were often at school during drop-off and pick-up times, there were constraints, which limited them from fully immersing themselves in classroom activities beyond this.

Of the ten parents interviewed, three made explicit reference to barriers to parental involvement such as job requirements and their own school duties, which prevented them from communicating with their children's teachers. One parent shared that her inherent disposition of being shy was the reason for her reluctance to communicate with her child's teacher frequently.

Despite noting some of the barriers to their involvement, many of the parents spoke of the "pull factors" which drew them to become more involved in school. In this regard, all the parents viewed their support of school activities as very good. They noted that special school functions such as Jamaica Day, Culture Day and Sports Day were important and provided wonderful opportunities for parents to become involved in the school. One of the parents, Pat, explained:

> "well ... activities ... Sports Day, Jamaica Day, dem Culture Day, anything dem av I am der ..." ("... their Culture Day and anything they have I am there ..."). (Pat, March 2018)

Resources

The findings indicate that a crucial determinant of parental involvement specifically relates to parents' resources, meaning not only financial strength but also parents' access to knowledge about how young children learn and develop. As it pertains to the latter, when asked how the school could help promote their involvement, all the parents stated that they could benefit from workshops geared towards parenting practices and how to better assist their child's overall development. Developing parenting skills was a common concern, as they believed the school could do more to help them develop these skills by having workshops or seminars on the initiative of the PTA, as they indicated a willingness to learn about parenting and handling children at the early childhood level.

As Andy concisely explained:

> we may think we know it all as parents but we have so much more to learn ... there is always room to learn something new. (Andy, March 2018)

Two were more specific about wanting workshops that could help them to assist their children academically.

Parents noted that the resources available to them were limited. They shared that access to support was very important as it was only then that parents could provide better support for their children. Parents who were unemployed noted that financial support would better help them meet their children's needs. Likewise, parents also shared that they would want more access to information on strategies they could use at home to assist their child.

Stemming from this, there was consensus among the parents about the usefulness of parenting workshops dealing with children at various developmental stages. Kim expressed:

> I think it would be very beneficial because we come up on things that you as a parent may never know. (Kim, March 2018)

Andy, concurring with Kim, shared a similar perspective:

> "It is human nature to compare our children, I think if we knew what we were to look for we would stop stressing the children and allow them to progress as they should, or be able to identify if sumn rieli rang wid di chail" (... or be able to identify if something is really wrong with the child"). (Andy, March 2018)

Max said he had prior experience with children of that age group, so he didn't think he would benefit from a workshop of this nature based on his prior experience.

Discussion

This study aimed to explore how parents of basic school children viewed the importance of their involvement in their children's academic achievement. The findings of this study support the view that parental involvement has a positive influence on a young child's academic achievement. The findings also address differences in the interpretation of "parental involvement" and the role of the school in supporting or fostering parents' involvement. As suggested by Barnett and Hustedt (2005), when the Headstart Programme was developed in the United States to improve children's readiness for school, a crucial premise of the programme was that parents were equal partners with the teachers in their child's educational development. The findings of this study also note that parents believe that when they play an active role in their children's education, it allows them to have insight into their children's developmental needs, and how as parents, they can better support these needs.

As suggested by Harris and Goodall (2007) and Epstein and Daubner (1989), parents play a crucial role in transmitting knowledge to their children. Parents in this study were aware of this role and positioned it as an essential aspect of their parenting. This study also noted that parents described the importance of parental involvement as being a valuable and influential platform to impart and develop knowledge and set the foundation for their child's learning and development. Parents were aware of the benefits their involvement could have on their child's academic development. They were able to identify that if they were involved with their child and maintained a relationship with the teacher and the school, their child's potential to succeed academically would increase. This was reiterated by one of the parents who participated in the study when she explained that she designed a classroom space at home to help her child.

Interestingly, as explained by Tucker-Drob and Harden (2012), research has noted that one of the ways parents play an important role in children's overall development is by providing activities and experiences which cognitively and affectively stimulate their children. This study also identified that parents often look to teachers as a means to identify what many of these stimulating activities should be.

The level of importance in this study is dependent on what parents understand to be included in the concept of parental involvement. Many parents viewed involvement as helping with the child's homework, occasionally visiting with the teacher and asking how the child is doing, making contributions to novelty days such as Jamaica Day or Career Day and volunteering. Only two of the parents interviewed specifically stated that they offered their services at school regardless of what was happening; all aspects of involvement are needed as best as the parent can offer it.

An important finding of this study was the need for parent support through parenting education. Similar to findings of Epstein and Daubner (1989) and Watson Williams (2011), our findings indicated that parents recognized the value of parent education. We identified that parents believed they would be better able to assist their child if they had greater knowledge of children and how they learn. The parents felt that their involvement could be improved by workshops that facilitated parenting seminars, an indication that parents felt there was still more that they could do to help their children but were not equipped to do so. PTA meetings are an appropriate medium to impart parenting tips to parents on how to become more involved in their children's development. It is via these meetings that professionals can promote learning in the home, which extends beyond the homework that is given.

Parents' employment status also affects their level of involvement. It is sometimes difficult for employed parents to find time to become involved in their child's academic development and exercise some of the elements that constitute parental involvement, such as volunteering or learning in the home. Unemployment, on the other hand, can fuel frustration in the parent – which causes them to become impatient and uninterested in the child's academic development. This was mentioned by a parent who is currently unemployed and noted that she sometimes became overly frustrated while helping her child at home, because of her own personal frustrations with worrying about financially supporting herself and her child.

The inability to provide resources to promote development due to financial constraints is another crucial barrier. Some parents are also in denial about the academic abilities of their children. Having a child with a learning disability is taboo in some communities, especially in some inner-city communities in Jamaica. This denial is fed by the lack of financial resources, and these resources are needed to support a child with a disability better, which in turn can help that child to succeed. It is this denial that limits parental involvement because they are unaware of how to help the child at the current developmental level.

Recommendations for Future Research

Based on the research conducted, we provide a short list of recommendations that could be undertaken to expand on the findings:

- Conduct a longitudinal study to determine whether an intervention programme (e.g., literacy programmes, parenting programmes) has prolonged effect on parents and how it influences the child's performance.
- Change the sampling method to include more fathers and other types of early childhood development programmes.
- Conduct a longitudinal study in Jamaica to find out if the parent's level of education influences the value placed on parental involvement.
- Collaborate with other researchers in the Caribbean to diversify the sample and compare the value placed on parental involvement within the region.

Conclusion

This research aimed to find out the perceptions of parents on the role of parental involvement in children's academic achievement at the basic school level. The review of previous research shows that there is a relationship between parental involvement and academic achievement, but there is limited knowledge about involvement at the beginning stages of formal education, that is, the basic school or pre-school level. The results indicate that there is value placed on parental involvement and the part it plays in a child's academic development. This value is dependent on their understanding of what parental involvement entails, their level of education and how well they think they can help the child. Unfortunately, as identified in the results, parents have to be encouraged and told how to be involved with their children for it to impact the child's academic development (Epstein & Daubner, 1989). "Some parents are not equipped for their role as caregivers and to provide a supporting environment for the development of their children" (PIOJ, 2009, p. 81). With this in mind, the relevant steps can be taken to promote involvement in schools as best as possible, inclusive of seminars and workshops.

As a part of achieving Goal 1 of Vision 2030 – "Jamaicans are empowered to achieve their full potential"; where education is concerned, parental involvement will have to be one aspect that they aim to improve, as it sets the foundation for the development of the child and aids and promotes early intervention where necessary so that the child is able to function optimally. As the results have shown, once there is an improvement in parental involvement, teachers note an improvement in student performance.

This study aimed to identify the gap in the local research and make recommendations to bridge the gap. The proposed interventions should not be limited to parents, as family involvement is equally important in Jamaican culture: the proposed interventions should also extend to other trusted persons within the child's microsystem.

References

Barnett, W.S. & Hustedt, J.T. (2005). Head start's lasting benefits. *Infants and Young Children,* 18(1), 16–24.

Bronfenbrenner, U. (1979). *The ecology of human development: Experiments by nature and design.* Harvard University Press.

Chamberlain, M. (2003). Rethinking Caribbean families: Extending the links. *Community, Work & Family,* 6(1), 63–76.

Cole, S.M. (2007). *An investigation into the relationship between parental involvement and the social and cognitive skills of first graders.* [Unpublished master's thesis]. The University of the West Indies, Mona.

———. (2020). Contextualising parental involvement at the elementary level in Jamaica. *International Journal of Early Years Education.* doi:10.1080/09669760.2020.1777844; https://doi.org/10.1080/09669760.2020.1777844

Denzin, N.K. & Lincoln, Y.S. (2005). Introduction: The discipline and practice of qualitative research. In N.K. Denzin & Y.S. Lincoln (Eds.), *The Sage handbook of qualitative research* (2nd ed., pp.1–32). Sage Publications.

Department for Children, Schools and Families. (2008). The impact of parental involvement on children's education. http://www.thecustodyminefield.com/research/dcsf_parental_involvement.pdf

Englund, M.M., Luckner, A.E., Whaley, G.J.L., & Egeland, B. (2004). Children's achievement in early elementary school: Longitudinal effects of parental involvement, expectations and quality of assistance. *Journal of Educational Psychology,* 96(4), 723–30. https://doi.org/10.1037/0022-0663.96.4.723

Epstein, J. & Daubner, S. (1989). Parent attitudes and practices of parent involvement in inner-city elementary and middle schools (Report No. 33, pp. 1–29). *Centre for Research on Elementary and Middle Schools.* http://files.eric.ed.gov/fulltext/ED314152.pdf

Fan, X. & Chen, M. (1999). *Parental involvement and students' academic achievement: A meta-analysis.* http://files.eric.ed.gov/fulltext/ED430048.pdf

Hackman, D.A., Betancourt, L.M., Gallop, R., Romer, D., Brodsky, N.L., Hurt, H., & Farah, M.J. (2014). Mapping the trajectory of socioeconomic disparity in working memory: Parental and neighborhood factors. *Child development, 85*(4), 1433–45.

Harris, A. & Goodall, J. (2007). *Engaging parents in raising achievement: Do parents know they matter?* http://dera.ioe.ac.uk/6639/1/DCSF-RW004.pdf

Jayakody, R. & Stauffer, D. (2000). Mental health problems among single mothers: Implications for work and welfare reform. *Journal of Social Issues, 56*(4), 617–34.

Morsy, L. & Rothstein, R. (2015). Five social disadvantages that depress student performance: Why schools alone can't close achievement gaps. Report. *Economic Policy Institute.*

Planning Institute of Jamaica [PIOJ]. (2009). *Vision 2030 Jamaica, National Development Plan* (Draft). http://jis.gov.jm/media/Vision-2030-Jamaica-Draft-Integrated-National-Development-PlanJanuary2009.pdf

Planning Institute of Jamaica [PIOJ] and the Statistical Institute of Jamaica [STATIN]. (2014). Jamaica survey of living conditions, 2012. PIOJ and STATIN.

Puckett, M.B. & Black, J.K. (2005). *The young child: Development from pre-birth through age eight* (4th ed.). Pearson.

Tucker-Drob, E.M. & Harden, K.P. (2012). Early childhood cognitive development and parental cognitive stimulation: Evidence for reciprocal gene–environment transactions. *Developmental Science, 15*(2), 250–59.

Samms-Vaughan, M. (2004). *The Jamaican pre-school child: The status of early childhood development in Jamaica.* University of the West Indies.

Shen, J., Washington, A.L., Palmer, L.B., & Xia, J. (2008). Effects of traditional and nontraditional forms of parental involvement on school-level achievement outcomes: An HLM Study using SASS 2007–2008. *The Journal of Educational Research, 107,* 326–37. https://www.doi.org/10.1080/00220671.2013.823368

Smith, D.E. & Ashiabi, G.S. (2007). Poverty and child outcomes: A focus on Jamaican youth. *Adolescence, 42*(168), 837–59.

Vygotsky, L. (1978). Interaction between learning and development. *Readings on the Development of Children, 23* (3), 34–41.

Watson Williams, C. (2011). Challenges to achieving generational transformation in Jamaica through parental involvement in children's education. *Caribbean Journal of Education, 33*(1), 61–78.

Chapter 5

Exploring the Impact of Parental Involvement on the Education of Students

The Case of Students with Two Types of Disabilities

SUSAN ANDERSON AND SHARLINE COLE

Introduction

The authors' combined experience working in Deaf Education, Guidance and Counselling, School Management, Educational Psychology and Special Education gave us insights into why school personnel sometimes do not accommodate parents and at times blame parents for not being involved in their children's education. School administrators sometimes do not understand the challenges parents face, and some parents sometimes feel overwhelmed by what they are told is expected of them. This contributes to some parents being reluctant to visit and volunteer. Parents complain that some schools stereotype the children and their parents, and this is reflected in the low expectations for students' academic success. Parents who believe that they are unfairly treated may not want to be involved.

Our interface with students who appeared to need more than what was being offered in the regular education system, with limited resources, was the cause of concern. Results from Cole's (2013) mixed-methods doctoral thesis, "An Investigation into the Impact of Parental Involvement on the Cognitive and Social Skills of Grade One Students in Jamaica", revealed that parental involvement is a critical element of success in all school types, more so in schools that cater to students with disabilities. In addition, anecdotal evidence shared by parents, teachers, principals and empirical data propelled us to explore parental involvement in two schools for the deaf and one school for the blind.

Many researchers have unearthed a preponderance of the evidence that parental involvement is critical to the educational success of students (Bempechat, 1992; Chen, 2020; Fan & Chen, 2001; Park, Stone, & Holloway, 2017; Sheldon & Epstein, 2005). McWayne and Marissa (2004) report that "parental involvement has been repeatedly identified as a protective factor for young, low-income children's positive development" (para. 1). Henderson and Mapp in Razalli et al. (2015) state that

> studies have shown students whose parents are actively involved in their education have obtained excellent results, passed the exam, good attendance in school, good social skills and behavior, adapted themselves well at school and managed to finish school. (p. 106)

Parental participation is important in the curriculum delivery at the early childhood level (Davies, 2008) and influences the cognitive development of students (Munroe, 2009; Ricketts & Anderson, 2009; Samms-Vaughan, 2004, 2008; Springer, 2004). The roles parents play in the education of their children are multifaceted, notwithstanding all the other challenges they face in the daily conduct of their lives. The participation of parents in special education is critical because children with disabilities need even more parental support and advocacy than other children in general education.

The Jamaica Disabilities Act of 2014 (which reflects international standards) states that individuals with disabilities should have equal access to privileges, interests, benefits and treatments that ensure they are not discriminated against and have equal access to education and training (Government of Jamaica, 2014). This means that educational institutions must provide an environment that caters to the individual needs of students with disabilities. In enforcing the Disabilities Act, parents should be active participants in their children's education, making the necessary adjustments to accommodate them in the Least Restrictive Environment (LRE). The LRE is "a system that places students in a normal and educational setting as possible whilst still meeting the special academic, social and physical needs" (Anderson, 2014, p. 60). According to the National Centre for Learning Disabilities (2004) in the Individuals with Disabilities Education Act (IDEA) of 2004, parental involvement is important in the development of the Individual Educational Plan (IEP) for students. Parents who are involved in the education of their children with special needs are more likely to have positive relationships with the schools and are more likely to feel empowered in influencing their children's success.

There is limited information in Jamaica on the impact of parental involvement in special education, which supports the assertion by Fan and Chen (2001) that there is limited empirical research on parental involvement and the outcome of students with disabilities. Anderson (2000) highlights the importance of encouraging parents who have children with disabilities to be involved in their children's education in order to ensure future success. However, the cost of special education services can be very expensive, which places parents from low socio-economic backgrounds at a considerable disadvantage. In addition, some parents may accept the treatment meted out to them by schools and the entities that offer services, because they do not have the requisite knowledge on how to help their children in accessing the required services. As a result, some may subject themselves and their children to treatment associated with the stereotypes, attitudes, beliefs and behaviours of people entrusted with the responsibility of providing support.

This research proposed to explore the impact of parental involvement in the education of students with two types of disabilities. The information from principals and teachers provided answers for the following research questions:

1. How are parents involved in the education of their children with disabilities?
2. What are the perspectives of school personnel on parental involvement in special education?
3. What accounts for parents' involvement or non-involvement in the education of their children with disabilities?

Parental Involvement in Special Education

Fan and Chen (2001) defined parental involvement as the different parenting behaviours and practices that influence children's academic outcomes. Parents are involved through communicating with their children's school, participating in school activities and ensuring that they provide adequate supervision for homework, for example. Additionally, Jeynes (2007) defines parental involvement as "parental participation in the educational process of their children" (p. 88). "Parental involvement is not only a partnership between teachers and parents, it should also include the school principal, it is essentially a partnership between parents and schools" (El Shourbagi, 2017, p. 136).

Theoretical Framework

Overlapping Spheres of Influence

Epstein's (2001) model of parental involvement explains the development and learning process of children through overlapping spheres of influence.

The partnership and collaboration between the family, school and community influence students' academic and psycho-social outcomes. The six types of parental involvement are parenting, volunteering, communicating, learning at home, decision making and collaborating with the community. Parenting includes creating a home environment that facilitates children's academic development. Parents participate in training and get involved in support programmes that are beneficial to children's overall development.

Effective communication is a two-way process that is critical to school and home collaboration. Schools communicate with parents through different modes about students' progress and the different school programmes. In addition, parents communicate with schools about their children's needs. It is expected that the school should meet the parents and use the most appropriate methods to communicate with families. Volunteerism is beneficial to parents, students and schools. Through volunteerism the schools are able to partner with parents as they assist the school or their children's teacher(s).

Schools can help parents to encourage learning at home by providing them with the necessary approaches and strategies they can utilize at home in helping their children with homework and other school-related matters. Being a part of the decision-making process empowers parents to become parent-leaders, active members of the parent-teacher association and provides them with a voice to express their concerns about what is good for their children's educational growth (Epstein, 2001). Whenever parents are involved in the decision-making process, they develop positive attitudes towards the school (Epstein et al., 2002).

Parental Involvement Model

Hoover-Dempsey and Sandler's Model of Parental Involvement suggests that parents become involved because they see it as their responsibility to secure their children's well-being and they have the necessary knowledge and skills to help them succeed. In addition, parental involvement is encouraged when parents are motivated because they believe that they have positive experiences with the school, with the teachers and in their ability to help (Hoover-Dempsey & Sandler, 1995; Hoover-Dempsey, Walker, & Sandler, 2005). Parents who believe that it is their role to help their children succeed and who have opportunities for involvement provided by the school are more likely to get involved (National Academies of Sciences, Engineering, and Medicine, 2016). Parents' ability to help is influenced by their level of efficacy, which contributes to them making "positive decisions about active engagement in their child's education; further they are likely to persist in the face of challenges or obstacles and work their way through difficulties to successful outcomes" (Hoover-Dempsey, Walker, & Sandler, 2005, p. 109). Parents who are efficacious in helping their children are more likely to offer consistent supervision.

Concurring with Epstein and Van Voorhis (2001), Hoover-Dempsey, Walker and Sandler (2005) state that parents develop a sense of well-being when they are invited by their children's teachers to be involved. This involvement helps parents to feel valued and build a sense of partnership between themselves and the teachers. Razalli et al. (2015) assert that "the involvement of parents in the IEP construction raised by the Epstein model is capable of delivering success in the achievement of pupils with special needs" (p. 109). However, from the perspective of the National Quality Framework for Early Childhood Education (n. d.), it is difficult to appeal to parents to be involved in the decision-making process. In addition, parents may not accept that their children have disabilities, and this denial could affect their level of involvement.

Parental Involvement in Children with Disabilities

In developing countries, parental involvement with children who have disabilities is often unstructured (Balasundaram, 1995). UNESCO (2006) in Balli (2016) reports that children with disabilities are often excluded from the benefits provided by the education system. With the passing of the Disability Act in Jamaica in 2014 persons with disabilities should have equal access to education and other services, such as physical access to buildings, appropriate transportation and accessing social services that they would not otherwise obtain because of stereotyping, prejudice and discrimination (Anderson, 2014). The IDEA of 2004 emphasizes the importance of parental involvement in special education, where parents are fully involved in the development of the IEP. An IEP is a plan developed by a team with the input of teachers, parents and children to ensure that children who are identified with disabilities receive specialized instructions and the related services that support children's learning. Brown (2005) asserts that participation in the IEP improves the involvement of parents in the education of their children with special needs.

Collaboration between the family and the school is important in the development of students with disabilities (Bowe, 2005; Morrisette & Morrisette, 1999; O'Shea & O'Shea, 2001; El Shourbagi, 2017). There should be communication between schools and parents about children's needs and the development of programmes that facilitate effective learning

(Gibb-Brown, 2005; IDEA, 2004). According to Anderson (2000) "every category of disability requires the full support of the family as the family is important in early childhood intervention" (p. 27). Afolabi's (2014) critical review of parental involvement in learners with special educational needs points out that students' learning is enhanced when parents are actively engaged in their children's learning outside of school and this contributes to improvement in learning outcomes. Balli (2016) agrees that parental engagement is critical in the education of children with special needs. However, parents of children with disabilities have lower levels of involvement (El Shourbagi, 2017). Hoover-Dempsey and Sandler (1995, 1997) assert that parents who believe that the education of their children is their role and responsibility in association with the school are more likely to be involved.

Parental involvement is critical to the cognitive and social development of students with disabilities because students (in particular those who are blind or deaf) may have challenges working at the pace of those without disabilities and in an environment that is restrictive (Allen & Schwartz, 2001). An environment that is restrictive is a space that does not accommodate the movement of persons who rely on a wheelchair, walker and cane and impedes communication via braille or sign language. Restrictions occur not only at school but also at home, because feedback to some children from family members and friends is not provided (Allen & Schwartz, 2001). There is an association between parents who are uninvolved and their children's socio-emotional development (Hetherington & Parke, 1999). Desforges and Abouchaar (2003) report that children of uninvolved parents are socially immature and irresponsible and their attachment to family members is somewhat disorganized, while children of involved parents are more resilient, more tolerant and exhibit fewer behavioural problems.

Factors Impacting Parental Involvement

In their exploratory model on barriers to parental involvement, Hornby and Lafaele (2011) identified parent-related factors, child-related factors and parent/teacher-related factors. The parent-related barriers include parent and family factors, parents' belief about parental involvement, parents' current life context, parents' perceptions of invitation to be involved and parents' social class and gender. The child-related factors include the age of the child and their exceptionalities and behavioural problems. The parent/teacher factors include differing agendas, attitudes displayed, language used and economic issues. Parents are more likely to be involved when they believe that the way they raise their children impacts their development and their academic outcome. Consistent with research conducted by Hoover-Dempsey and Sandler (1997) on parents' role construction, how parents view their role influences their involvement. Some parents believe that their role is to take their children to school, and it is the school's responsibility to take over the education of their children (Hornby & Lafaele, 2011). Additionally, parents who believe that they can help their children to succeed will influence their involvement. Dollahite (2004) reports that fathers experience significant challenges when raising and being involved with their children with special needs because of the unique needs of the children. Fathers are likely to face more challenges than mothers because they tend to spend less time interacting, communicating and playing with their young children. This is important for children with disabilities because the interactions impact language development, play, social-emotional development and their ability to purposefully explore objects.

The family structure affects the level of parental involvement. This is evident where parents are working, as it limits the time spent with their children. In addition, family discord which may contribute to separation and divorce, resulting in an increase in single parenting (Hornby & Lafaele, 2011), could also negatively influence parental involvement.

The educational level of parents also affects their involvement. Boonk et al. (2018) conclude (based on various reviews of research) that "higher educated mothers are in general more successful in their involvement activities compared to lower educated mothers" (p. 36). Parents with higher levels of education are more likely to be involved, are more efficacious and are more likely to participate in the decision-making process of their children's education (Hoover-Dempsey, Walker, & Sandler, 2005; Hornby & Lafaele, 2011; Razalli et al., 2015). El Shourbagi (2017) made reference to a number of school-related barriers which tend to have a chilling effect on parental involvement. Some parents may feel intimidated by school personnel; others may feel that their opinions are not taken into consideration when decisions are being made about their children's education. In addition, some parents feel that when meetings are being scheduled, enough consideration is not given to setting meeting times that would be convenient to them (El Shourbagi, 2017).

Research Method

Cole (2013) previously conducted mixed-methods research that examined parental involvement and its impact on the cognitive and social skills of grade students attending schools that provide general and special education, in which the initial findings suggested that a more in-depth look into students with disabilities and how they navigate the system was necessary. Cole's (2013) research found that the education system (as configured at that time) was not necessarily designed for students with disabilities. More importantly, it revealed that both mothers and fathers spoke about their involvement with their children (Cole, 2013). This suggested the need for a more in-depth understanding from the stakeholders' perspectives. Therefore, a qualitative case study was employed to conduct the current research, utilizing the rich data collected from principals, teachers and parents of schools with two types of disabilities in understanding the impact parents have on their children's education.

Qualitative studies seek to explore, understand and explain participants' experiences, perspectives, beliefs and values about a particular phenomenon (Bogdan & Biklen, 2003; Smit, 2010). Researching the influence of parental involvement qualitatively provides richness and depth in understanding. Additionally, the qualitative approach (unlike the quantitative approach) can provide reasons for particular results.

Using the case study approach provides a holistic and in-depth examination of parental involvement from the perspectives of parents, teachers, principals, guidance counsellors and special education specialists. Cozby and Bates (2012) state that "case studies are valuable in informing us of conditions that are rare and thus providing unique data of some psychological phenomenon" (p. 122). This applies especially to students attending special-needs schools that cater to the auditory and visually impaired.

The data were collected through the use of interviews. Participants shared their experiences of and approaches to parental involvement of students who are blind or deaf. Interviews are one of the most important sources of case study information, because during an interview clarifications can be obtained and participants can provide their perspectives on the area of interest (Qu & Dumay, 2011). For the purpose of this research, semi-structured open-ended interviews were used. In an open-ended interview, the researcher can ask for the informant's opinion on events or facts. This can corroborate previously gathered data (Tellis, 1997).

A purposive sample was used to select the three schools with two types of disabilities based on their characteristics. The rural school accommodated students who boarded on campus and those who travelled daily, while the urban school only accommodated students who commuted daily. The school for the blind accommodated both boarding and commuting students.

Three principals, three teachers and six parents were interviewed. For the purpose of anonymity and easy identification pseudonyms were used. The principals were Ms Love (urban school for the deaf), Ms Green (rural school for the deaf) and Mr Black (school for the blind), while the teachers were Ms Minot (urban school for the deaf), Mrs Biggs (rural school for the deaf) and Mrs Brown (school for the blind). The parents were Ms Black and Ms White (urban school for the deaf), Ms Tiff and Mr George (rural school for the deaf) and Ms Jenn and Mr Barrett (school for the blind).

Using different cases ensured that the data were collected from multiple sources, which enhanced the consistency of the research. Additionally, member checking was also done to confirm transcriptions, and triangulation was employed. Triangulation is "the idea that looking at something from multiple points of view improves accuracy" (Neuman, 2006, p. 149). The triangulation methods were in-depth semi-structured interviews and focus group discussions with the participants that contributed to the accuracy of the findings.

Findings

Parental Involvement in the Cognitive and Social Outcomes of Children with Disabilities

It was heart-warming to engage with the parents as they shared about their involvement in the school life of their children. What was even more encouraging was the involvement of fathers, since the general consensus locally is that fathers (especially of children with disabilities) tend to avoid such participation. The fathers interviewed were willing to learn about their children and understand how best to help.

Parents revealed that their involvement in their children's school life took the form of volunteering in activities such as parent meetings organized by the school, meeting their children's friends and getting to know them, as well as regular visits to the school. They commented on the other activities they engaged in such as homework facilitation (which requires reading to the children), singing songs and playing with them (even when there are communication challenges like the use of sign language). Parents also spoke about keeping a positive attitude in the face of their own depression (which can sometimes accompany the realities of raising a child with a disability).

As we engaged parents from the three schools, they disclosed that not only did they participate in school life, but they actively followed through at home, as benefitting from occasional training arranged by the schools empowered them to continue the behaviour at home. It was evident that these parents were devoted to their children and this enhanced positive attachment with them. Ms Jen (whose child attends the school for the blind) said, "I am trying, I am trying my best because I did not have the support when I was younger, probably if my mother found out about this school shi wud sen mi (send me)".

In the main, the parents reported that they would like their children to achieve more than they did and as such are motivated to be more proactive in seeing to their well-being – regardless of ability. Miss Black, a proud mother, disclosed the following as she beamed with pride about her daughter, who is deaf:

> For me, the way I see Ella now, she can become a doctor or a teacher. She is very helpful, she is very loving, if she sees a little baby, she would want to help the baby ... she knows when the biebi ungri, shi mix fiidin far di biebi (she knows when the baby is hungry, she mixes feeding for the baby), she makes sure the baby is clean, she is sensible. From ever since, they told me to be careful about what you are doing around Ella, because you might think she doesn't understand, she understands.

The parents argued that those parents who fail to see the light at the end of the tunnel sometimes do not know what to do, so they give up too easily. According to these parents, the schools act as a source of strength, facilitating their involvement. Without this they would be at a loss, especially for those children boarding at the institutions. Parents were allowed to visit, and the principals encouraged this by being open and accommodating them as "partners". They were taught coping skills and were encouraged to express themselves freely. Parents spoke positively about teachers who knew them by name and treated them with respect. These teachers had their telephone numbers and sometimes called them to keep the communication flowing. They encouraged them as parents to call when necessary. This made them feel a sense of belonging. Mr George, whose son attends the rural school for the deaf, reported:

> When I first come up here it was one of the most nervous day[s] of my life but Miss Bev, I took Miss Bev's number and would call Miss Bev and then I start[ed] talking to Miss Madden and then after visiting the school and si im plieying an im api, trus mi (see him playing and him happy, trust me) the environment, everyone, I like up here, is wonderful.

Commenting on the cognitive skills of students in special schools, Mrs Biggs (the teacher from the rural school for the deaf) shared enthusiastically about her "special" parents, those she could rely on to work with their children. She spoke glowingly of the father of one student:

> Daniel is doing well at school as a result of his family support. His father visits regularly and can't wait for weekends and holidays to pick up his son; he is better with sign language than the other parents and does not miss meetings put on by the school.

Ms Minot (a teacher from the urban school for the deaf) was equally expressive and corroborated Mrs Biggs' report:

> It's a well-known fact that children who do have parents that can communicate with them perform better and it shows I think not only at this level, practically at every level. Those parents that communicate with children and have a kind [of] a rapport with them ... for example, if you come home and you ask how is your day – that kind a thing – the children do, generally, perform.

Ms Love, the principal from the urban school for the deaf, spoke about a student who could do much better if the parent would use sign language at home. She stated, "one of those kids that would benefit more and would perform much better if her mother was fluent in sign language, because I'm presuming that at home she would be able to communicate using sign language". Parents' proficiency in sign language is an important predictor of success for students who are deaf. If their first language or communication at home is not sign language, they will experience communication barriers and are more likely to experience difficulties at school.

Perspectives of School Personnel on Parental Involvement in Special Education

Principals and teachers in this study considered themselves to be custodians of their children with special needs. They believed that active parental involvement is the hallmark of every successful school and as such they formally encouraged parental participation during registration and throughout other events/activities in all aspects of the school. The schools had policies (written or understood) on parental involvement that sought to engage parents in the tripartite relationship, where teachers (schools), parents and students are actively engaged in the education of students. Ms. Green (principal from the rural school for the deaf) reported that her school has a parental involvement policy that is informed by the Ministry of Education. She further said, "we exercise an open door policy where parents are encouraged to visit the child's class where they feel free to obtain information on their child's performance".

Parental and family empowerment is critical to the positive development of students, more so with parents who have children with special needs. The schools seek to provide parents and families with the appropriate information that will benefit their children and provide ongoing training and support to families. All the principals and teachers interviewed were in agreement that parents who have the requisite knowledge are in a much better position to help their children. In addition, they have to consider the context of the parents (socio-economic background, distance from school and parents with disabilities themselves) and provide the necessary resources for them to attend the sessions. All three schools have ongoing seminars for parents on understanding and working with their children. The principal and teacher from the school for the blind reported that sometimes the parents were provided with bus fare and lunch to encourage attendance. The principal and teacher believe that because of the challenges parents may have, they should continue to educate them about the different needs such as helping them to navigate the physical space and to provide them with coping strategies. Examples of coping strategies taught to parents are deep breathing and positive thinking. Ms Brown (the teacher from the school for the blind) reported that

> Parents are given the adequate information so they will be able to help their children. For example, the occupational therapist came in for those children who have a physical handicap; we would have the seminars to help them to learn how to deal with that, things that they can do to help the child to learn.

Ms Love, the principal from the urban school for the deaf, highlighted programmes developed and implemented by the Jamaica Association for the Deaf (JAD) that help parents develop the necessary skills in communication and understanding children who are deaf. Similar sentiments were shared by Ms Minot. She noted that in addition to the programmes implemented by JAD, the school provides sign language classes for the parents.

The schools try to help parents to understand their children, their level of cognitive and social development and their needs. The expectations of the parents and the school should be clearly communicated to all parties involved. Time is spent with the parents to develop the students' IEP so that parents can work with children at home in accordance with the agreed objectives.

Being custodians also involves providing the necessary support for the students after school, because some parents may not be equipped with the necessary knowledge to reinforce what was done at school. The principals and teachers felt that working with a child who has a disability has its challenges because it requires different curriculum adaptations, accommodations and support based on the needs of the students. They cannot take for granted that someone is at home who can provide the necessary scaffold for what was taught at school. Mr Black, principal of the school for the blind, stated:

> If you are a teacher and you have something that you really want to share with the parent of that child with regard to your instruction and you can't find that parent, there is nothing more frustrating to a teacher, a classroom teacher when you are not able to speak or sit with a parent to discuss a child.

Similar sentiments were shared by Ms Love, the principal of the urban school for the deaf. She said that "because there is no sustenance at home you can't support what is learned at school and pretty soon the students themselves are realising that they have non-signing parents".

In addition, it takes patience, commitment, selflessness and longer work hours to work with children who have disabilities. Mr Black (the principal for the school for the blind) stated:

> We have much more to do, we need to do much more. For example, if you are a teacher here, you have to understand that whatever is set out for you to do here is going to be times two of the regular schools.

Like Mr Black, Ms Love suggested that some students tend to stay late at school because that is where they feel understood. She highlighted the incongruence between home and school, where at home, "mada no ondastan mi, sista no ondastan mi, prefa stiey a skuul an taak" (mother don't understand me, sister don't understand me, prefer stay at school and talk), "everybody has a need for belonging, a sense of connection that's how they try to connect" (Ms Love). Whenever students are not understood at home, they are likely to find other avenues outside of the home to share or express their feelings or opinions, and the school can provide such an environment.

Parents' Involvement or Non-involvement in the Education of Children with Disabilities

The context of parents is a significant feature that influences their involvement. All participants were in agreement that parents' ability to help their children and their knowledge about their child's disability influenced the quality of their involvement. Ms Minot, teacher from the urban school for the deaf, asserted that

Parents who are ashamed of the children being Deaf, they keep them at home, they don't carry them out and expose them to certain things. And you know that a child loves when a child is exposed, because they are locked away at home and that has to do with the parents educational level, not carrying the child out and expos[ing] them to certain things, because you know that the children never go certain place[s]. They don't have the experience, because the parents say well piipl a go laaf afta mi chail an may caal im a dumi (people are going to laugh after my child and may call him a dummy). When you have the parents having a much higher level of education, some of the stigmatism can be reduced and they are able to help them.

Furthermore, the public does not seem to understand individuals who are deaf. Their concern was raised by Ms Love, the principal from the urban school for the deaf:

> I hate when they are ridiculed in society or made a mockery of and then you do the gestures that are meaningless without trying to understand, so that is what I have for the public – try and understand so you can care.

Taking care of a child with a disability is very costly. Mr Black said that parents may be "willing to participate in the education of their children but because of poverty they can't afford the technology". The interview with the parents confirmed that financially it is difficult providing the best for their children. The parents also added that they seek help from different organizations as a result of the information provided to them by the schools and their primary health-care provider (public health clinics). Ms Jen reported that the support and assistance she received from personnel motivated her in wanting to motivate her children to excel. She added:

> I know that the disability is not the end of it. They can be big men, big women, big women who grow up to teach. It is not the end of the world, so I have to explain that to them for them to understand, because I know it is going to be hard for them to accept it. Therefore, encouraging that having a disability is not the end of the world, because there are people in worse situations. (Transcribed from Jamaican Creole to Jamaican English)

All participants agreed that the distance from their homes to school negatively impacted their involvement. Two of the schools offered boarding facilities, and for the rural school for the deaf boarding was compulsory. However, visiting the school regularly could be prohibitive because of the location, travel cost and time taken from work to visit. Ms Jen and Mr Barrett (parents of students at the school for the blind) telephoned whenever they could not visit because of financial constraints and work-related obligations.

Mr George, the parent from the rural school for deaf, stated that although he communicated regularly with the school by phone he still visited because he needed to communicate with his son. He reiterated that his son is deaf, and he needs his son to feel safe and be adjusted at school because as a father he will always be there. In addition, he stated that location and time would not affect him because he can drive to the school as it facilitates visits outside of contact time. He found it meaningful for the family that his son spent time with them. In addition, the new phone gadgets can facilitate face-time chat using sign language.

For Ms Tiff, the other parent with a child attending the rural school for the deaf, the distance from the school was a limitation. She had to take a bus and then a taxi to the school, which was costly. This made it more difficult because she was actively searching for a job. She needed to work because she is a single mother with three children and no financial support from the father of the children. She regrettably said, "like today, every child [is] supposed to enrol in school and because of the financial crisis she can't go to school. The others can go to school because they live near".

Parents from the urban school for the deaf shared similar concerns in relation to financing. They also reported that they lived far from school, and although urban bus fares may be cheaper, they can get only route taxis, which are a bit more expensive.

Discussion

Most parents with children with disabilities believe that their children can do well academically and socially, making their involvement critical to their success. The findings from all the stakeholders revealed that parents get involved by working with their children at home, accepting invitations to volunteer at school and attending the different meetings and sessions put on by the schools.

Parental involvement at home includes helping with homework, learning sign language for parents who have children who are deaf and participating in recreational activities. Through these activities they can develop the necessary cognitive and social skills required for adjusting to school and the general environment. Although parents of children with disabilities may encounter more challenges working with them, as Dollahite (2004) pointed out, there are benefits to the children and the parents when they are involved. Anderson (2000, 2014) and Balli (2016) found that parental involvement is critical to the success of students with disabilities. Getting involved is at times influenced by one's level of competence in helping the child, especially if one does not know how to communicate using sign language or how to read braille. Hoover-Dempsey and Sandler (1997) looked at the parents' role construction about their belief as parents and how efficacious they felt in helping their children. In addition, Hornby and Lafaele (2011) found that some parents may leave it entirely up to the schools because they believe they do not have the necessary skills and knowledge to work with their children.

Some parents need to be invited to be involved, which can be done by asking parents to volunteer and attend seminars and training sessions to help their children. Volunteerism is considered to have a significant influence on the success of schools. Epstein (2001; Epstein et al., 2002) saw volunteerism on the part of parents in their children's school as a medium for parents to develop self-confidence and to feel empowered. Epstein felt that volunteerism contributed to greater commitment to schools on the part of parents. Participating in the different training sessions empowered and positively contributed to defining their roles as parents and improving their ability to help their children. It is also important to note that parents who have children with disabilities need to be empowered through training and having one-on-one dialogue with them, because the challenges that they encounter may negatively affect their emotional well-being. Parents' emotional well-being impacts their thoughts and behaviour and may place children at a disadvantage in receiving the best psycho-emotional support. Empowerment sessions conducted by the school could provide parents with some of the necessary skills for coping and improve their involvement in their children's education.

From the perspective of school personnel, working with parents who have children with disabilities is challenging, notwithstanding the small class sizes. Schools sometimes have to train parents on how to work with their children at home based on the severity of the disabilities. Principals and teachers play multiple roles in ensuring the active involvement of parents. The parents consider them to be the experts from whom all the relevant information should come. They are considered the first point of contact when there are challenges.

School personnel encourage parental participation through the different training sessions and empower them with the necessary skills to work with their children. Such empowerment includes having the parents actively involved in developing the IEP for the students. This reinforced Razalli et al.'s (2015) report that when parents are actively involved in the development of the IEP there is greater student success.

The principals and teachers also highlighted that the context of the parents should be taken into consideration when working with them.

The different experiences influence the decisions and approaches taken. Therefore, involvement is encouraged based on the needs of the children and sometimes the family. A number of cases were identified where parents were provided with lunch and bus fare to attend parenting sessions. This is because some parents encountered difficulties engaging in full-time employment, which placed them at a financial disadvantage. The location of the school (e.g., those that were residential) could also impact how much they could get involved. Therefore, schools must facilitate them whenever they can and have one-on-one sessions to provide and explain the necessary information.

Educating the students does not end at dismissal time for the teachers; the schools facilitate the students' development and academic success through extra work, because some students have limited support at home. Therefore, the collaboration between home and school that Bowe (2005), Morrisette and Morrisette (1999), O'Shea and O'Shea (2001) and El Shourbagi (2017) reported as important for children with disabilities may be absent.

Parents' involvement is impacted by their belief in their ability to help their children, the type of disability of their children, educational and socio-economic reality and the distance to the school from their house. According to Hoover-Dempsey and Sandler (1997), if parents do not think they have the requisite knowledge and skills to help, they may not help. Parents of children with disabilities, in this case children who are deaf or blind, may think that they are not competent enough in sign language or braille to offer meaningful assistance to their children. Parents who reported that they were able to help made the effort to learn the language, and their children were allowed to share their skills with other family members.

On the other hand, being ashamed of, or in denial of, the existence of a child's disability could influence help-seeking behaviour. It could also be assumed that a parent's educational level can influence how much help is sought. Boonk et al. (2018) reported that parents' educational level (in particular, that of the mother) influences their involvement. The two fathers interviewed reported that they were actively involved, while the four mothers felt that there could be greater involvement. Of note, all the mothers whose children attended the schools for the deaf felt that they should do more but did not feel competent enough to help. Such findings are similar to that of the JAD (2015) that parents with limited or no sign language experience found it difficult to communicate with their children.

Socio-economic reality impacts how much parents can get involved and how often parents can visit their children's schools. The well-being of the family is affected by its socio-economic background. Homes with limited finances to send children to school (in this case little or no money to pay for boarding their children in special-needs schools) face an extra barrier to parental involvement. In addition, the location of the schools can further inhibit involvement. Parents who are challenged financially may not be able to visit or volunteer in their children's school. Additionally, some of these parents were unemployed and were actively seeking employment. Therefore, they had to make difficult decisions about how often to visit the schools. Additionally, if the parents are working, they may find it difficult to take a day from work to attend school and scheduled meetings for fear of losing one day's pay.

Conclusion

Parental involvement is multidimensional and requires the tripartite relationship, the input of teachers (schools), parents and students to improve the outcomes of all students. Special-needs schools require consistent support from the Ministry of Education, the Parenting Commission, Parent Teachers Associations and other stakeholders to understand the needs of the parents and help to mitigate the challenges they face. Parents of children with disabilities should take a more active role in their children's education and partner in the development of the IEP for their children. When they are involved in the development of the IEP, they can better work with their children in meeting the different targets agreed on for their children's success. In addition, parents of children who are deaf should seek to learn sign language to improve communication at home and improve their sense of efficacy in helping their children. A working partnership between parents and school is always more likely to produce satisfactory results.

References

Afolabi, O.E. (2014). Parents' involvement in inclusive education: An empirical test for psycho-educational development for learners with special educational needs (SENs). *International Journal of Educational and Policy Studies, 6*(10), 196–208.

Allen, K.E. & Schwartz, I.S. (2001). *The exceptional child: Inclusion in early childhood education* (4th ed.). Thompson Learning.

Anderson, S.R. (2000). *In pursuit of personal excellence: Educational barriers, opportunities and experiences of Jamaican students with disabilities.* [Unpublished doctoral dissertation]. University of the West Indies, Mona.

———. (2014). *Climbing every mountain: Barriers, opportunities and experiences of Jamaican students with disabilities in their pursuit of personal excellence*. Arawak Publications

Balasundaram, P. (1995). Fostering parental involvement. In B. O'Toole and R. McConkey (Eds.), *Innovations in developing countries for people with disabilities* (pp. 29–28). Lisieux Hall Publications. http://www.aifoeng.it/archives/disability/books/1995_innovations_book.pdf

Balli, D. (2016). Importance of parental involvement to meet the special needs of children with disabilities in regular schools. *Academic Journal of Interdisciplinary Studies, 5*(1), 157–52.

Bempechat, J. (1992). The role of parent involvement in children's academic achievement. *The School Community Journal, 2*(2), 31–41.

Bogdan, R.C. & Biklen, S.K. (2003). *Qualitative research for education: An introduction to theories and methods* (4th ed.). Pearson Education Group.

Boonk, L., Gijselaers, H.J.M., Ritzen, H., & Brand-Gruwel, S. (2018, June). A review of the relationship between parental involvement indicators and academic achievement. *Educational Research Review, 24*, 20–30. http://dx.doi.org/10.1016/j.edurev.2018.02.001

Bowe, F.G. (2005). *Early childhood special education: Birth to eight* (3rd ed.). Thompson and Delmar Learning.

Brown, K.M. (2005). *How parents of exceptional children describe their relationships with education professionals*. [Unpublished doctoral dissertation]. Virginia Polytechnic and State University.

Chen, G. (2020). *Parental involvement is key to student success*. https://www.publicschoolreview.com/blog/parental-involvement-is-key-to-student-success

Cole, S.M. (2013). *An investigation into the impact of parental involvement on the cognitive and social skills of grade one students in Jamaica*. [Unpublished doctoral dissertation]. University of the West Indies, Mona.

Cozby, P.C. & Bates, S.C. (2012). *Methods in behavioral research* (11th ed.). McGraw Hill.

Davies, R. (2008). *The Jamaica early childhood curriculum for children birth to five years: A conceptual framework*. The University of the West Indies-Mona. The Dudley Grant Memorial Trust.

Desforges, C. & Abouchaar, A. (2003). *The impact of parental involvement, parental support and family education on pupil achievement and adjustment: A literature review*. Department for Education and Skills.

Dollahite, D.C. (2004). A narrative approach to exploring responsible involvement of fathers and their special-needs children. In R.D. Day and M.E. Lamb (Eds.), *Conceptualizing and measuring father involvement* (pp. 109–28). Lawrence Erlbaum.

El Shourbagi, S. (2017). Parental involvement in inclusive classrooms for students with learning disabilities at Omani schools as perceived by teachers. *Journal Psychology Cognition, 2*(2), 133–37.

Epstein, J.L. (2001). *School, family, and community partnerships: Preparing educators and improving schools*. Westview.

Epstein, J.L., Sanders, M.G., Simon, B.S., Salinas, K.C., Jansorn, N.R., & Van Voorhis, F.L. (2002). *School, family, and community partnerships: Your handbook for action* (2nd ed.). Corwin Press. https://www.govinfo.gov/content/pkg/ERIC-ED467082/pdf/ERIC-ED467082.pdf

Epstein, J.L. & Van Voorhis, F. (2001). School programmes and teacher practices of parental involvement in inner city and elementary middle schools. *The Elementary School Journal, 91*(3), 289–305.

Fan, X. & Chen, M. (2001). Parental involvement and students' academic achievement: A meta-analysis. *Educational Psychology Review, 13*(1), 1–22.

Gibb-Brown, K.M. (2005). *How parents of exceptional children describe their relationships with educational professionals*. [Doctoral Dissertation]. http://scholar.lib.vt.edu/theses/available/etd-12022005-112707/unrestricted/KM_Brown.pdf

Government of Jamaica. (2014). *The disability act, 2014*. https://www.japarliament.gov.jm/attachments/341_The%20Disabilities%20bill%202014%20No.13.pdf

Hetherington, E.M. & Parke, R.D. (1999). *Child Psychology: A contemporary viewpoint* (5th ed.). McGraw Hill.

Hoover-Dempsey, K.V. & Sandler, H.M. (1995). Parental involvement in children's education: Why does it make a difference? *Teachers College Record, 97*, 310–31.

———. (1997). Why do parents become involved in their children's education? *Review of Educational Research, 67*(1), 3–42.

Hoover-Dempsey, K.V., Walker, J.M.T., & Sandler, H.M. (2005). Parents' motivation for involvement in their children's education. In E.N. Patrikakou, R.P. Weisberg, S. Redding, & H.J. Walberg (Eds.), *School-family partnerships for children's success* (pp. 40–56). Teachers College Press.

Hornby, G. & Lafaele, R. (2011). Barriers to parental involvement in education: An explanatory model. *Educational Review, 6*(1), 37–52.

Jamaica Association for the Deaf [JAD]. (2015). *The impact of deafness on the family*. https://www.jamdeaf.org.jm/articles/the-impact-of-deafness-on-the-family

Jeynes, W. (2007). The relationship between parental involvement and urban secondary school student academic achievement: A meta-analysis. *Urban Education, 42*, 82–110.

McWayne, C. & Marissa, O. (2004). Parent involvement and the social and academic competencies of urban kindergarten children. *Family Involvement Research Digest*. https://archive.globalfrp.org/publications-resources/browse-our-publications/parent-involvement-and-the-social-and-academic-competencies-of-urban-kindergarten-children

Morrisette, D.L. & Morrisette, P.J. (1999). Rethinking parental participation in special education. *International Electronic Journal for Leadership in Learning, 3* (14).

Munroe, G.C. (2009). *Parental involvement in education in Jamaica: Exploring the factors that influence the decision of parents to become involved in the education of their children*. [Doctoral dissertation]. University of Toronto. http://proquest.umi.com/pqdlink?Ver=1&Exp=10-18-2016&FMT=7&DID=1904061901&RQT=309&attempt=1&cfc=1

National Academies of Sciences, Engineering, and Medicine. (2016). *Parenting matters: Supporting parents of children ages 0-8*. The National Academies Press. doi: 10.17226/21868. https://www.ncbi.nlm.nih.gov/books/NBK402024/pdf/Bookshelf_NBK402024.pdf

National Centre for Learning Disabilities. (2004). Individuals with Disabilities Education Act (IDEA): IDEA parent guide. https://www.ncld.org/wp-content/uploads/2014/11/IDEA-Parent-Guide1.pdf

National Quality Framework for Early Childhood Education. (n.d). Research digest standard 3 parents and families. http://siolta.ie/media/pdfs/Research%20Digest%20-%20Parents%20and%20Family.pdf

Neuman, W.L. (2006). *Social research methods qualitative and quantitative approaches* (6th ed.). Pearson Education.

O'Shea, D.J., O'Shea, L.J., Algozzine, R., & Hamilton, D.J. (2001). *Families and teachers of individuals with disabilities: Collaborative orientations and responsive practices*. Allyn & Bacon.

Park, S., Stone, S.I., & Holloway, S.D. (2017). School-based parental involvement as a predictor of achievement and school learning environment: An elementary school-level analysis. *Children and Youth Services Review, 82*, 195–206.

Qu, S.Q. & Dumay, J. (2011). The qualitative research interview. *Qualitative Research in Accounting & Management, 8*(3), 238–64. https://www.doi.org/10.1108/11766091111162070

Razalli, A.R., Mamat, N., Hashim, A.T.M., Ariffin, A., Rahman, A.A., & Yusuf, N.M. (2015). Epstein model application for measuring parents' participation level in the individual education plan (IEP) students with special needs. *Australian Journal of Basic and Applied Sciences, 9*(25): 105–10.

Ricketts, H. & Anderson, P. (2009). *Parenting in Jamaica, a study conducted on behalf of PIOJ*. Policy Research Unit–Planning Institute of Jamaica.

Samms-Vaughan, M. (2004). *The Jamaican pre-school child: The status of early childhood development in Jamaica*. Planning Institute of Jamaica.

———. (2008). Comprehensive longitudinal studies of child health, development and behaviour in Jamaica: Findings and policy impact. *West Indian Medical Journal, 57*(6), 639–44.

Sheldon, S.B. & Epstein, J.L. (2005). Involvement counts: Family and community partnerships and mathematics achievement. *The Journal of Educational Research, 98*(4), 196–206.

Smit, B. (2010). Doing research in comparative education. In E. Lemmer & N. Van Wyk (Eds.), *Themes in South African education*. Heinemann.

Springer, P.A. (2004). *An investigation into the current perceptions of parental involvement at the primary school level in Barbados*. [Unpublished master's thesis]. University of the West Indies, Cave Hill.

Tellis, W. (1997). Application of a case study methodology. *The Qualitative Report, 3*(3), 1–19. http://www.nova.edu/ssss/QR/QR3-3/tellis2.html

Chapter 6

The Impact of Early Parental Involvement on Academic Outcome

SHARLINE COLE

Introduction

It is generally accepted that parental involvement at home and at school, as well as time spent helping with homework and other activities, often improves the chances of childhood academic success (Chowa et al., 2013). "Parental involvement has been shown to be an important variable in children's education, and more schools are trying to encourage increased involvement" (Khajehpoura & Ghazvini, 2011, p. 1208). In early childhood education, this academic success can be demonstrated in the form of improved scores on school-based assessments and standardized tests, and the ability to progress successfully to higher grades of learning. To increase the likelihood of parental involvement in the academic activities of their children, it is important to understand the motivators for parental involvement and to create an informed system of support that will encourage parental involvement and consequently the academic success of children.

Understanding the impact of parental involvement at the different stages in primary education is critical in determining students' outcome as they transition through each grade. Much has been reported on the achievement gaps in Jamaica's public school system (USAID/MOE Partnership for Improved Reading Outcomes, 2014; Watson Williams & Fox, 2013). However, there is little evidence that connects the achievement gap as students' transition through primary school with the influence of parents. Hayakawa et al. (2013) asserted that the achievement gaps evident at the early childhood level can continue through primary school if there are deficiencies in early parental involvement. Samms-Vaughan (2004) reinforced the importance of early development of cognitive skills in children's future success. There are long-term benefits to parental involvement at the preschool level as students show improved reading and numeracy skills.

The purpose of this study is to examine the impact of early parental involvement on the academic outcomes of students from entry in grade 1 to exit at grade 6. The influence of parental involvement was assessed at grade 1 through the Grade One Individual Learning Profile (GOILP), at grade 4 with the Grade Four Literacy and Numeracy Tests and at grade 6 with the Grade Six Achievement Test (GSAT). In addition, parents' and teachers' reports of parental involvement were compared with students' academic outcomes in the different assessments.

The research sought to answer the following questions:

1. What is the extent of the relationship between parental involvement and students' academic outcomes over the three assessment periods in GOILP, GFLT/GFNT and GSAT?
2. What is the difference in students' academic outcomes and parental involvement between males and females?
3. To what extent do parental involvement, invitation to be involved and the efficaciousness of parents predict the academic outcome of students at the primary level?

Literature Review

Parental involvement is multidimensional and has been defined by different researchers (Epstein, 2001; Hoover-Dempsey & Sandler 1997; Fan & Chen, 2001). Epstein (2001) asserted that parental involvement embodies six types: parenting, communicating, learning at home, volunteering, decision making and collaborating with the community. Hoover-Dempsey and Sandler (1997) explained that parents' perception of their roles as parents determines their level of involvement. Fan and Chen's (2001) report on parental involvement considered the practices and behaviours of parents that encouraged academic success. All three researchers' definitions concur with that of Jeynes (2007), which states that the active participation of parents in the education of children is considered parental involvement. In addition, Campbell et al. (2017) described parental engagement as the "attitudes, values and behaviors of parents that promote their child's learning and educational outcomes" (p. 1). Therefore, the construct of parental involvement is context dependent, because the different parenting behaviours and practices influenced the attitudes and role construction of parents.

The types of parental involvement that occur can be either school initiated or parent initiated (Driessen, Smith, & Sleegers, 2004). School-initiated parent involvement includes the school presenting a welcoming environment and the creation of opportunities for parents to participate in school life; this can be done in the form of parent workshops or seminars (Đurišić & Bunijevac, 2017). Examples of tangible resources are notes sent home, invitations to partake in the decision making of the school's governance and opportunities to communicate and exchange resources with other parents (Driessen, Smith, & Sleegers, 2004). Parent-initiated involvement entails the parent helping with homework, regularly enquiring about their children's progress at school and initiating communication with the school about the progress of their children (Driessen, Smith, & Sleegers, 2004). In early childhood, parent-initiated involvement can also be demonstrated by parents' use of opportunities presented in the home and community to reinforce concepts presented in the classroom (Driessen, Smith, & Sleegers, 2004).

In discussing the impact of parental involvement on children's academic outcome, an examination of the variables that motivate parents to become involved in the first place is important. Two theories that discuss motivators for parental involvement specifically include Epstein's Overlapping Spheres of Influence (Đurišić & Bunijevac, 2017; Epstein, 2001) and Hoover-Dempsey and Sandler's Model of Parental Involvement (Green et al., 2007; Hoover-Dempsey & Sandler, 1997).

Epstein's Overlapping Spheres of Influence

Epstein's Overlapping Spheres of Influence explores six types of parental involvement that serve as a guide to schools and teachers wanting to develop partnerships that benefit students (Đurišić & Bunijevac, 2017, Epstein et al. 2002). These are the following: parenting, learning at home, communicating, volunteering, decision making and collaborating with the community. Epstein views these partnerships as the process in which the stakeholders involved support each other to ensure the motivation, learning and success of students (Đurišić & Bunijevac, 2017; Epstein et al., 2002; Epstein, 2001).

For Epstein, partnership ensures the effective parenting necessary in the home environment to support children's learning and provides parents with the appropriate support through training and capacity building in order to benefit children's outcomes. It also encourages learning at home by equipping parents with the tools and resources to help their children at home with homework activities. It is therefore important that parents are provided with the curriculum to be taught at school and with guidance on how to help with homework at the early childhood level and beyond (Epstein et al., 2002).

To encourage success, schools need to communicate with parents about the progress of their students. Therefore, based on the particular situation of each parent, different modes of communication are used (Epstein et al., 2002). The communication is typically done by sending notes home from school, arranging individual parent-teacher meetings/consultations and, more recently, the use of email or mobile applications (WhatsApp group chats).

Parents are more likely to be involved if they believe that they have a say in the decision-making process of their children's welfare. Parents can play an active role when they are members of the Parent Teachers Association (PTA) and are involved in other aspects of school governance. Furthermore, parents who make themselves available through volunteerism and respond to school and teacher invitations to volunteer provide an environment that empowers parents and will positively influence their involvement (Epstein et al., 2002).

Successful schools encourage community involvement and collaboration. The school and the community engage in activities that support learning and support the school and learning environments overall (Epstein et al., 2002). The collaboration between school and community ensures that the resources are effectively used to enable overall development of the community and the school and to encourage students' success.

Hoover-Dempsey and Sandler's Parental Involvement Model

The Hoover-Dempsey and Sandler Model explains the multiple influences on a child's life that result in the child's achievement, even into adulthood (Green et al., 2007). The prime motivators include motivational beliefs, parental self-efficacy and school and teacher invitations (Hoover-Dempsey & Sandler, 1997).

Parents construct their roles based on their belief of what their role should be in their children's schooling or the specific tasks that they believe they are responsible for as parents and caregivers. This "role construction" is formed from the parent's community, culture and social influencers as it relates to schooling and can change over time (Green et al., 2007). Parents also tend to construct this role based on tasks carried out by their own parents when they were children (Hoover-Dempsey et al., 2005). For example, if a parent's perception of their role construction does not include attending PTA meetings or doing homework, but rather involves providing finances for extra classes and financial support, then that parent would consider themselves actively involved and would expect an increase in the likelihood of academic success.

Parents' sense of efficaciousness (the belief that they can have a positive impact on their children's academic performance) influences their involvement (Hoover-Dempsey & Sandler, 1997). Yamamoto, Holloway and Suzuki (2016) conducted a study among Japanese and American families and found that "mothers who feel efficacious about their parenting may feel more motivated to interact with children and support their children's academics at home" (p. 60). If a parent believes that they may be a deterrent to positive academic outcomes or that they have nothing to offer in the form of homework help or teacher communication, then they will surely not be motivated to perform perceived parental roles related to schooling. Parents who did not finish schooling themselves or who are unfamiliar with their child's school curriculum may refrain from offering help if they do not believe their help will have a positive outcome (Lueder, 2011).

Parents are more likely to be involved if they are invited by the school and in particular their children's teachers. This serves as an indicator that the teachers value the parents' contribution to the children's academic success (Green et al., 2007). In addition, Shajith and Erchul (2014) found that parents are more likely to respond positively to specific invitations from teachers.

Cognitive Development

Significant to academic achievement is the development of the necessary cognitive skills from early childhood to primary level education. Children develop language and other competencies through their internal processing and interaction with others (Slavin, 2012). This interaction with others, mainly parents, extended family and teachers, contributes to cognitive development (Berk, 2010; Rutherford, 2011).

Children who are nurtured in an enriched environment that facilitates language acquisition and the necessary academic knowledge are more likely to do better in school (Piaget, 1972, 1990; Vygotsky, 1978). It is important that the knowledge acquired and processed from parents, teachers and the immediate environment is clear, and that students can build on existing information which is reflective of the curriculum in schools.

From the perspective of Piaget, children should be taught based on their age-related stages, while Vygotsky asserted that children can be taught anything at any age and therefore their interactions with others promote cognitive development (Berk, 2010). Children's development is therefore context dependent (Bowe, 2005), and their academic outcome is dependent on the enriched environment provided by home and school.

A study by Alves, Gomes, Martins and Almeida (2017) among a sample of Portuguese preschool children revealed that family characteristics are stronger predictors of pre-schoolers' academic achievement than the type of school. Finn et al. (2014), however, reported that students' cognitive skills and academic outcomes can improve through targeted intervention.

The Impact of Parental Involvement on Academic Achievement

Early parent involvement has been shown to have more of an impact at the elementary/early childhood level (Strawhun et al., 2014; Wilder, 2014). Another study revealed that "parent involvement in elementary school provides long-lasting benefits to children throughout high school" (Jaiswal & Choudhuri, 2017, p. 114). Parents who create positive learning environments are usually knowledgeable and supportive of the schools' curriculum. They work as advocates for their children and are part of the decision-making process early in their children's education (Jethro & Aina, 2012). Empirical studies conducted by Fernández-Alonso et al. (2017) and Kimaro and Machumu (2015) found that parental involvement is a predictive factor for students' academic outcomes. Jethro and Aina (2012) stated that "the most accurate prediction of a student's achievement in school is not income or social status, but the extent to which that student's parent is able to create a home environment that encourages learning and to express high expectations for their children's achievement and future careers" (p. 196).

While parent participation in school organizations has proven to be beneficial, some studies have found that home-based involvement seems to have more of an impact than parent participation in school organizations (Altschul, 2011; Epstein, 2001; Hayes, 2012; Hoover-Dempsey et al., 2001). These forms of parental involvement are more significant and have more of an impact earlier on in a child's academic career (Altschul, 2011). Jaiswal and Choudhuri (2017) have come to the conclusion (based on reviews of multiple authors and findings) that "parental involvement, whether at home or at school, has a positive relationship with students' academic performance" (p. 118). A study by Fernández-Alonso et al. (2017) among 26,543 Spanish students attending public schools revealed that there is improved academic performance when parents are involved at home. They also reported that parents who have control over the education of their children are more likely to see improvements at school. Guo et al. (2018) suggested that parental involvement in the form of supervision is more likely to increase when children's academic performance is below standard.

Đurišić and Bunijevac (2017) support the general perception of parental involvement and its effects on academic achievement. They found that parents who read to their children, invest in extra classes or tutoring where necessary and who have a vested interest in helping with homework see better results in the academic success of their children. Furthermore, communication about parental expectations of students was found to improve the likelihood of academic achievement (Altschul, 2011). In addition, Park and Holloway (2017) found that parental involvement was associated with children's achievement in mathematics and reading, with consistent improvement in mathematics performance across grades. Parents' high expectation for academic achievement was found to be the strongest motivator for academic achievement (Wilder, 2014). "Mothers with less mathematics preparation and less confidence about their mathematics skills were less likely to participate effectively in tutoring sessions" (Park & Holloway, 2017, p. 11). Furthermore, parents seek additional information from schools to help children with mathematics as they advance through the grades (Park & Holloway, 2017). In an earlier study, Sheldon and Epstein (2005) found that students' improvement in mathematics over time at the elementary level was a result of schools implementing quality mathematics programmes that focused on parent and family involvement.

With most researchers on parental involvement reporting the benefits of parental involvement in student academic outcomes, McDowell, Jack and Compton (2018) report that although invitations from schools to be involved had a significant relationship with parents' role construction and their sense of efficacy, there was no significant relationship with student achievement. Kimaro and Machumu's (2015) sequential exploratory study of 288 students and 125 teachers at the primary level found that factors such as parent-teacher face-to-face contact and desirable communication also contributed to positive student outcomes. Therefore, being involved is contextual and dependent on parents' perception of parental involvement, how they feel about their role as parents and the influence of schools in terms of how parental involvement is encouraged.

Jaiswal and Choudhuri's (2017) reviews of empirical studies concluded that with the different constructs that researchers used to measure parental involvement, it is difficult to say what construct or combination of constructs on parental involvement contribute to students' positive academic performance. Of significance is Cousins and Mickelson's (2011) study exploring black parents' beliefs about their participation in their children's education, which found that black parents were motivated to be involved in their children's education "even if they felt unwelcomed" (p. 12).

Children's Gender, Parental Involvement and Academic Outcomes

Exploring the effects of parental involvement based on children's gender can reveal the gaps that exist at home and in schools and provide opportunities for parents to be involved in their children's education. Fathers' and mothers' demonstration of interest contributed to their sons' and daughters' belief that they could attain academic success and fostered an increased likelihood of attaining university-level education (Campbell et al., 2017). Campbell et al. (2017) also found that fathers' interest in the early childhood education of girls had a positive effect on educational attainment in adolescence and at the university level.

Research by Houtenville and Smith-Conway as reported by the University of New Hampshire (2008) found that "parents seemed particularly interested in the academic achievements of their daughters. They discovered parents spent more time talking to their daughters about their school work during dinnertime discussions" (line. 1). The literature on boys was found to be more mixed. Cooper et al., in Jafarov (2015), reported that parents who have male children in elementary school are called to school more often about bad behaviour. In addition, mothers are more often likely to contact teachers concerning boys' performance than they would about the performance of their daughters (Deslandes & Potvin, in Jafarov, 2015). Moon and Hofferth's (2016) study, which examined the achievement of boys and girls from immigrant families, suggests that parental involvement at home benefits boys more than girls – particularly from the elementary level to grade 5. They reported that "parental involvement had a significantly greater association with boys' reading and mathematics test performance during the earlier elementary years than during the later elementary years" (p. 10). Pires et al. (2017) found that parental involvement that provides instrumental support was more likely to influence the academic outcome of boys, while affective support influenced the academic outcome of girls. Altschul (2011) stated that parents' academic support measured along with the support of teachers did not significantly affect academic achievement for boys and was less effective in achievement for girls. What was evident is that girls' capacity for self-control does not require constant monitoring by parents, as is required by boys (Guo et al., 2018). Future studies considering academic achievement based on the gender of children may want to explore this claim.

Methods

Design

This research employed a panel longitudinal design that collected data at three points of students' primary education. In understanding and comparing students' outcome, over time, a panel design was considered appropriate because the same participants would be measured at different points across time or years (Blossfeld, Schneider, & Doll, 2009). This research is a follow-up of the quantitative phase of the author's doctoral thesis "An Investigation into the Impact of Parental Involvement on the Cognitive and Social Skills of Grade One Students in Jamaica" (Cole, 2013) that looked at parental involvement and its impact on grade 1 students' cognitive and social skills. This paper sought to investigate the impact of parental involvement on students' academic outcomes, where the variables of significance from the author's previous study were used as elements in understanding students' outcomes in high-stakes assessments in the Jamaican context. Three data collection points were used at the beginning of grade 1 (wave 1), end of grade 4 (wave 2) and the end of grade 6 (wave 3).

Participants

The sample consisted of 116 students; 56 males and 60 females matched with a parent consecutively selected from 2 inner-city primary schools in the Kingston Metropolitan Region. The sample was followed through the six years of their primary education, where data were collected from the standardized assessment developed and administered by the Ministry of Education at the beginning of grade 1 and the end of grades 4 and 6. In wave 1, data were collected at the beginning of grade 1 from the parents and teachers. Parents completed questionnaires on parental involvement, while teachers completed surveys on parental involvement for each student along with the scores from the students' GOILP. At wave 2, the grade 4 assessments (Grade Four Literacy and Numeracy) and at wave 3 (the GSAT) results were collected.

Procedure

Permission was granted by the schools and the participating parents. The parents and teachers completed questionnaires on parental involvement from their perspectives. In addition, the scores from the GOILP, Grade Four Literacy and Numeracy and GSAT were collected for each student.

In wave 1, the students' names and schools were matched with the questionnaires received from parents and teachers and the students' Grade 1 Individual Learning Profile Scores. A listing with the names of the students and their respective schools was prepared for further data collection.

The schools were informed of the possibility that future data on the students would be collected based on the results. It was agreed that the grades 4 and 6 results were the best results to be used because these assessments were standardized for Jamaican students, and all schools at the primary level sat these exams on the same date and time. In addition, parents were similarly enthusiastic that their children do well to enter grade 1 and excel on grade 4 and grade 6 assessments. Mastery on the Grade Four Literacy Test guarantees eligibility to sit the GSAT,[1] and high performance at GSAT guarantees placement in high schools of choice. Therefore, grade 4 literacy and numeracy results represent wave 2, and grade 6 results represent wave 3.

Instrument

The Parental Involvement Questionnaire developed by Hoover-Dempsey and Sandler (1997) was used to collect the data on parental involvement. The instrument had five subscales that measured parental involvement (teacher and parent), invitation to be involved (teacher and parent) and efficaciousness of parents in helping their children.

Responses on the general involvement of parents were collected from teachers and parents. The teachers' report of parental involvement subscale had a total of sixteen questions which asked teachers to rate parents on particular parental involvement strategies. The rating was based on teachers' belief about parents being involved in specific parental involvement activities. The instrument (subscale) had a 6-point Likert-type response that ranged from none to all. The data collected on this scale was computed and then recoded into four responses representing never, low, moderate and high.

---

[1] Replaced by the Primary Exit Profile (PEP) in 2019 that uses a series of assessments to assess students' knowledge with an increased emphasis on twenty-first-century skills (Ministry of Education, Youth and Information).

Parents' report of their involvement had eight questions that asked parents to rate how often they engaged in particular activities related to their children's learning. A 6-point Likert-scale response was used to capture parents' responses, ranging from never to 1 or more times each week. The data were computed and based on the responses further recoded into three categories: low, moderate and high.

The invitation to be involved subscale sought responses from both teachers and parents. Teachers' report of invitation to parents to be involved sought to capture the teachers' responses on how often they invited parents or involved parents in activities that were beneficial to their children's outcomes. The scale had a total of fourteen questions that utilized a 6-point Likert scale response, ranging from never to 1 or more times each week. Parents' report on invitation from teachers to be involved asked parents to indicate how often they were invited by their children's teachers to be involved in activities beneficial to their children's outcomes. This scale had a total of six questions with a 6-point Likert-type response similar to that of the teachers' scale.

Teachers were asked to report on their level of agreement and disagreement on their beliefs about parents' efficacy for helping their children to succeed. The scale asked if parents had the necessary influence, knowledge and skills to help their children succeed. This aspect of the instrument had seven questions with responses on a 6-point Likert scale, ranging from disagree very strongly to agree very strongly. The data for the scale were further computed and then recorded into three responses: low, moderate and high.

The instrument with its corresponding subscales was considered to be reliable; however, when the Cronbach Alpha was disaggregated for the different scales, teachers' report on parents' efficaciousness had a reduced C-Alpha (table 6.1).

Three assessments developed by the Ministry of Education Youth & Information were used. The GOILP is a formative assessment that seeks to determine if students were ready for grade 1, while the grades 4 and 6 assessments are summative in nature, done at the end of the grade for transitioning and placement. The Grade Four Literacy Test captures word recognition, comprehension and the communication task, while the Grade Four Numeracy Test measures six strands of mathematics, namely, number representation, number operation, measurement, geometry, algebra and statistics. The GSAT assessed students' performance in language arts, communication task, mathematics, science and social studies. All three assessments are standardized instruments administered to all Jamaican students in the respective grades.

Table 6.1 C-Alpha for Variables Measuring Parental Involvement

Variables	# of Questions	Original C-Alpha	Final C-Alpha
Teachers' belief about parent efficacy for helping their children	7	.79	.64
Teachers' report of parental involvement	16	.89	.87
Teachers' report of invitation to parental involvement	14	.89	.94
Parents' report of their involvement	8	.85	.80
Parents' report on invitation from teacher to be involved	6	.82	.88

The GOILP is administered to students at the beginning of grade 1 and captures information on students' general knowledge, concept of numbers, oral language, reading and writing. The scores students received on the different areas were then converted to readiness levels, which are organized in four categories: proficient, developing, beginning and not yet.

The Grade Four Literacy and Numeracy Tests are administered to students at the end of grade 4. The literacy test assesses students' mastery on word recognition, comprehension and communication task. The numeracy assessment tests students in number representation and operation, measurement, geometry, algebra and statistics. The raw scores were converted to the level of mastery in each component, then to a final mastery level in the respective tests (literacy and numeracy).

The GSAT was administered to students in March, with assessment in language arts, communication task, mathematics, science and social studies. The overall performance in this test determined their high school placement. Students were awarded raw scores which were converted to percentages. Therefore, students could score up to 100 per cent on each assessment.

All three assessments were recorded as interval/ratio measures that provided the scores for each student. In addition, the parental involvement scales were computed into interval/ratio measures to conduct the necessary inferential statistics and then to nominal measures to facilitate appropriate descriptive analysis. The assumptions for parametric tests were not met; therefore, Spearman rho correlation was used to investigate the relationships among the specified variables. Independent samples t-tests (Mann Whitney) were used to determine gender differences and Multiple Regression to investigate the impact of parental involvement on academic outcome. In addition, cross-tabulation and chi-square were used to investigate the differences between parental involvement and academic outcome based on students' gender.

Results

Teachers' report of parental involvement was moderate, accounting for 75 per cent, while parents' report of their involvement ranged between moderate and high representing 40 per cent and 58 per cent, respectively. Teachers report that most of the parents were efficacious in helping their children to succeed, where 33 per cent reported moderate and 65 per cent reported high (figure 6.1).

Invitation to be involved revealed some differences between reports from teachers and parents. More parents (accounting for 33 per cent) reported that they were never invited to be involved by the teacher, 22 per cent reported once per month and 17 per cent reported 1 or more times per week. From the teachers' report, parents were invited once every one to two weeks, once per month and one or more times each week, accounting for 44 per cent, 36 per cent and 13 per cent respectively (table 6.2).

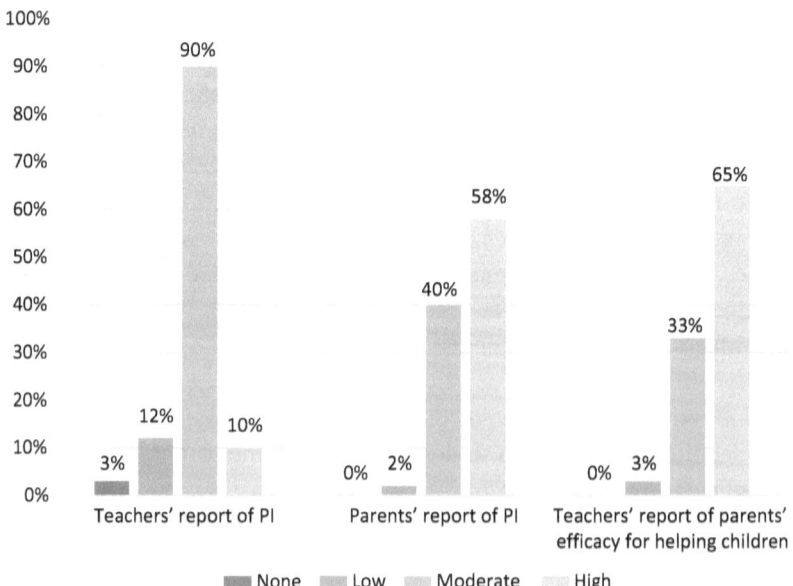

Figure 6.1 Report of parental involvement and parent efficaciousness.

Table 6.2 Report on Invitation to Be Involved

Study Variables	Never	Once This Year	Once Each Term	Once per Month	Once Every 1–2 Weeks	1+Times Each Week
Parents' report of teachers inviting them to be involved	38 (33%)	12 (10%)	10 (9%)	26 (22%)	10 (9%)	20 (17%)
Teachers' report of the invitation for parents to be involved	2 (2%)		9 (8%)	42 (36%)	48 (44%)	15 (13%)

Table 6.3 Descriptive Results of Academic Outcome

Assessments	Mean	Std. Deviation	Minimum	Maximum
Grade 1 Individual Learning Profile	111.37	25.262	9	144
Grade 4 Literacy	83.10	14.277	25	100
Grade 4 Numeracy	70.04	20.074	19	99
Average GSAT	72.90	16.833	32	98

The students had generally high performance on the GOILP and the Grade Four Literacy Test and moderate performance on the Grade Four Numeracy and GSAT, as represented by the mean and standard deviation in table 6.3.

Question 1: Relationship between parental involvement and students' academic outcomes

In determining the relationship between parental involvement and students' academic outcome, Spearman rho correlation was used, revealing low relationships. Teachers' report of parental involvement had a low relationship with GOILP ($r=.264$, $n=116$, $p<0.01$), and parents' report of their involvement had a negatively low relationship with GOILP ($r=-.250$, $n=116$, $p<0.01$) and Grade Four Numeracy Test ($r=-.197$, $n=116$, $p<0.05$) (see table 6.4).

Teachers' report on their invitation to parents to be involved revealed no significant relationship with students' performance. On the other hand, negative correlations were recorded for parents' report on invitation from teachers to be involved with GOILP ($r=-.377$, $p<0.01$), Grade Four

Literacy ($r=-.492$, $p<0.01$), Grade Four Numeracy ($r=-.415$, $p<0.01$) and GSAT ($r=-.345$, $p<0.01$) (see table 6.4). According to parents' reports, the findings suggest that parents whose children had higher scores were least likely to be invited by teachers, while parents of children with lower scores were more likely to be invited to be involved. This occurred across the three assessment periods.

Teachers' report on parents' efficacy for helping children had a positive relationship across the two assessment periods. There were low correlations between teachers' report of parents' efficacy for helping children at grade 1 based on GOILP results ($r=.379$, $p<0.01$), Grade Literacy ($r=.275$, $p<0.01$) and Grade Four Numeracy ($r=.261$, $p<0.01$). It can be assumed that parents' efficaciousness declined as students moved from grade 1 to grade 4.

Question 2: What is the difference in students' academic outcomes and parental involvement between males and females?

A Mann Whitney U test was conducted to determine if there were statistical differences between the gender of students with parental involvement and their academic outcomes. The results suggest differences in teachers' reports of parental involvement $z=-2.364$, $p<0.05$ where parents with male children ($m=66.13$) were more involved than those who had female children ($m=51.38$). Teachers' reports of their invitation to parental involvement also had significant differences ($z=-2.080$, $p<0.05$) between males and females, where parents of male students were invited to be involved more ($m=65.21$) than the parents of female students

Table 6.4 Correlation between Parental Involvement and Academic Outcomes

	Grade 1 - GOILP	Grade 4 Literacy	Grade 4 Numeracy	GSAT
Teachers' report of parental involvement	.264**	.137	.090	.165
Parents' report of their involvement	-.250**	-.197*	-.147	-.015
Invitation from teacher to be involved	-.141	.068	-.013	.061
Parents report of teachers invitation to be involved	-.377**	-.492**	-.415**	-.345**
Teachers' report of parent efficacy for helping children	.379**	.275**	.261**	.121

** Correlation is significant at the 0.01 level (2-tailed).

($m=52.24$). The findings therefore suggest that based on the teachers' reports, the parents of male students are more likely to be involved and are more likely to be invited to be involved.

Further crosstab analysis was done to determine the level of parental involvement and students' outcomes according to the gender of students. In addition, a chi-square test of independence was performed to examine the significant relationships among the variables. In relation to teachers' reports of parental involvement and students' outcome in grade 1, it was significant for males, X^2 (9, $n=56$) = 19.025, $p<.01$. Teachers reported that parents of males who were rated as proficient and developing were moderately involved. For students' outcomes in literacy, it was also significant for males, X^2 (6, $n=54$) = 11.075, $p<.05$. Male students of moderately involved parents who scored 71 per cent and above accounted for 89 per cent. Parents' reports of their involvement in relation to GSAT results were significant for males, X^2 (6, $n=47$) = 7.89, $p<.05$, which suggests that 70 per cent of the males with high parental involvement scored 71 per cent and over.

Teachers' reports on the invitation to parents to be involved was significant for female results in grade 4 numeracy scores, X^2 (10, $n=56$) = 24.01, $p<.05$) and for males in GSAT scores, X^2 (10, $n=47$) = 23.116, $p<.05$). This therefore suggests that parents were never invited to be involved, which represents 66 per cent of the females who scored 71 per cent and over. For males, 95 per cent scored 71 per cent and above for parents who were never invited to be involved.

Teachers' reports of their beliefs about parents' efficacy for helping their children and students' outcome in grade 1 were significant for both males – X^2 (6, $n=56$) = 24.239, $p<.01$) and females, X^2 (6, $n=56$) = 14.578, $p<.05$. The data suggest that 72 per cent of the males who were proficient at grade 1 had parents who were considered to be highly efficacious, while 67 per cent of the females at the same level had parents who were considered highly efficacious. Similar results occurred across grade 4 literacy and numeracy tests for both males and females. Results of the literacy tests suggest that of the males (X^2 (4, $n=54$) = 13.458, $p<.05$) and females (X^2 (4, $n=57$) = 10.307, $p<.05$) who scored 71 per cent and above, 98 per cent of their parents were considered highly efficacious. The results were somewhat different for females in the assessment of the numeracy results. For females, only 59 per cent of those who scored 71 per cent and above had parents who were considered very efficacious (X^2 (4, $n=56$) = 14.855, $p<.05$), while 78 per cent of males scoring 71 per cent and above had parents who were considered highly efficacious (X^2 (2, $n=51$) = 11.740, $p<.05$).

Teachers' report of parent efficaciousness with regard to GSAT scores was only significant for males (X^2 (4, $n=44$) = 7.843, $p<.05$). Of the males who scored 71 per cent and above, 76 per cent of their parents were reported to be highly efficacious.

Question 3: To what extent do parental involvement, invitation to be involved and the efficaciousness of parents predict the academic outcome of students at the primary level?

Multiple regression analysis was conducted to examine if parental involvement, invitation to be involved and parents' efficaciousness in helping students to succeed significantly predicted students' academic outcomes entering grade 1 and exiting grades 4 and 6.

Parents' and teachers' report on the following in the regression analysis accounted for 43.1 per cent of the variance in the GOILP scores: parents' reports of their involvement, invitations from teachers to be involved, teachers' report of parental involvement, invitations to parents to be involved and the efficaciousness of parents (F(5, 107) = 16.232, $p<.001$). This suggests that parental involvement impacts students' outcome at grade 1. Further examination of the individual predictors suggests that teachers' reports of parents' efficaciousness in helping children, teachers' reports of parental involvement and parents' reports on their invitation from teachers to be involved were statistically significant. The report on parents' efficaciousness had a higher Beta value ($\beta=.377$, $p<.001$) than teachers' report of parental involvement ($\beta=.248$, $p<.05$), while parents' reports on invitations from teachers to be involved negatively predicted students' outcome at grade 1 ($\beta=-.321$, $p<.001$). This therefore suggests that parents who are able to help their children contribute to them doing well at grade 1.

Approximately 43 per cent (42.9%) of the variance in the Grade Four Literacy scores was explained by analysing the following: parents' report of their involvement and how often they were invited to be involved by teachers, teachers' report of parental involvement, how often teachers invited parents to be involved and teachers' report of the efficaciousness of parents in helping their children succeed (F(5, 106) = 15.934, $p<.001$). This suggests that parental involvement impacts students' outcomes in grade 4 literacy.

Further examination of the individual predictors suggests that teachers' report of parents' efficaciousness in helping children and parents' report on their invitation from teachers to be involved were statistically significant. The report on parents' efficaciousness had a higher Beta value ($\beta=.444$, $p<.001$) than the parents' report on their invitation from the teacher to be involved, which negatively predicted students' outcome in literacy at grade 4 ($\beta=-.422$, $p<.001$). This therefore suggests that parents who are able to help their children contribute to them doing well in literacy at grade 4.

For the Grade Four Numeracy Test using parents' report of their involvement, invitation from teachers to be involved and teachers' report of parental involvement, invitations to parents to be involved and parents' efficaciousness as predictors, the results of regression analysis suggest that 30.1 per cent explained the variance in scores received on the numeracy assessment ($F(5, 104)=8.938$, $p<.001$). This suggests that parental involvement impacts students' outcomes in the grade 4 numeracy assessment.

Further examination of the individual predictors suggests that teachers' report of parents' efficaciousness in helping children and parents' report on their invitations from teachers to be involved were statistically significant. Parents' report on invitation from teachers to be involved had a higher Beta value, although negative ($\beta=-.401$, $p<.001$) than teachers' report on parents' efficaciousness to help children ($\beta=.359$, $p<.001$) in grade 4 numeracy. This therefore suggests that parents who are able to help their children contribute to them doing well in numeracy at the grade 4 level. However, the parents of children who are doing well are invited less often by teachers. It can be assumed that parents who knew how to help their children required less input and invitations from teachers.

At wave 3, the GSAT results were collected to determine if parents' reports of their involvement, invitation from teachers to be involved and teachers' reports of parental involvement, invitations to parents to be involved and parents' efficaciousness, predicted students' performance. The results of the regression analysis suggest that 23.5 per cent explained the variance in scores received on the GSAT assessment ($F (5, 94)=5.781$, $p<.001$). This suggests that parental involvement impacted on students' outcomes in GSAT now PEP. Further examination of the individual predictors suggests that teachers' report of parents' efficaciousness in helping children and parents' report on their invitation from teachers to be involved were statistically significant. Parents' report on invitation from teachers to be involved had a higher Beta value, although negative ($\beta=-.359$, $p<.001$) than teachers' report on parents' efficaciousness to help children ($\beta=.270$, $p<.05$) in GSAT. This therefore suggested that parents who are able to help their children contributed to them doing well in GSAT. However, the parents of children who do well are invited less often by teachers. It can be assumed that parents who know how to help their children required less input and invitation from teachers.

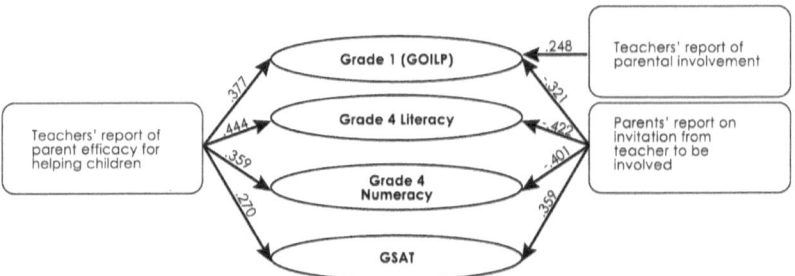

Figure 6.2 Parental involvement variables predicting students' outcome.

The model in figure 6.2 suggests that only teachers' report of parents' efficaciousness had a direct impact on the outcome of students throughout grades 1–6; and reports of parental involvement only impacted students' outcome in grade 1. In addition, invitation to be involved had an indirect effect on students' outcome throughout grades 1–6, and teachers' reports on parents' efficacy in helping children to succeed declined at grade 6 (see figure 6.2).

Discussion

Early parental involvement significantly impacted students' academic outcomes as they transitioned to different grades. The moderate to high scores in the different assessments were significantly related to teachers' report of parent efficaciousness, invitation from teacher to be involved and teachers' report of parental involvement.

According to the findings, parental involvement is expected to be high at the elementary level, because at the beginning of primary education parents are expected to be highly involved and efficacious in helping their children to succeed. Additionally, parents' sense of efficacy is related to students' performance throughout their primary education. Parents' sense of efficacy is socially constructed as a result of personal experiences and children's success. It is important to parents that they have positive experiences in helping their children to succeed, as this makes them more likely to continue throughout their children's schooling. The findings are consistent with the results of Alves et al. (2017) that parent and family characteristics have a significant impact on students' outcomes. This therefore suggests that students (with the help of parents) can excel, regardless of the school that they attend. This is the view shared by Berk (2010) and Rutherford (2011), that family engagement in children's learning is important to academic outcome.

Parents get involved in their children's education because they believe it is their responsibility. It is hoped that being involved will contribute to their children's academic success. Teachers reported that parents who had boys were more involved than those who had girls. This is consistent with the findings of Jafarov (2015) that parents of male students were more involved than those of girls. To further explain this phenomenon from the Jamaican perspective, girls tend to outperform boys, and boys' success requires constant and consistent supervision from both parents and teachers to motivate them to excel. Guo et al. (2018) stated that girls do not require constant supervision because they are capable of sustained self-control and improved self-regulation, thus reinforcing the finding that males require more instrumental support (Pires et al., 2017). In addition, parents of male students are more likely to be invited to be involved. Consistent with the findings of Pires et al. (2017) and Guo et al. (2018) that males may require more supervision and consistent support in achieving their academic outcomes, this necessitates consistent parental engagement and support, as well as compliance with teachers' invitations to be involved.

Parents' role construction as parents will determine their willingness to visit school when invited to be involved. Furthermore, if visiting the school is reflected in increased performance, they will visit when invited. Therefore, parents who are interested in their children's success are more likely to accept invitations from teachers to be involved. In addition, teachers are least likely to invite parents to be involved when their children are performing according to the standard set by the school. This suggests that parents who are equipped with the necessary parenting skills and who can facilitate learning at home consistent with Epstein's (2001) explanation of parental involvement are more likely to positively influence their children's academic outcomes. The findings are also reflective of the views outlined by Hoover-Dempsey et al. (2005) that how parents feel about their role as parents impacts on their children's success. When schools provide a welcoming environment and opportunities are provided for parents to participate, as suggested by Đurišić and Bunijevac (2017), they are more likely to be involved when they are invited to do so. This affirms the findings of Green et al. (2007) that teachers who value the input of parents will invite them to participate in different school-related activities that will benefit the students.

Parents play a significant role in helping children to transition into a new school and into different grades. The findings from the teachers' report of parents' efficaciousness to help children succeed, although small (.27–.38), had a direct impact on students' performance on their GOILP, Numeracy and GSAT and moderately predicted literacy outcome. According to Hoover-Dempsey et al. (2005), parents who believe they have the necessary knowledge, training and skills to help their children to succeed will do so. However, as students transition through the grades, the content gets more difficult and efficaciousness may decline, while parents may not help as much because they believe that they are not competent enough to help. In Jamaica, the Grade Four Literacy, Numeracy and GSATs are high-stakes examinations. Most parents usually make great effort to help when they have the necessary skills and knowledge, and where they cannot help, they seek help from others in the form of extra lessons and one-on-one tutoring. The positive impact between parents' sense of efficaciousness and helping their children to succeed at the different levels confirms the findings of Yamamoto, Holloway and Suzuki (2016) that parents who feel efficacious are more likely to help.

Conclusion

Teachers' report of parental involvement, parent efficaciousness and invitation to be involved are statistically significant predictors of students' academic outcomes throughout primary education. Involvement and parents' efficaciousness were positively associated with academic performance, while invitation from teachers to be involved had a negative association. Parental involvement benefits students' outcomes; this reinforces Epstein's six types of involvement. According to Epstein (2005), when parents take an active role in the education of their children and schools communicate with them, they will get involved. In addition, schools can encourage active parental engagement when they provide parents with the necessary skills to help their children, and the parents are involved in the decision making that will benefit their children. Moreover, how competent parents feel about helping their children to succeed (Hoover-Dempsey & Sandler, 1997) is a strong indicator of how much they will get involved.

Schools should seek to orient parents as their children transition through the different grades and communicate their expectations for involvement in their children's education and academic success. In addition, parents can be empowered by being provided with practical approaches, for example, workshops, consistent with their children's stages of development and grade level, and this in turn will improve their academic outcomes. A communication network that encourages parents' participation and provides positive feedback could also be created, and this would increase the level of involvement when parents are invited to be involved.

References

Altschul, I. (2011). Parental involvement and the academic achievement of Mexican American youths: What kind of involvement in youths' education matter most? *Social Work Research, 35*(3), 159–70.

Alves, A.F., Gomes, C.M., Martins, A., & Almeida, L.S. (2017). Cognitive performance and academic achievement: How do family and school converge? *European Journal of Education and Psychology, 10,* 49–56.

Berk, L.E. (2010). *Development through the lifespan* (5th ed). Allyn & Bacon.

Blossfeld, H., Schneider, T., & Doll, J. (2009). Methodological advantages of panel studies: Designing the new national educational panel study (NEPS) in Germany. *Journal for Educational Research Online, 1*(1), 10–32.

Bowe, F.G. (2005). *Early childhood special education: Birth to eight* (3rd ed.). Thompson and Delmar Learning.

Campbell, A., Povey, J., Hancock, K., Mitrou, F., & Haynes, M. (2017). Parents' interest in their child's education and children's outcomes in adolescence and adulthood: Does gender matter? *International Journal of Educational Research, 85,* 131–47.

Chowa, G.A.N., Masa, R.D., & Tucker, J. (2013). *Parental involvement's effects on academic performance: Evidence from the YouthSave Ghana experiment.* https://openscholarship.wustl.edu/cgi/viewcontent.cgi?article=1728&context=csd_research

Cole, S.M. (2013). *An investigation into the impact of parental involvement on the cognitive and social skills of grade one students in Jamaica.* [Unpublished doctoral dissertation]. The University of the West Indies, Mona.

Cousins, L.H. & Mickelson, R.A. (2011). Making success in education: What black parents believe about participation in their children's education. *Current Issues in Education, 14*(3), 1–17.

Driessen, G., Smith, F., & Sleegers, P. (2004). *Parental involvement and educational achievement.* Institute of Applied Social Sciences, Radboud University; Department of Education, University of Amsterdam.

Đurišić, M. & Bunijevac, M. (2017). Parental involvement as an important factor for successful education. *CEPS Journal 7*(3), 137–53.

Epstein, J.L. (2001). *School, family, and community partnerships: Preparing educators and improving schools.* Westview Press.

Epstein, J.L., Sanders, M.G., Simon, B.S., Salinas, K.C., Jansorn, N.R., & Van Voorhis, F.L. (2002). *School, family, and community partnerships: Your handbook for action* (2nd ed.). Corwin Press. https://www.govinfo.gov/content/pkg/ERIC-ED467082/pdf/ERIC-ED467082.pdf

Fan, X. & Chen, M. (2001). Parental involvement and students' academic achievement: A meta-analysis. *Educational Psychology Review, 13*(1), 1–22. Plenum Publishing Corporation.

Fernández-Alonso, R., Álvarez-Díaz, M., Woitschach, P., Suárez-Álvarez, J., & Cuesta, M. (2017). Parental involvement and academic performance: Less control and more communication. *Psicothema, 29*(4), 453–61. doi: 10.7334/psicothema2017.181

Finn, A.S., Kraft, M.A., West, M.R., Leonard, J.A., Bish, C.E., Martin, R.E., Sheridan, M.A., Gabrieli, C.F.O., & Gabrieli, J.D.E. (2014). Cognitive skills, student achievement tests, and schools. *Psychological Science, 25*(3), 736–44.

Green, C.L., Walker, J.M.T., Hoover-Dempsey, K.V., & Sandler, H.M. (2007). Parents' motivations for involvement in children's education: An empirical test of a theoretical model of parental involvement. *Journal of Educational Psychology, 99*(3), 532–44.

Guo, X., Lv, B., Zhou, H., Liu, C., Liu, J., Jiang, K., & Luo, L. (2018). Gender differences in how family income and parental education relate to reading achievement in China: The mediating role of parental expectation and parental involvement. *Frontiers in Psychology, 9*, 1–12.

Hayakawa, M., Englund, M.M., Warner-Richter, M., & Reynolds, A.J. (2013). Early parent involvement and school achievement: A longitudinal path analysis. *Dialog, 16*(1), 200–04.

Hayes, M. (2012). Parental involvement and achievement outcomes in African American adolescents. *Journal of Comparative Family Studies, 43*(4), 567–82.

Hoover-Dempsey, K. & Sandler, H. M. (1997). Why do parents become involved in their children's education? *Review of Educational Research, 67*(1), 3–42.

Hoover-Dempsey, K.V., Battiato, A.C., Walker, J.M.T., Reed, R.P., DeJong, J.M., & Jones, K.P. (2001). Parental involvement in homework. *Educational Psychologist, 36* (3), 195–209. https://doi.org/10.1207/S15326985EP3603 _5.Hoover-Dempsey, K.V., Walker, J.M.T., Sandler, H.M., Whetsel, D., Green, C.L., Wilkins, A.S., & Closson, K. (2005). Why do parents become involved? Research findings and implications. *The Elementary School Journal, 106*, 105–30.

Jafarov, J. (2015). Factors affecting parental involvement in education: The analysis of literature. *Khazar Journal of Humanities and Social Sciences, 18*(4), 35–44.

Jaiswal, K.S. & Choudhuri, R. (2017). A review of the relationship between parental involvement and students' academic performance. *The International Journal of Indian Psychology, 4*(3), 110–23.

Jethro, O.O. & Aina, F.F. (2012). Effects of parental involvement on the academic performance of students in elementary schools. *International Journal of Academic Research in Business and Social Sciences, 2*(1), 196–202.

Jeynes, W.H. (2007). The relationship between parental involvement and urban secondary school student academic achievement-A meta-analysis. *Urban Education, 42*(1), 82–110.

Khajehpoura, M. & Ghazvini, S.D. (2011). The role of parental involvement affect in children's academic performance. *Procedia Social and Behavioral Sciences, 15*, 1204–08.

Kimaro, A.R. & Machumu, H.J. (2015). Impacts of parental involvement in school activities on academic achievement of primary school children. *International Journal of Education and Research, 3*(8), 483–94.

Lueder, D.C. (2011). *Involving hard-to-reach parents: Creating family/school partnerships.* Rowman & Littlefield.

McDowell, K., Jack, A., & Compton, M. (2018). Parent involvement in pre-kindergarten and the effects on student achievement. *The Advocate, 23*(6). https://doi.org/10.4148/2637-4552.1004

Moon, U.J. & Hofferth, S.L. (2016, April 1). Parental involvement, child effort, and the development of immigrant boys' and girls' reading and mathematics skills: A latent difference score growth model. *Learn and Individual Differences, 47,* 136–44. Author's manuscript. doi:10.1016/j.lindif.2016.01.001.

Park, S. & Holloway, S.D. (2017). The effects of school-based parental involvement on academic achievement at the child and elementary school level: A longitudinal study. *The Journal of Educational Research, 110*(1), 1–16. doi: 10.1080/00220671.2015.1016600

Piaget, J. (1972). *The psychology of the child.* Basic Books.

———. (1990). *The child's conception of the world.* Littlefield Adams.

Pires, H.S., Candeias, A.A., Grácio, L., Galindo, E., & Melo, M. (2017). The influence of family support according to gender in the Portuguese language course achievement. *Frontiers in Psychology, 8,* 1–8.

Rutherford, M.D. (2011). *Child development: Perspectives in developmental psychology.* Oxford University Press.

Samms-Vaughan, M. (2004). *The Jamaican pre-school child: The status of early childhood development in Jamaica.* Planning Institute of Jamaica.

Shajith, B.I. & Erchul, W.P. (2014). Bringing parents to school: The effect of invitations from school, teacher, and child on parental involvement in middle schools. *International Journal of School and Educational Psychology, 2*(1), 11–23.

Sheldon, S.B. & Epstein, J.L. (2005). Involvement counts: Family and community partnerships and mathematics achievement. *The Journal of Educational Research, 98*(4), 196–206.

Slavin, R.E. (2012). *Educational psychology: Theory and practice* (10th ed.). Pearson.

Strawhun, J., Olson, A., Kane, L., & Peterson, R.L. (2014). *Parent & family involvement. Strategy Brief.* Student Engagement Project, University of Nebraska-Lincoln and the Nebraska Department of Education. https://k12engagement.unl.edu/strategy-briefs/Parent%20%26%20Family%20Involvement%2011-15-14_0.pdf

University of New Hampshire. (2008, May 28). Parental involvement strongly impacts student achievement. *Science Daily.* Retrieved July 11, 2022 from www.sciencedaily.com/releases/2008/05/080527123852.htm

USAID/MOE Partnership for Improved Reading. (2014, June). *Closing the gender gap: A guide for improving the literacy performance of boys and girls at the primary level.* https://pep.moey.gov.jm/wp-content/uploads/2018/10/June-2014-Final-Revised-Guide-_-Gender-Strategies.pdf

Vygotsky, L.S. (1978). *Mind and society: The development of higher mental processes.* Harvard University Press.

Watson Williams, C. & Fox, K. (2013). *School effectiveness in Jamaica: What do successful schools look like?* https://ncel.gov.jm/sites/default/files/school_effectiveness_in_jamaica.pdf

Wilder, S. (2014). Effects of parental involvement on academic achievement: A meta-synthesis. *Educational Review, 66*(3), 377–97. http://dx.doi.org/10.1080/00131911.2013.780009

Yamamoto, Y., Holloway, S.D., & Suzuki, S. (2016). Parental engagement in children's education: Motivating factors in Japan and the U.S. *School Community Journal, 26*(1), 45–66.

Section 3

Chapter 7

A Survey Design of the Rate of Parental Involvement and Reported Academic Performance of Grade 10 Students

NATALIA WRIGHT, SHENHAYE FERGUSON AND SARAN STEWART

Introduction

One can argue that the home is deemed a habitat where a child first learns while the school is viewed as an institution that facilitates a child's continuous learning. Hawes and Plourde (2005) argued that parents who are involved in their children's lives, especially at an early age, are at an advantage and tend to develop important life skills and lead productive adult lives. Additionally, research has found that parents occupy a vital role in their children's education, thus impacting their academic outcomes (Barge & Loges, 2003; Driessen, Smit, & Sleegers, 2005; Hawes & Plourde, 2005). More specifically, there is a positive relationship between parental involvement and students' academic achievement (Driessen, Smit, & Sleegers, 2005; Griffith, 1996), though for some schools, it remains a scarce commodity. The president of the Jamaica's National Parent Teachers Association (PTA) noted that the attendance rate of parents at parent teachers' meetings in most schools in Jamaica is 20 per cent to 30 per cent (Reynolds, 2008). Additionally, some of the country's students receive limited to no educational support from parents (Troupe, 2017). Troupe further admitted that the most difficult task in her capacity as a principal of a Jamaican high school was to obtain the involvement of parents in the institution's educational programmes. This could be related to Harris and Goodall's (2008) study that described some parents as "hard to reach" (p. 285), explaining that these were parents who would visit the schools only when it was mandatory to do so.

Schools cannot work in a vacuum if optimum students' successes are to be realized (Wright, 2014). Ultimately, there needs to be an integrated approach to learning which includes parents, schools and communities. This vision of collaboration is based on Epstein's theory of overlapping spheres of influence (Epstein, 1995). This theory was adopted in this empirical study as the lens through which parental involvement will be measured. There are six principles of parental involvement based on Epstein's (1995) and Sanders and Epstein's (1998) research: (1) parenting, (2) communicating, (3) volunteering, (4) learning at home, (5) decision making and (6) collaborating with the community. The community sphere of the model was not utilized in this study as it did not play a significant role in attaining the purpose of this research, since its focus is on examining the rate of parental involvement and academic performance. Hence, data was collected from parents and students and not community members.

Accordingly, the purpose of this chapter is to present the findings of a pilot study that examined the extent to which the principles of parental involvement impact grade 10 students' academic performance. Notably, the terms "parents" and "guardians" will be used interchangeably throughout the study. The independent variable, parental involvement, is defined as the rate of participation of parents in school activities and school-related activities at home, which is a composite variable of the five constructs of Joyce Epstein's model (1995). The dependent variable, students' academic performance, is defined as students' self-reported grades received on their end-of-term examinations. The research topic was simplified into the following research questions:

1. Is there a statistically significant relationship between the parental involvement variables (parenting, communicating, volunteering, learning at home and decision making) and students' reported academic performance?
2. To what extent is there a statistically significant impact of parental involvement on students' reported academic performance at the grade 10 level?

Research Hypothesis. This study was guided by the following null hypothesis:

H_o: There is no difference between students' academic performance and parental involvement.

To address the research questions, we first presented the findings from the review of the literature and articulate a theoretical framework using Epstein's theory. Second, we utilized two survey instruments for the study sharing the results of the responses followed by a discussion of the findings and implications.

Literature Review

A review of the literature provided a myriad of definitions for parental involvement. For some researchers it is defined as "a direct effort, provided by the parent, in order to increase educational outcomes of their children" (Avvisati, Besbas, & Guyon, 2010, p. 4); a partnership between parents and schools (Epstein, 1995); and, being involved in activities like "volunteering at school, communicating with teachers and other school personnel, assisting in academic activities at home, and attending school events" (Hill & Taylor, 2004, p. 161). Jeynes (2005a) defined it as "parental participation in the educational processes and experiences of their children" (p. 245). Fan (2001) alluded to Bloom's (1980) definition of parental involvement "as parental aspirations for their children's academic achievement" (p. 29). Schools may define it as being a "provider-receiver model with conventional parent activities like teacher conferences and attendance at school fundraisers" (Stein, 2009, p. 1). For the purposes of this study, we decided to use Epstein's Overlapping Spheres of Influence, given the robust quantitative research carried out with the theory along with the approved use of the researcher's instrument.

Epstein's Factors that Influence Parental Involvement

Epstein established six principles of parental involvement that have been generated from over twenty-four studies between 1981 and 2018 that mirror the collaboration between schools and parents (Becker & Epstein, 1982, Epstein, 1995; Sui-Chu & Willms, 1996; Driessen, Smit, & Sleegers, 2005; Griffiths-Prince, 2009; "Naperville Community Unit School District 203", 2013; Hives, 2017; Troupe, 2017; Hicks, 2018). The principles are described in the subsequent listing based on Epstein (1995) and Sanders and Epstein (1998):

1. Parenting: this is where schools assist parents/families with parenting and child-rearing skills and overall assist them to be better parents and aid in creating a positive home environment to enhance the learning and development of children as students. Activities may include workshops, family support programmes, home visits, parent education and training courses (Epstein, 1995).
2. Communicating: schools should design effective forms of communication to inform parents about students' progress and school programmes from home to school and school to home. Activities may include parent conferences, language translators to

help families who need it and clear information on school policies and programmes (Epstein, 1995).
3. Volunteering: this involvement allows families to give their help, time and talent in support of the school, students and teachers by participating in school activities such as school renovation and Labour Day projects.
4. Learning at home: schools provide information, guidance and activities to families about how to help and monitor students with learning at home. These activities include homework- and curriculum-associated activities.
5. Decision making: include parents in the school's decision-making process and management of the school through a medium such as PTA meetings.
6. Collaborating with community: identifying and integrating community resources and services that will help to strengthen school programmes, parenting and children's learning and development. Activities may include "information for students and families on community programmes and services, participation of alumni in school programmes for students, service to the community by students, families and schools" (Epstein, 1995, p. 704).

Parental Involvement and Its Impact on Students' Academic Performance

Parental involvement can be influenced by factors such as school background characteristics (degree of urbanization, number of pupils and composition of pupil population) and the socio-economic and ethnic origin of pupil, which may in turn affect the performance of students (Driessen, Smit, & Sleegers, 2005; Griffith, 1996). Usually, the more favourable these factors, the more involved parents are (Driessen, Smit, & Sleegers, 2005; Harris & Goodall, 2008). Houtenville and Conway (2008) found that parental effort had a strong positive effect on academic performance depending on the resources of the school. In other words, parental effort was greater if the school had adequate resources to support students. Therefore, the school's characteristics and overall socio-economic status impact how involved parents are in their children's education (Jeynes, 2005a,b; Sanders, Epstein, & Connors-Tadros 1999). Further to this, Shoaga and Rasheed's (2019) study observed that there was a significant positive relationship between parental involvement and academic performance.

Students' educational success is influenced by parental engagement in learning (Desforges & Abouchaar, 2003; Fan & Chen, 2001; Shaw,

2008). Driessen, Smit and Sleegers (2005) noted specifically that parental involvement at home will lead to better academic performance. Interestingly, Fernández-Alonso et al. (2017) found that parental involvement, although desirable, does not guarantee better results academically for students. However, their study found that "students whose parents exhibited a more distal or indirect profile of family involvement tended to demonstrate better results than those from homes with a more controlling style" (p. 453).

Bhargava and Witherspoon (2015) examined parental involvement for students in grades 7 to 11 in a Maryland county in the United States. They found that parental involvement was crucial in the educational success of students at this level. They further argued that parents may reduce their involvement based on the fact that at the high school level students are given more autonomy. However, these parents manifest their involvement by maintaining strategies "that allow them to scaffold independence in youth and promote youth decision making ability (e.g., communicating the value of education)" (Bhargava & Witherspoon, 2015, p. 1702).

Harris and Goodall (2008) conducted a research for twelve months which found a positive effect on students' learning outcome when parents were engaged in learning at home. Notably, Bower and Griffin (2011) stated that this involvement at home could range from parents checking in with students on homework being done, asking students to tell them about their day, liaising with teachers, engaging with what they learn in class, asking about upcoming projects and providing support emotionally and also physically depending on the assignment. Chen (2003) postulated that there is a positive relationship between students' academic performance and parents who are involved in their child's reading at home (as cited in Shute et al., 2011). Fan (2001) found that parents' supervision of children at home, which is similar in meaning to Epstein's variable *learning at home*, has the weakest impact on academic achievement. He noted that these students were not doing well at school in the first place. Thus, at the point of parental involvement, students were already underperforming. Similarly, Driessen, Smit and Sleegers (2005) examined students' success in English language and mathematics and noted that parental involvement might not be useful in children's academic life at the point where the child is already failing or is deemed problematic.

Jeynes (2005a) posited that parents who communicate with their children about school, check homework and attend school functions help to improve students' academic performance. Harris and Goodall (2008) revealed that volunteering in school-related activities by parents has different effects on achievement. Fan's (2001) study highlighted a more precise result indicating that volunteering has a positive but small impact on students' academic growth. Additionally, Sanders, Epstein and Connors-Tadros (1999) mentioned that volunteering and decision making as parental involvement constructs have significant, independent and positive impacts on parents' reported participation in school activities. They further stated that these two constructs are likely to encourage student's success (Sanders, Epstein, & Connors-Tadros, 1999). Conversely, Okpala and Smith (2001) noted volunteering was not significant to students' academic achievement. Based on these studies, it is uncertain of the effect that volunteering has on students' academic achievements.

Shaw (2008) who collected data from career and technical students found that the most prevalent types of parental involvement based on Epstein's theory are parenting and learning at home; this she attributed to the structure of the institution she studied which was a Career and Technology Center. Sanders, Epstein and Connors-Tadros (1999) found that many schools do not educate families on how to provide learning at home to their children, but that if schools implement partnership practices, then parents can become more involved in their adolescents' lives. The authors also stated that high schools that implement programmes of partnership will see greater parent participation both at school and at home regardless of the parents' educational backgrounds.

Methodology

Research Design

A survey design approach was employed in this quantitative study to explain the extent to which parental involvement impacts students' academic performance in grade 10. This approach afforded us the opportunity to contextually pilot an internationally tested survey instrument which provides strong baseline data to discern the scope and prevalence of the rate of occurrence of parental involvement, as well as its relationship with academic performance, in a Jamaican high school.

Population and sample. This research drew on the population of grade 10 students ($n = 307$) and their parents ($n = 307$) at an upgraded co-educational high school in Clarendon, Jamaica, where there were 101 males and 206 females. A single-stage sampling design was used in this study since all grade 10 students were chosen from the school's population, in addition to their parent/guardian who they identified as being most involved in their academic life. Additionally, the systematic probability sampling method was used where every second student was selected from a list generated until the desired student sample size of 150 was realized. Data was collected from students and their parents/guardians so that an association could be made between the data from both sampled groups. This study has a sample size of 193, more specifically, 125 students and 68 parents with consideration given to the practicality, time and economic constraints of the study.

Instrumentation. For the purpose of this study, the survey items were adapted from Shaw (2008), Davis (2000) and NM Family/Parent/Involvement Initiative (n.d.) which they originally adapted from Epstein's (1995) research. The student survey consisted of fifty items and the parent survey had fifty-four items.[1] Each survey has items on participants' demography and the topic being examined which are based on the adopted theoretical framework. The first five items on the students' survey represented their demographic information, while the others covered their academic performance and the research topic. The parent survey had the first ten representing demographic information, and the others were based on the research topic. Likert-scale responses were mainly used on both survey instruments,[2] and academic performance was measured at a continuous level from 0 to 100 per cent. These instruments were tested to obtain their reliability and validity through an instrument-pilot study.

Reliability. Internal consistency was used to measure the reliability of the surveys by using Cronbach's alpha which was computed using the Spearman's correlation formula in SPSS.

Refer to table 7.1 for the reported reliability for the students' and parents' surveys were .853 and .887 respectively which are acceptable as they are above .7 (Pallant, 2005).

Validity. The validity of the instruments was measured using face and content validity. Based on a review of the survey items, satisfactory feedback was given by an expert researcher and also from its original developer, Joyce Epstein. These reviews gave the assurance that the instruments had face validity. Content validity of the surveys was established through the information gathered from various literature (Davis, 2000; Driessen, 2005; Shaw, 2008) that used Epstein's (1995) overlapping spheres of influence

---

[1] Please email the authors at wright.success@gmail.com to access the details of survey instruments completed by parents and students.
[2] Ibid.

Table 7.1 Participants' Response Rate and Reliability Coefficient of Surveys

Participants	Pilot Study		Actual Study	
	Response Rate	Reliability Coefficient	Response Rate / Sample Size	Reliability Coefficient
Students	(100%)	.742	100% / 125	.853
Parents/Guardians	83%	.846	54% / 68	.887

Table 7.2 Defined Constructs for Parental Involvement Framework

Constructs	Descriptions
Parenting	Schools assist parents with parenting and child-rearing skills.
Communicating	Schools design effective forms of communication.
Volunteering	Schools allow families to participate in school activities.
Learning at home	Schools provide information and activities to families about monitoring students' home learning.
Decision making	Schools include parents in its decision-making process.

framework to research the relationship of parents, community and school for the benefit of the students.

Variables. The independent variable, parental involvement was defined as the participation of parents in school activities and school-related activities at home which includes the five constructs defined in table 7.2. These constructs are based on Epstein (1995) and Sanders and Epstein (1998). The dependent variable, students' academic performance was defined as students' self-reported grades received on their end of term examinations. This was measured using students' responses to items related to academic performance via surveys.

Data Analysis

The parametric techniques of Pearson Product Moment Correlation and multiple linear regression were used to analyse the data. In answering the first research question, the Pearson Product Moment Correlation was employed to examine the relationship between the parental involvement constructs (*parenting, communicating, volunteering, learning at home* and *decision making*) and students' academic performance. As a result, the strength and direction of the relationship between the variables were obtained between +1 and −1. Multiple linear regression was used to analyse the second research question in revealing the impact of parental involvement on students' academic performance. From this analysis, the relative contribution of each parental involvement subscale on the dependent variable was statistically known, along with the variance of the model as a whole on the dependent variable. Additionally, descriptive statistics were used to analyse aspects of the data such as participants' demographics and selected items on each subscale.

Ethical Considerations

Both the University of the West Indies and the principal of the participating school gave permission to undertake this study. Consent was granted by parents/guardians, which allowed data to be collected from their child/ward. Anonymity and confidentiality were maintained throughout the study. American Psychological Association (APA) guidelines were also adhered to which included proper referencing and citations.

Limitations

This study drew on 193 participants which can be made generalizable to the sampled population but not to other school populations. However, it can serve as a pilot of the instruments, which can provide strong baseline data for future studies in a similar context.

Results

The research questions and null hypothesis guiding this study are as follows:

1. Is there a statistically significant relationship between the parental involvement variables (parenting, communicating, volunteering, learning at home and decision making) and students' reported academic performance?
2. To what extent is there a statistically significant impact of parental involvement on students' reported academic performance at the grade 10 level?

H_o: There is no difference between students' academic performance and parental involvement.

Descriptive Statistics

Profile of student participants. The data indicated that most of the 125 student participants reside in Clarendon (98.4 per cent) and were females (68 per cent). They ranged between the ages 14–15 (55.2 per cent) and 16–17 (44.8 per cent) with most of them living in nuclear families (40 per cent, $n = 124$) followed by extended families (30.6 per cent) and single-parent families (26.6 per cent). A small per cent of 2.4, however, reported that they lived with siblings (*see* table 7.3).

Students' academic performance. This was measured using students' self-reported grades obtained on their end of term examinations. Items used on the students' survey which measured students' academic performance were the average percentage range of students' academic performance and students' average percentage score on their last report card. Both items had responses measuring from 0 to 100 per cent. A majority (85 per cent) of students reported that on average their academic performance ranged from 60 per cent to 79 per cent, while 12 per cent and 3 per cent performed at 80 per cent to 89 per cent, and 40 per cent to 59 per cent respectively. Additionally, most (73 per cent) students reported receiving scores between 60 per cent and 79 per cent on their last report card with the least (2 per cent) receiving 90 per cent to 100 per cent.

Profile of parent participants. The parents' demographic data summarized in table 7.4 indicated that mothers were more involved in

Table 7.3 Descriptive Statistics of Students' Demographic Background

		Frequency	Per Cent	Valid Per Cent	Cumulative Per Cent
Gender	Male	40	32.0	32.0	32.0
	Female	85	68.0	68.0	100.0
Age	14–15	69	55.2	55.2	55.2
	16–17	56	44.8	44.8	100.0
Family Structure	Single	33	26.4	26.6	26.6
	Nuclear	50	40.0	40.3	66.9
	Extended	38	30.4	30.6	97.6
	Siblings	3	2.4	2.4	100.0

their child/children's lives than any other family member or guardian as they accounted for 71.2 per cent of the sixty-six participants who responded to this item, followed by fathers with 16.7 per cent. The majority of persons who completed this survey were in the age range of 41 to 50 (48.3 per cent, $n = 67$). The data also showed that most respondents were from nuclear families (47.1 per cent), were employed (75 per cent) and that they lived in the parish of Clarendon (98.5 per cent, $n = 68$). Most respondents had a high school level education (36.4 per cent, $n = 66$) and vocational or training education (31.8 per cent). Only 23 per cent of them had tertiary level education.

Rate of parental involvement. The majority of respondents, students (92.7 per cent, $n = 124$) and parents (98.5 per cent, $n = 68$) agreed that school/parent partnership is important to students' academic success (*see* figure 7.1). The highest percentage of parents/guardians at 34.8 per cent ($n = 68$) disagreed that their child likes school, while 32.8 per cent ($n = 124$)

Table 7.4 Descriptive Statistics of Parents' Demographic Background

		Frequency	Per Cent	Valid Per Cent	Cumulative Per Cent
Relationship	Mother	47	69.1	71.2	71.2
	Father	11	16.2	16.7	87.9
	Stepmother	1	1.5	1.5	89.4
	Grandparents	2	2.9	3.0	92.4
	Guardian	2	2.9	3.0	95.5
	Other	3	4.4	4.5	100.0
Age	21–30	5	7.4	7.5	7.5
	31–40	19	27.9	28.4	35.8
	41–50	33	48.5	49.3	85.1
	51–60	8	11.8	11.9	97.0
	61–70	1	1.5	1.5	98.5
	71–80	1	1.5	1.5	100.0
Family Structure	Single	15	22.1	22.1	22.1
	Nuclear	32	47.1	47.1	69.1
	Extended	20	29.4	29.4	98.5
	Siblings	1	1.5	1.5	100.0

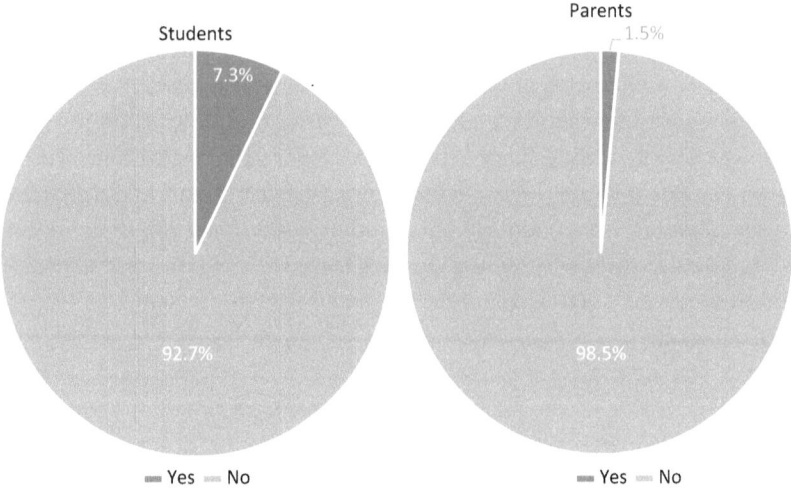

Figure 7.1 Is school/parent partnership important to students' academic success?

being the highest for students agreed that they like school. Also, 10 per cent of the students reported that they do no homework and a total of 63 per cent reported that they spend one hour or less doing the same.

Forty per cent of the sixty-eight parents reported that they have "never" volunteered in school activities with 50 per cent saying that they do not do so often. Twenty-nine per cent of parents also reported that sometimes they are needed at home, while 24 per cent stated that they were rarely needed at home. Fifty-seven per cent of them ($n = 63$) reported that the distance from school does not affect their ability to attend school activities, while 18 per cent say sometimes and 6 per cent say regularly they are affected by this. A total of 50 per cent ($n = 66$) of parents agreed and strongly agreed that they go to PTA meetings often and 33 per cent slightly agreed, 11 per cent disagreed and 6 per cent strongly disagreed that they attend PTA meetings often.

Parenting. One of the items that was used to measure this variable asked if "the school conducts workshops or provides information for parents on child development". The results indicated that 34 per cent of the students strongly agreed to this statement, while 15.2 per cent disagreed ($n = 125$). The majority of parents agreed (31 per cent) to this with 29 per cent disagreeing ($n = 67$). Another item that was used focused on whether the school helps parents to be involved in students' education. Most students (63 per cent, $n = 124$) and parents (46 per cent, $n = 68$) strongly agreed to this with the lowest of 4 per cent parents disagreeing.

Communicating. The item "the school develops communication for parents, who do not read or see well" had 50 per cent students (*n* = 122) and 42 per cent parents responding "disagree" (*n* = 62). The mean for the students' data of 2.33 and parents' data 2.42 also reinforced that students and parents do not agree that their school encourages this. This was followed by 19 per cent of students and parents strongly disagreeing. Most students (39.5 per cent, *n* = 124) and parents (38.5 per cent, *n* = 65) strongly agreed that their school establishes clear two-way channels of communication from home to school and from school to home. Twenty-nine per cent of students also agreed, and 35.4 per cent parents agreed to this statement. A minority of students (11.3 per cent) and parents (9.2 per cent) disagreed that their school establishes clear two-way channels of communications from home to school and from school to home.

Students' responses to whether their parents/guardian were contacted if they were having academic or behavioural problems at school revealed that 25 per cent and 69.4 per cent agreed and strongly agreed, respectively. For this item, the parent data showed a total of 9 per cent strongly disagreeing and disagreeing, while 32.8 per cent agreed with the highest percentage of 58.2 strongly agreeing (*n* = 67). This item also had a mean statistics of 4.60 for the students' data and 4.37 for parents' data which further highlights that the majority of the respondents strongly agreed that the school contacted parents if their child/children had academic or behavioural concerns.

Volunteering. One of the items used to measure this subscale focused on how the school provides a variety of ways for parents/guardians to volunteer at school which revealed that 37 per cent students (*n* = 123) and 32 per cent parents (*n* = 67) were in agreement (*see* figure 7.2). Also, 30 per cent of the students slightly agreed to this with the least being 4 per cent for strongly disagreed, while 30.3 per cent of parents slightly agreed with this statement with the least being 3 per cent for strongly disagreed. Another item used to assess this subscale was *"school schedules events at different times during the day and evening so that all families can attend some throughout the year"*. The highest percentage of students (26 per cent, *n* = 125) disagreed with this statement (*see* figure 7.3), while the highest percentage of parents (29 per cent, *n* = 65) strongly agreed which highlights that both responding groups had contrasting views. Another item used examine if parents who volunteer in school activities are celebrated, both participating groups had the highest percentage strongly agreeing to this with 39 per cent for students (*n* = 125) and 38 per cent for parents (*n* = 66). Strongly disagreed

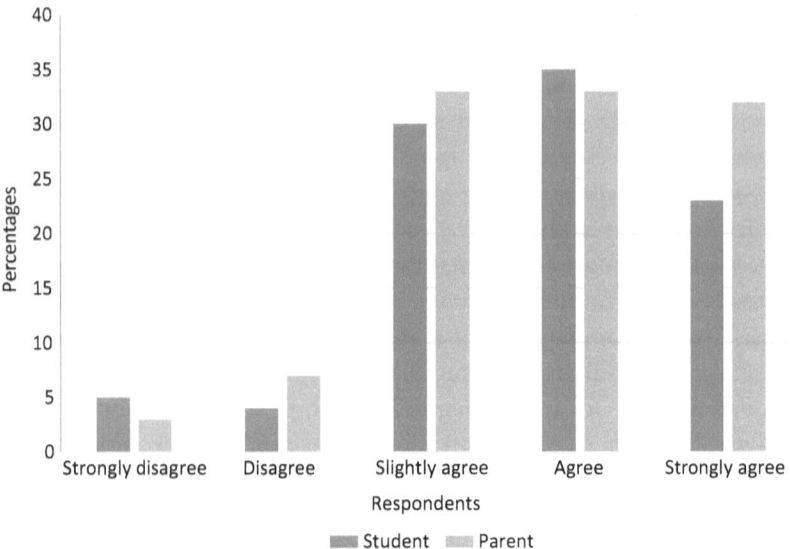

Figure 7.2 My school provides a variety of ways for my parents/guardians to volunteer at my school.

had the least percentage for students (3 per cent) and disagreed had the least percentage (2 per cent) for parents.

Learning at home. For this construct, 37 per cent of the students slightly agreed that the school provides information to families on how to monitor and discuss school work at home ($n = 123$), while for parents it was 32 per cent that agreed to this ($n = 66$). Both groups had the least responses for strongly disagreed with the students being 4 per cent and parents being 3 per cent. Based on the results an equal number of students responded "strongly agree" and "slightly agree" accounting for 28 per cent each to the survey item "the school provides ongoing information to families on how to assist children with skills that they need to improve" ($n = 123$). This item had the most response rate of 29 per cent for "agree" and the least response rate for "strongly disagree" of 2 per cent for students. A total of 54 per cent parent respondents strongly agreed and agreed that the school provides ongoing information to them on how to assist children with skills that they need to improve, while a total of 16 per cent strongly disagreed to this statement. Most students (61 per cent, $n = 123$) and parents (69 per cent, $n = 67$) strongly agreed that the "parents talk to their child about the importance of school", while 2 per cent of the parents disagreed that they do this and 3 per cent of students strongly disagreed that parents do this.

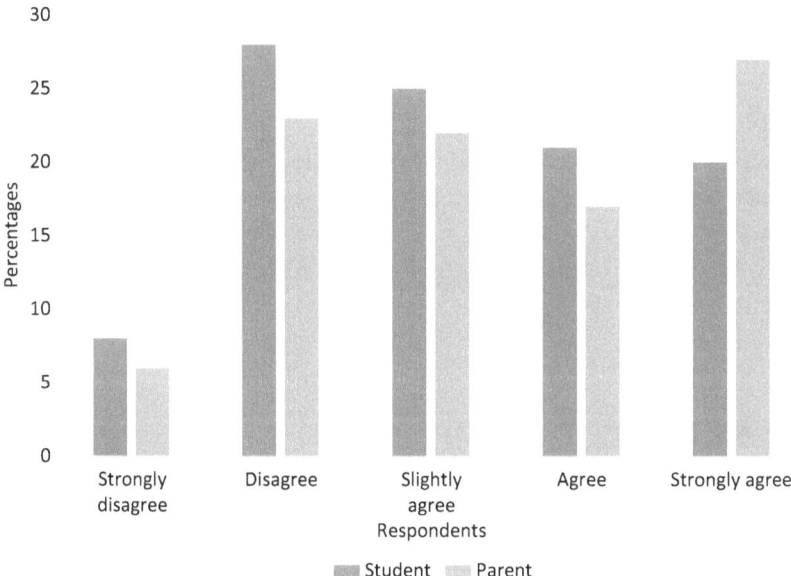

Figure 7.3 School schedules events at different times during the day and evening so that all families can attend some throughout the year.

A majority of both students (38 per cent, $n = 120$) and parents (40 per cent, $n = 67$) strongly agreed that "parents talk to the child/children about doing homework". A total of 48 per cent students and 55 per cent parents agreed and slightly agreed to this with a minority of 6 per cent students strongly disagreeing and 2 per cent parents disagreeing. Most students (59 per cent, $n = 122$) and parents (68 per cent, $n = 67$) strongly agreed that discussion takes place between the two groups about the child/children's grades on tests and report cards. One per cent of the students and 5 per cent of parents disagreed with this. However, 59 per cent of students strongly agreed ($n = 124$) that their parents checked that they attend school. Additionally, 65 per cent of parents strongly agreed that they check that their child/children attend school.

Decision making. Students equally strongly agreed and agreed (23 per cent, $n = 124$) that their school includes parents in its decision-making process about how the school operates, while 16 per cent strongly disagreed with this. A majority of parents, on the other hand, disagreed with this statement (36 per cent, $n = 67$) with the least strongly agreeing (10 per cent). The majority of the students strongly agreed (46 per cent, $n = 122$) and agreed (31 per cent) that parents are asked to help in dealing with problems that face the school. On the contrary, most parents disagreed (31 per cent) to this statement with 13 per cent being the least, slightly agreeing to it.

Empirical Results for Inferential Statistics

All assumptions for multiple linear regression were tested and met to ensure that the results produced using this analytical technique were credible.

There is a linear relationship between academic performance and parental involvement. This occurs where there is a straight-line relationship between residuals and dependent variables (Pallant, 2005).

Parents' Data

Both data sets were tested for all assumptions. The P-Plot was normal and variances along the best fit line remains congruent as the data moves against line. Test for homoscedasticity was met as indicative of normal distribution of the data.

Both data sets collected showed a normal distribution.

RQ1: Is there a statistically significant relationship between the parental involvement variables (parenting, communicating, volunteering, learning at home and decision making) and students' reported academic performance?

Based on the students' data the results of all constructs have statistically negative low correlations with academic performance; however, all except *parenting* were statistically significant with the dependent variable. This occurred at the 95 per cent confidence interval and at the .05 significance level. The relationship between *communicating* and academic performance showed a Pearson's Correlation of −.209 at a significant value of .019 ($r = -.209, n = 125, p = .01 < .05$), with *volunteering* there was a Pearson's Correlation of −.302 at a significance level of .001 ($r = -.302, n = 125, p = .001 < .05$), *learning at home* and the dependent variable had Pearson's Correlation of −.221 at a significance value of .013 ($r = -.221, n = 125, p < .05$) and *decision making* and academic performance had a Pearson's Correlation of −.257 at a significance level of .004 ($r = -.257, n = 125, p = .004 < .05$).

The parents' data showed *communicating* and *learning at home* having statistically positive significant relationships between them and students' perceived academic performance at the 95 per cent confidence interval and .05 significant level. *Communicating* and academic performance had a Pearson's Correlation of −.389 at a significance value of .001 ($r = -.389, n = 68, p = .001$), and the relationship between *learning at home* and the dependent variable had a Pearson's Correlation of −.249 at a significance of .040 ($r = -.249$, $n = 68$, $p = .040 < .05$).

A closer look at both correlation results showed most of the constructs having a weak positive to moderately positive Pearson's Correlation with each other which is a good indication as they were designed to measure different constructs. According to Frankfort-Nachmias and Leon-Guerrero (2016), a correlational value of .20 and less is said to be a weak positive correlation and demonstrates an almost negligible relationship, while a correlation of .20 to .40 is considered a weak to moderate positive relationship which indicates there is a relationship although moderate.

RQ2: To what extent is there a statistically significant impact of parental involvement on students' reported academic performance at the grade 10 level?

Students' Results. The multiple linear regression model explained 12 per cent of the variance in students' perceived academic performance with $r^2 = .116$ (see table 7.5). Based on the results in table 7.6, parental involvement is a statistically significant predictor variable of students' reported academic performance at a 95 per cent confidence interval and at the .05 significance level ($F(5, 119) = 3.123$, $p < .05$). Therefore, the null hypothesis was rejected as there is evidence that parental involvement impacts students' perceived academic performance. However, none of the five constructs made any

Table 7.5 Model Summary for Parental Involvement

Model	R	R Square	Adjusted R Square	Std. Error of the Estimate	Durbin-Watson
1	.341[a]	.116	.079	1.578	1.786

a. Predictors: (constant), decision making, communicating, parenting, learning at home, volunteering.

Table 7.6 ANOVA for Parental Involvement

Model		Sum of Squares	df	Mean Square	F	Sig.
1	Regression	38.901	5	7.780	3.123	.011[a]
	Residual	296.491	119	2.492		
	Total	335.392	124			

a. Predictors: (constant), decision making, communicating, parenting, learning at home, volunteering.

statistically significant unique contribution to the prediction of students' perceived academic performance.

Limitations

This is a single-site study that limits the data to the particular socio-economic and other ecological factors of the school and district the students and their families reside. These factors could pose threats to the external validity of the study and therefore is being used as a pilot. Students' academic performance was measured using students' self-reported information based on related items on their survey instruments which can be very subjective. Hence, the reported grades may be contrary to their actual grades received on their summative examinations. This study drew on 125 students and 68 of their parents in one co-educational upgraded high school which can only speak to the reliability of the instrument and the feasibility of conducting this study on a larger scale within the same or similar context. Another limitation was that teachers' voices were not accounted for in this study. This would have provided for data triangulation from all three participating groups making the study more robust. Another limitation is the timeline of the study. This survey designed study was conducted in 2015, and as such although relatively dated, it is still contextually relevant and reliable to assess the rate of parental involvement in a Jamaican high school.

Discussion

The first research question sought to ascertain the relationship between the parental involvement constructs and academic performance. The findings from the students' survey indicated there was a significant relationship between the parental involvement constructs (except *parenting*) and students' perceived academic performance. In addition, the parent data revealed statistical significant relationships between two of the five constructs (*communicating* and *learning at home*) and students' perceived academic performance. The second question revealed that parental involvement significantly predicts students' reported academic performance.

This study found parental involvement to be significant to students' perceived academic performance both for the students' and parents' data ($p = .011$; $p = .021$). While it concurred with other research studies (Griffith, 1996; Driessen, Smit, & Sleegers, 2005), it differed from the findings of Fan and Chen (2001) and Desforges and Abouchaar (2003) who stated that parental involvement is the most significant contributor to students' academic success. Parental involvement in this study did not predict a very large variance in academic performance (12 per cent for students). Consequently, we would advise against using parental involvement alone as a single determinant of students' academic success as agreed by Desforges and Abouchaar (2003) and Shute et al. (2011).

Additionally, Avvisati, Besbas and Guyon (2010) support the view that when students matriculate into high school, they receive less parental involvement in comparison to their former educational years. This connects with Bhargava and Witherspoon (2015), who argued that as students get older, they have more autonomy especially as they transition to high school or to their adolescence stage. Also, as argued by Harris and Goodall (2008) and Jeynes (2005b), students who received higher levels of parental involvement performed academically better than their counterparts whose parents were less involved. Notably, the grade 10 students of this study believed that parental involvement had a small impact on academic performance; however, it was still seen as an important factor in students' academic success.

The regression model was statistically significant when observed to see whether or not the five constructs were predicting the outcome variable. All were not unique predictors, since students believed none were predictors of their academic achievement. This is irrespective of their beliefs that their parents are involved in their academic life and being satisfied with parental involvement in their school and education. Students agreed (63 per cent) that they spend one hour or less on homework in the evenings, while 10 per cent admitted to not doing homework at all. Another reason could be that most students did not seem to like school very much as a total of 57 per cent disagreed and slightly agreed to liking school. Therefore, we could possibly argue that students are lacking motivation in school.

Communicating was found to have a relationship with students' outcomes where students believed it explained 4 per cent of the variance in the dependent variable, while parents believed it explained 15 per cent. *Communicating* and *decision making* were not widely mentioned in much of the literature, but this study found that students believed *decision making* had a strong relationship to their academic success and contributes 7 per cent of the difference between the two variables.

Parents believed *communicating* to be the main attributing factor to their child/children's academic performance. This could be due to a total of 91 per cent of them agreeing and strongly agreeing that they are contacted if their child/children were having academic or behavioural problems at school. Also, a total of 74 per cent agreed and strongly agreed that the school establishes clear two-way channels of communication from home to school and vice versa. Though 61 per cent of parents disagreed that the school develops communication for parents, who do not read or see well, it is evident that the school makes great effort to foster *communication* between itself and home. It should be noted, however, that more effort is needed to bridge the gap to facilitate effective communication with parents at various educational and socio-economic levels and those with disabilities.

The subscale *parenting* had no significance on students' outcome for both groups and is contrary to Shaw's (2008) findings, which had *parenting* as one of the most prevalent types of parental involvement. When correlated, the results were significant as 98 per cent and 62 per cent of the difference between *parenting* and academic performance was not explained in the students' and parents' data respectively. It can be argued then that *parenting* might not be very important in the grades students received.

From the results gathered, the lack of parenting may be fuelled by many parents being self-employed (34 per cent) or having full-time employment (37 per cent) or most of them having secondary level education (36 per cent). Harris and Goodall (2008) highlighted that the educational background of parents has a significant impact on time spent with students. Despite the reason(s), it is the students who are at a disadvantage as they would receive less meaningful involvement from their parents both at home and at school. It was also observed that some students (44 per cent) and parents (36 per cent), though not to a large degree, believed that the school could assist parents more in developing a home environment that supports learning. This is vital to students' academic success, because if homes are not equipped to reinforce what is taught in schools, then the consequences faced may be detrimental not only to students and the education system but to the Jamaican economy as a whole.

Notably, parents' responses were more favourable in relation to the construct *learning at home*. Similarly, this was one of the two prevalent types of parental involvement constructs in Shaw's (2008) study. Primarily, both students' and parents' findings confirmed that it was significantly related to academic outcomes with a variance of 5 per cent and 6 per cent, respectively. Even though the majority of parents had only a secondary level education, they were highly involved in their child/children's education in ways such as talking to them about homework and the importance of school; discussing grades on tests and report cards; and checking to ensure that their child/children attended school. Irrespective of their educational background, many parents invested time with their child/children in these ways which was highlighted by Harris and Goodall (2008) as having a significant impact on students' performance. Jeynes (2005a) added that parents, who communicate with their children in these ways and attend school functions, assist in the development of students' academic performance.

In order to gather participants' views on the research topic, it was important to note their perceptions of Epstein's (1995) vision of school/parent partnership on students' academic success. Most participants strongly agreed that such relationships are important. Despite this, parents are not fully involved in the schools' activities as the findings revealed that 50 per cent of the parents do not attend PTA meetings often. In comparison, 40 per cent have never volunteered in school activities, and 50 per cent indicated that they rarely participated.

Students believed that *volunteering* has a very high significant relationship at $p = .001$ to academic performance, but it must be mentioned that a very small percentage (9 per cent) explains both variables. Parents, on the other hand, believed that *volunteering* does not have any significant relationship to the dependent variable, which is not alarming since Okpala, Okpala and Smith (2001) had similar results, and neither did they believe that it contributes to academic success. The findings showed that most parents were not always or regularly needed at home and that they had no major problems with transportation cost and availability. Additionally, parents had no issue with the staff/school climate, distance from home to school, inability to leave work or the time frame in which announcements are received. Nevertheless, they minimally volunteered or attended PTA meetings. Consequently, we observed that the parents believed that the school/parent partnership is important, but that parents do little to enhance this relationship or even to encourage their children to succeed academically by being more involved in their education, specifically where volunteering is concerned.

Roksa and Potter (2011) postulated that attending school events and PTA meetings were ways of parental involvement. Parents not attending and/or volunteering in school activities and events are no fault of the school since both parents and students on average, agreed that the school fosters *volunteering* as a parental involvement construct. In addition, the parents' data confirmed that 50 per cent of parents did not volunteer in school activities often, while 40 per cent had never done so. Twenty-nine per cent of parents reported that they were needed at home, while 57 per cent stated that the "distance from school does not affect their ability to volunteer for school activities". The study found that parents/guardians perceived the school/parent partnership as being important, yet 50 per cent did not volunteer.

As mentioned before, this study was piloted using a contextually relevant and reliable instrument that can be used to ascertain baseline data for a larger study. The rate of parental involvement and its correlation to students' academic performance is not a new debate. However, this study is indicative of the fact that more research within the Jamaican context is needed to determine how this relationship between parents and schools could be strengthened and to increase the rate of parental involvement. A larger study of several schools could yield significant findings that would assist with developing an ideal model of parental involvement that would have a positive impact on students' academic performance.

Conclusion

A myriad of studies states that parental involvement impacts students' academic performance (Fan & Chen, 2001; Houtenville & Conway, 2008; Chowa et al., 2013 and Fernández-Alonso et al., 2017). This study further confirms that it is an important factor in students' academic success. In some cases, parents take on passive roles or abdicate their parenting roles, particularly, when it concerns students' education. Harris and Goodall (2008) opined that some parents are reluctant or unable to work with schools. Parents are valuable and children are dependent on parents to reap better academic success and no longer are they to stand aside or be accessories to their academic pursuit. One way of accomplishing this is through attending school activities and events and frequently volunteering. As suggested by Bhargava and Witherspoon (2015), there needs to be a multidimensional approach to parental involvement, for example, "home-based involvement; distinguishes between specific forms of school-based involvement (i.e., school-based communication and volunteerism); and incorporates academic socialization" (p. 1715). A sad reality is that a total of 69 per cent of the parents in this study admitted that they have never or seldom engaged in school activities and volunteering. This study can highlight to parents that their involvement impacts their child/children's academic success and that volunteering is also a way of being involved.

The findings showed that communication might not be effective for all parents especially those who do not read or see well as this was not highly facilitated by the school. Thus, using effective means of communication for all parents is critical for more effective ways of two-way communication between parents and the school. As such, the school's method of communicating with parents needs to be widened. The findings showed that this could be done by sending electronic messages to parents via text messaging, voice notes, emails, and phone calls where possible, as most parents reported never receiving messages from the school in these ways. This will assist in catering to parents from diverse educational and socio-economic backgrounds, as well as those with disabilities. Schools should also keep in mind that parents are to be involved in its decision-making process since ultimately it will affect their children academically. Lastly, many students reported not spending enough time completing homework. One suggestion could be that teachers provide students with tasks that require parents' participation at home, which would encourage parental involvement.

To conclude, the influence of parental involvement in children's education should never be one that is underestimated. After all, the socialization of children is a dual relationship between parents (home) and educational institutions. We encourage all stakeholders to see that teaching and learning do not only take place within the classroom but also outside. Building a community and emphasizing parental involvement are necessary steps to close the gap between students' performance and academic achievement. Furthermore, developing and sustaining these relationships will be effective and will ensure that students are continuously supported throughout their educational journey.

References

Avvisati, F., Besbas, B., & Guyon, N. (2010). Parental involvement in school: A literature review. http://www.jstor.org/stable/24703051

Barge, K. & Loges, W. (2003). Parent, student, and teacher perceptions of parental involvement. *Applied Communication Research Journal*. https://doi-org.du.idm.oclc.org/10.1080/00909880320000064597

Becker, H.J. & Epstein, J.L. (1982). *Influences on teachers' use of parent involvement at home*. Center for Social Organizations of Schools: John Hopkins University. https://du.idm.oclc.org/login?url=https://www-proquest-com.du.idm.oclc.org/reports/influences-on-teachers-use-parent-involvement-at/docview/63562597/se-2?accountid=14608

Bhargava, S. & Witherspoon, D. (2015). Parental involvement across middle and high school: Exploring contributions of individual and neighborhood characteristics. *Journal of Youth and Adolescence*, 44(9), 1702–19.

Bower, H. & Griffin, D. (2011). Can the Epstein model of parental involvement work in a high-minority, high-poverty elementary school? A case study. *Professional School Counseling*, 15(2), 77–87. doi:10.5330/PSC.n.2011-15.77

Davis, D. (2000). Supporting parent, family, and community involvement in your school. https://sedl.org/txcc/resources/strategies/ayp/ParentInvolvement10/ParentInvolvementHandout4.pdf

Desforges, C. & Abouchaar, A. (2003). The impact of parental involvement, parental support and family education on pupil achievements and adjustment: A literature review. http://bgfl.org/bgfl/custom/files_uploaded/uploaded _resources/18617/desforges.pdf.

Driessen, G., Smit, F., & Sleegers, P. (2005). Parental involvement and educational achievement. *British Educational Research Journal*, 31(4), 509–32. doi: 10.1080/01411920500148713

Epstein, J.L. (1995). School/family/community partnerships: Caring for the children we share. http://online.missouri.edu/exec/data/courses2/ coursegraphics/2226/L5-Epstein.pdf

Fan, X. (2001). Parental involvement and students' academic achievement: A growth modeling analysis. *The Journal of Experimental Education*, 70(1), 27–61. http://www.jstor.org/stable/20152664

Fan, X. & Chen, M. (2001). Parental involvement and students' academic achievement: A meta-analysis. *Educational Psychology Review*, 13(1). http://www .jstor.org/stable/23358867

Fernández-Alonso, R., Álvarez-Díaz, M., Woitschach, P., Suárez-Álvarez, J., & Cuesta, M. (2017). Parental involvement and academic performance: Less control and more communication. *Psicothema*, 29(4), 453–61.

Frankfort-Nachmias, C. & Leon-Guerrero, A. (2016). *Social statistics for a diverse society* (8th ed.). Pine Forge.

Griffith, J. (1996). Relation of parental involvement, empowerment, and school traits to student academic performance. *The Journal of Educational Research*, 90(1), 33–41. http://www.jstor.org/stable/27542066

Griffiths-Prince, M. (2009). *Cultivating parental involvement in middle schools: A case study*. https://files.eric.ed.gov/fulltext/ED529869.pdf

Harris, A. & Goodall, J. (2008). Do parents know they matter? Engaging all parents in learning. *Educational Research*, 50(3), 277–89. http://cmapspublic .ihmc.us/rid=1JTG44B1H-W7WF5G-1BSN/ArticleDoParentsKnowTheyMatter .pdf

Hawes, C. & Plourde, L. (2005). Parental involvement and its influence on the reading achievement of 6th grade students. *Reading Improvement*, 42(1), 47–57. https://du.idm.oclc.org/login?url=https://www-proquest-com.du.idm.oclc .org/scholarly-journals/parental-involvement-influence-on-reading/docview /62152142/se-2?accountid=14608

Hicks, S.B. (2018). *A case study: Exploring African American parental involvement of students with disabilities in transition planning in an urban school district* (ProQuest No. 10947986) [Doctoral dissertation, Ohio University]. ProQuest Dissertations and Theses Global.

Hill, N.E. & Taylor, L.C. (2004). Parental school involvement and children's academic achievement: Pragmatics and issues. *Current Directions in Psychological Science*, 13, 161–64. http://www.jstor.org/stable/20182940

Hives, B.A. (2017). *Parental engagement: A study of urban, K-8 parents' and teachers' perceptions and experiences in a K-8 school in Ohio.* (ProQuest No. 10688393)

[Doctoral dissertation, Concordia University Chicago]. ProQuest Dissertations and Theses Global.

Houtenville, A. & Conway, K. (2008). Parental effort, school resources, and student achievement. *Journal of Human Resources, 43*(2), 437–53.

Jeynes, W.H. (2005a). A meta-analysis of the relation of parental involvement to urban elementary school student achievement. *Urban Education, 40*(3), 237–69. doi: 10.1177/0042085905274540

———. (2005b). The effects of parental involvement on the academic achievement of African American youth. *The Journal of Negro Education, 74*, 260–74. https://du.idm.oclc.org/login?url=https://www-proquest-com.du.idm .oclc.org/scholarly-journals/effects-parental-involvement-on-academic/docview /222131053/se-2?accountid=14608

NM Family/Parent/Involvement Initiative. (n.d.). http://www.surveymonkey.com /s.aspx?sm=pCDueJj3maVVOe3NvWUhDg_3d_3d

Okpala, C.O, Okpala, A.O., & Smith, F.E. (2001). Parental involvement, instructional expenditures, family socioeconomic attributes, and student achievement. http://web.a.ebscohost.com.rproxy.uwimona.edu.jm/ehost /pdfviewer/pdfviewer?sid=d555a68d-8225-4d65-9f5e-77bf4d90f626 %40sessionmgr4004&vid=1&hid=4104

Pallant, J. (2005). SPSS Survival Manual: *A step by step guide to data analysis using SPSS for windows version 12.* http://www.academia.dk/BiologiskAntropologi/ Epidemiologi/PDF/SPSS_Survival_Manual_Ver12.pdf

Reynolds, A. (2008, May 26). National parent-teachers' association of Jamaica - Boosting education through parent involvement. *Jamaica Gleaner.* http://old .jamaica-gleaner.com/gleaner/20080526/lead/lead6.html

Roksa, J. & Potter, D. (2011). Parenting and academic achievement: Intergenerational transmission of educational advantage. *Sociology of Education, 84* (4), 299–321. doi: 10.1177/0038040711417013

Sanders, M.G. & Epstein, J.L. (1998). School-family-community partnerships in middle and high schools: From theory to practice. http://www.csos.jhu.edu/ crespar/techReports/Report22.pdf

Sanders, M.G., Epstein, J.L., & Connors-Tadros, L. (1999). Family partnerships with high schools: The parents' perspective. http://files.eric.ed.gov/fulltext/ ED012275.pdf

Shaw, C. (2008). A study of the relationship of parental involvement to student achievement in a Pennsylvania career and technology Center. file:///C:/Users/ User/Downloads/parent_involvement.pdf

Shoaga, O.O.M. & Rasheed, S. (2019). The socio-economic variables, parental involvement and academic performance of pupils. *Annual Journal of Technical University of Varna, 3*(1), 21–27.

Shute, V.J., Hansen, E.G., Underwood, J.S., & Razzouk, R. (2011). A review of the relationship between parental involvement and secondary school students' academic achievement. *Educational Research International,* 1–10. doi: 10.1155/2011/915326

Stein, L.B. (2009). The influence of parent and community involvement on local school councils in Massachusetts. http://scholarworks.umass.edu

Sui-Chu, E. & Willms, J.D. (1996). Effects of parental involvement on eighth-grade achievement. *Sociology of Education, 69*(2), 126–41.

Troupe, K.T. (2017). *Motivations influencing home support engagements in Jamaican high schools.* https://scholarworks.waldenu.edu/cgi/viewcontent.cgi?article=5509&context=dissertations

Wright, N. (2014, November 6–8). *The extent to which parental involvement impacts the academic achievement of tenth grade students* [Paper presentation]. International Conference on Urban Education, Montego Bay, Jamaica.

Chapter 8

An Investigation into the Scope and Prevalence of Parental Involvement at a Rural High School in Jamaica

NATRECIA WHYTE LOTHIAN AND TASHANE HAYNES-BROWN

Introduction

Educating a child requires a multifaceted approach which includes school, home and community. "One cannot overstate the great deal of importance placed on parental involvement in the educational arena" (Robinson & Harris, 2014, p. 2). Several researchers contend that parental involvement in education makes a difference and yields significant improvement in students' academic achievement (Epstein 1992; Eccles & Harold 1993; Catsambis 1998; Fan & Chen 2001; Robinson & Harris, 2014; Sheldon & Epstein, 2005; Hill & Tyson, 2009; Wei et al., 2019). However, research on parental involvement, though plentiful, has focussed predominantly on parental involvement in the elementary or primary school population rather than on high school students (Hill & Taylor, 2004; Henderson & Mapp, 2002; Muhammad et al., 2013). Furthermore, research indicates that parental involvement in high school is declining (Epstein & Connors, 1995; Eccles & Harold, 1996; Catsambis & Garland, 1997; Hill & Taylor, 2004, Wei et al., 2019).

This is a troubling trend because it is perhaps at this level that parental involvement is most critical. According to Robinson and Harris (2014), parental involvement in the lives of older children is considered important in reducing school delinquency, improving discipline and increasing the likelihood that students matriculate to college. Likewise, Krane and Klevan (2019) state that due to the demand for increased effort in academic complexity and achievement at the upper secondary level, many students struggle with these demands as well as motivation, achievement and mental health issues. Parents' continued involvement can potentially mitigate the impact of these challenges on academic achievement, especially for students at the upper secondary level.

Parental Involvement at the High School Level

Unfortunately, parents are often unaware of the positive impact their continued involvement at the high school level could potentially have on their children's academic success. Likewise, secondary schools sometimes do not have any data on the scope and extent of parents' involvement in their children's academic lives. One possible reason for the lack of focus on parental involvement at the high school level is that high school students are generally perceived to be more mature and independent. However, parental involvement is critical at the secondary level because students at this level present a different challenge owing to the plethora of changes that they undergo. Many adolescents are more vulnerable to distractions and peer pressure owing to their quest to define themselves, and this can potentially create problems with delinquency and disruptive behaviours. Psychologist Erik Erikson classified this stage as *identity versus role confusion* (Berk, 2001). At this stage in their development some adolescents have a proclivity to easily lose academic focus (Hill & Tyson, 2009). This is an issue that is of great concern, since this stage of their education plays a critical role in decisions for their future. Wang, Hill and Hofkens (2014) contend that although students become more independent as they progress through the grade levels and parent-teacher interactions seem less needed, parental involvement in a child's education during the secondary school years plays an essential role in developing positive academic, behavioural and emotional outcomes.

Background to the Study

Over the years, administrators and teachers in the Jamaican context have observed that, at the secondary level, the greatest level of involvement for some parents is during the registration and orientation period at grade 7. As the students advance to higher grade levels (fourth and fifth forms) parents' involvement generally wanes. This is the time when parental support is in fact most critical as it can be an important determining factor in their future career success. For many high school students in Jamaica, the end of year five (fifth form) marks the end of their formal education. At the end of year five, the students sit their Caribbean Secondary Education Certificate (CSEC) exams that have traditionally been considered benchmark exams which serve to identify students suitable for higher education and to determine the fitness of students for certain types of jobs (Griffith, 2015). An important component of these exams is the School-Based Assessment

(SBA) that requires students to complete a major project or assignment which contributes to their final grade in the CSEC exams (Griffith, 2015). The progressive nature of the SBA component allows parents to support their children at home as they work towards completion. In fact, Griffith (2015) states that some students develop and demonstrate the skills that the SBA seeks to assess owing to their access to informed and knowledgeable parents. This suggests that parental involvement at home can impact on the quality of the SBA assignment completed by students.

Unfortunately, the parental support necessary to provide students with this advantage in completing SBAs is often absent, and this is possibly one of the reasons for the less than desirable overall CSEC results. Generally, in more than 70 per cent of Jamaican high schools, at least half of their grade 11 students do not pass five CSEC subjects, including math and English, at a single sitting (Francis, 2014). While several factors could account for these results, lack of parental involvement is a major contributor to students' failure in these benchmark exams. This is an issue that the Ministry of Education in Jamaica has noted as a crippling issue for years. In 2008, then minister of education Andrew Holness stressed the need for greater parental involvement in education (Jamaica Information Service [JIS], 2008). He expressed concern for the lack of active participation by parents in their children's educational development, stating that "the efforts by the Ministry and other sector stakeholders and interests in the development of the education system would amount to nothing unless parents played their part in the process" (Jamaica Information Service [JIS], 2008). In 2011, a study commissioned by the Ministry of Education revealed that based on a sample of 300 parents, approximately 50 per cent had never attended a Parent Teacher Association (PTA) meeting, while 65 per cent had neither initiated nor met with a teacher in regard to their child's academic performance (*Jamaica Observer*, 2011). These findings suggest that lack of parental support is a major problem affecting students' academic outcomes.

In a bid to remedy this problem, some initiatives have emerged such as the Coalition of Better Parenting (CBP), the National Parent-Teacher Association of Jamaica (NPTAJ), Parenting Partners Caribbean (PPC) and the Parent's Place project. While these initiatives are a step in the right direction, researchers such as Munroe (2009) and Watson-Williams (2011) contend that there are certain factors at play in the Jamaican context that limit parental involvement. Munroe (2009) argues that the state of parental involvement in education in Jamaica is not owing to a lack of parental interest but the result of a range of factors related to the social context, driven by issues such as poverty and social status. Nelson (2018) also supports this position, contending that for many Jamaican parents attendance at PTAs and helping their children with homework are luxuries that they cannot afford because

> low-wage earners, the income bracket many parents are in, don't get much time off to go to PTA meetings. And if they can get the time off, every hour spent away from work is money lost, which, in some cases, might mean an entire day's salary/wage. Quite often, they work long hours, even doing two jobs, to make ends meet and are, therefore, unable to get home before their children fall asleep or have energy to do much when they get home. (Nelson, 2018)

Sadly, this is the reality for many parents and schools in the Jamaican context. It is also an indication that schools need to become creative in their attempts to improve parental support.

The Valley High School of Jamaica

The Valley High School of Jamaica is a co-educational institution located in a rural community in the parish of St. Mary in Jamaica. The school was built to accommodate 500 students; however, the growing student population has resulted in the school changing to a shift system. Over 1,300 students are currently enrolled and there are 68 teachers on staff along with a principal, 2 vice-principals, 3 guidance counsellors, a dean of discipline and a work experience coordinator. There are ten academic departments, and the students at Valley High School are equipped with at least one of the following Technical and Vocational Education and Training (TVET) skills: food and beverage server, masonry, welding, electrical installation, cosmetology and general construction.

The socio-economic activity of the community consists mainly of farming, retailing and seasonal tourism employment (in the local tourism sector, overseas and cruise line employment). The school caters to many students from lower socio-economic backgrounds, with 676 students receiving government assistance through the Programme of Advancement Through Health and Education (PATH), a social intervention programme that targets the most needy and vulnerable in society. The PATH programme assists students by providing them with daily lunches and a select few obtain daily transportation service to and from school. Some of the students can also be classified as "barrel children" (Brown & Grinter, 2012) after the circular brown fibre or blue plastic shipping containers used to send material support to those children whose parents move abroad, most likely for work. Many of the parents of the children from the Valley High School are employed overseas in the tourism sector, and this makes the school-parent relationship even more difficult to establish.

The absence of parents due to employment overseas, the heavy demands of parents' jobs and their socio-economic backgrounds certainly have implications for the scope and level of parental involvement in the school. Another countervailing factor that contributes to this issue is that the school operates on a shift system which results in fewer contact hours for student learning and teachers having to communicate with large numbers of parents from both shifts about their children's progress, general conduct and academic performance. With these issues affecting the Valley High School it was important to examine parental involvement to provide the school's administration with data to inform decisions targeting improving parental involvement.

Purpose and Research Questions

The purpose of this descriptive study was to investigate the scope and prevalence of parental involvement at grade 11 in an upgraded high school in rural Jamaica using a sample of 119 parents. This was accomplished by answering the following main question and sub-questions:

1. What is the scope and prevalence of parental involvement among parents of students from a rural high school in Jamaica?

    i) What are the ways in which parents are involved in their children's education in grade 11 in a rural high school in Jamaica?
    ii) How prevalent is parental involvement in homework among the grade 11 parents?
    iii) What proportion of parents are satisfied with their parental involvement in the academic life of their children?
    iv) What are the reported factors affecting parents' level of involvement?

The findings of this study are of importance because an assessment of the ways that parents are involved and parents' evaluation of their satisfaction with their parental involvement is critical for administrators in determining how to improve parental involvement in their children's academic pursuits. By exploring the extent that parents are involved in homework and their assessment of opportunities provided by the school to support their involvement at home, administrators can identify areas of weakness and make informed decisions about methods that can encourage greater parental involvement at home. As stated by Anfara Jr. and Mertens (2008), schools must seek and find methods to increase the participation of parents in their children's education. If the same enthusiasm that parents display at the start of high school was also displayed at grade 11, students' academic achievement would possibly be much better.

Theoretical Perspective

This study draws upon the works of Epstein (1995) and Hoover-Dempsey and Sandler (1995). The theoretical perspectives proposed by these authors build on the work of Bronfenbrenner (1979) who posits that human development cannot be adequately understood without significant reference to the social systems that work to limit or enhance developmental processes and outcomes. The microsystems and mesosystems proposed by their ecological theory are key considerations in understanding these frameworks. In the context of this study, the home and the school are considered microsystems, and the interactions between the home and school that work together to aid in the development of the children reflect the mesosystem (see Bronfenbrenner, 1979). Given that the "how and why" of parents becoming involved in their children's academic life are socially constructed, frameworks building on the ecological theory provide a useful lens for understanding the prevalence and scope of parental involvement as examined in this study.

Epstein's Framework

The framework developed by Epstein (1995) delineates the relationship between schools, families and communities as one of the overlapping spheres of influence. This emphasis on interrelated spheres of influence draws on a major component of the ecological theory known as the mesosystem, which Bronfenbrenner (1979) explains as being "the interrelations among two or more settings in which the developing person actively participates (such as, for a child, the relations among home, school, and neighbourhood peer group; for an adult, among family, work, and social life)" (p. 25). Aligned with this understanding of the mesosystem, Epstein's framework identifies six types of educational involvement and encourages schools to develop activities that involve schools, families and communities within the six types. These six types (parenting, communicating, volunteering, learning at home, decision making and collaborating with the community) are considered critical in building positive school-home partnerships.

However, only the five types relating to the microsystem were included in this study, since the focus was on home-school partnership. Collaboration with the community was beyond the scope of this study.

The core idea of this framework (see Epstein 2002) is that schools play a critical role in implementing activities for all six types of involvement and in so doing can help parents become more involved at school and at home in various ways that meet student needs and family schedules (Epstein & Salinas, 2004). This framework places the school at the heart of creating opportunities for parental involvement. Consequently, "parent involvement has been described as a prescriptive school centric process in which school staff direct the nature and extent of parents' involvement" (Mills et al., 2018, p. 35).

Parent involvement has traditionally been defined as parents engaging in school-based activities such as attending parent-teacher conferences and school events related to their child's education (Epstein, 1995). However, when these three agencies work together success is more likely, as there are frequent interactions among schools, families and communities; and more students are likely to receive positive messages about the importance of school, of working hard, of thinking creatively, of helping one another and of staying in school (Epstein, 2002). The positive messages that children believe about the importance of school have been identified by some authors as a type of parental involvement described as *academic socialization*. According to Hill and Tyson (2009), academic socialization mainly includes communicating with children about parents' expectations, academic advice and faith in their education. This suggests that in addition to Epstein's (1995) six types of parental involvement, there are variations reflecting other types of involvement that may be more parent centred (Mills et al., 2018). Therefore, if this model is to be successful, schools must seek input from parents, students and the community to help them address challenges and improve plans, activities and outreach – thus establishing families as productive partners in their children's school success (Epstein & Salinas, 2004). In keeping with this need for a more parent-centred focus, Hoover-Dempsey and Sandler (1995) proposed one such framework.

Hoover-Dempsey and Sandler's Framework

In their definition of parental involvement, Hoover-Dempsey and Sandler (1995), like Epstein (1995), incorporate a broad range of parental activities including "reviewing the child's work and monitoring child progress, helping with homework, discussing school events or course issues with the child, providing enrichment activities pertinent to school success, and talking by phone with the teacher" (Hoover-Dempsey & Sandler, 1995, p. 6). They elaborate further on the concept of parental involvement in their model, explaining that a parent and their decisions about involvement are influenced by constructs focussed primarily on the person – the individual parent. This is in keeping with the ecological theory which advanced the idea that processes and outcomes cannot be understood without the social systems that work to limit or enhance them (Bronfenbrenner, 1979). They further proposed that the factors undergirding parents' decisions and students' perceptions of mechanisms used by parents and students' attributes are critical to interpreting the types of involvement. The student-related factors were beyond the scope of this study. In keeping with the focus on understanding the role of parent-related factors in the types and levels of involvement, this study examines Levels 1 and 2 of the frameworks (Hoover-Dempsey & Sandler, 1995). At Level 1 in the Hoover-Dempsey and Sandler's (1995) Framework specific variables such as parents' construction of parental role, their sense of efficacy, invitations and demands from children and the school create patterns of influence at critical points in the parental involvement process. Level 2 is concerned with the idea that parents' choices of involvement forms (the types of involvement) are influenced by parents' skills and knowledge, the time available to parents given the demands of the family and their jobs and the invitations from their children and the school. Levels 3, 4 and 5 were beyond the scope of this study. These three levels focus on students' perceptions of the learning mechanisms used by parents and the student proximal attributes that are conducive to achievement.

While the types of involvement proposed by Epstein are critical to decisions about how schools and communities can foster parental involvement, it is also imperative that parental involvement is understood in conjunction with a focus on the parents and the factors undergirding their level of involvement. By examining both the types of parental involvement – as outlined by Epstein (1995) – and the factors influencing the levels and types of involvement, as stated by Hoover-Dempsey and Sandler (1995), a more comprehensive interpretation of the results of this study was facilitated. Thus, taken together, these frameworks – Epstein (1995) and Hoover-Dempsey and Sandler (1995) – provided a more comprehensive understanding of the topic being investigated in this study.

Literature Review

Several studies have indicated that parental involvement through high school takes many forms, with homework being one of the most prevalent types of involvement (Epstein, 2007; Hattie, 2008; Hill & Tyson, 2009; Jeynes, 2005; Krane & Klevan, 2019; Wang & Sheikh-Khalil, 2014; Wei et al., 2019). This literature review examines the findings of previous studies on the most prevalent types of involvement – parents' involvement in homework and parents' assessment of their satisfaction with their level of parental involvement – and the factors affecting parental involvement. The data for this review incorporated research from local and international literature.

Types of Parental Involvement

Internationally, Epstein's (1995) framework has been widely used to develop surveys capturing parental involvement. However, these studies have found different types of parental involvement to be most prevalent in their contexts. For example, a study conducted with 200 students in Tehran, Iran, found that home-based involvement, such as talking with the child at home about school or engaging in educational activities outside of school, was most prevalent and this type of involvement resulted in better grades (Khajehpour & Ghazvini, 2011). Likewise, Mahuro, Hungi and Lamb (2016), using a sample of 2,669 students in Uganda, found that parenting and communicating were the most prevalent forms of involvement, and these significantly increased students' numeracy and literacy scores. Yulianti, Denessen and Droop (2018), using a sample of 2,151 Indonesian parents, found that parents were more strongly involved in their children's learning at home than at school, and that higher levels of educational attainment yielded higher levels of involvement relating to parenting, communicating, volunteering and learning at home. Although these studies show that different forms are prevalent in different contexts, learning at home involving academic socialization seems to be the most common way that parents are involved in their children's academic life.

There are several meta-analyses in the international literature that not only identify the most prevalent types of parental involvement but also the types that are of significance to students' academic success. For example, Wilder (2014), based on the findings of a meta-synthesis, found that although all types of parental involvement are prevalent, parental expectations have the strongest relationship with educational achievement. Parental expectation is described broadly as part of academic socialization. As explained by Hill (2001), parental academic socialization is concerned with parents' beliefs about education, expectations and behaviours that influence their children's academic and school-related development. Therefore Wilder's (2014) analysis suggests that academic socialization is positively correlated with students' academic performance. Similarly Castro et al. (2015), in analysing types of parental involvement, found that the strongest associations between parental involvement and academic achievement were related to high academic expectations, developing and maintaining communication with children about school activities and helping them to develop reading habits, while supervision and control of homework and parental attendance at school activities do not appear to be especially related to children's academic achievement. Results by Benner, Boyle and Sadler (2016), from an Educational Longitudinal Study using a sample of 15,240 grade 10 students, found that of the types of involvement, school-based involvement and academic socialization were both related to higher educational attainment. These results taken together suggest that participation in various school-based activities and academic socializations have a significant influence on students' academic success.

While the international literature is inundated with research on parental involvement, the data on parental involvement in the Jamaican and Caribbean contexts are sparse, with only a few studies available. Among these, Murphy (2002) surveyed a sample of 219 parents in Jamaica and found that the most prevalent types of parental involvement reflected academic socialization, with over 80 per cent of parents reporting that their involvement primarily involved communicating with their children about school; the importance of school; and their future, career and work. In her case study, Watson-Williams (2011) found that parents were more involved in school-based activities than home-based activities. In the Caribbean region, a few studies were found. For example, a study by Marshall, Browne and Fongkong-Mungal (2014) conducted with 160 secondary level students in Barbados addressed students' perceptions of parental involvement. This study revealed that over 80 per cent of the students perceived their parents as exhibiting high levels of parental involvement in the form of encouragement, modelling, reinforcement and instruction. Another study conducted in Trinidad by Johnson and Descartes (2017) with a sample of 128 students sought to explore the relationship between parental influence and academic achievement in primary school students and found that all parents exerted influence over their children's academic lives. They also concluded that low levels of performance may be due to factors associated with the family background, such as students from single-parent families, students who live with guardians or stepmothers and having parents with an educational background below pre-degree (Johnson & Descartes, 2017).

These studies conducted in the Caribbean varied in scope and focus, using different frameworks to identify the types of involvement. Further, the small number of studies available indicate the dearth of local and regional data on parental involvement at the secondary level, and this further highlights the need for this research. As stated by Hagiwara and Davis (2018), little research exists on parental involvement among Jamaicans, and while Jamaican parents' experiences and contributions may be subsumed in information about black parents in general, there is a need for further research because the common values and beliefs shaping parental involvement are "rooted in and bounded by nationality" (p. 20).

Parental Involvement in Homework

Parents' involvement in students' homework is one of the most common types of involvement (Hattie, 2008), and it provides direct ways of creating structures at home that support children's learning (Walker et al., 2004). However, the results relating to its impact on academic success seem inconclusive. Several studies have found that parental involvement in homework has a negative impact on academic achievement (Benner, Boyle, and Sadler, 2016; Hill & Tyson, 2009; Xu et al., 2010). For example, Xu et al. (2010), based on the analysis of longitudinal data from 11,820 students, found that parental involvement in homework had a negative effect on academic achievement. On the other hand, studies have found a positive relationship between parental involvement in homework and academic achievement (Aries & Cabus, 2015; Hoover-Dempsey et al., 2001; Park, Byun, & Kim, 2011). Park, Byun and Kim (2011), in a longitudinal analysis of data from 6,400 students, found that when parents are involved in checking and correcting homework it can have a positive relationship to students' academic achievement. In their meta-analysis, Aries and Cabus (2015) concluded that large differences could occur in the outcomes of parental involvement in homework and academic achievement when specific types of direct parental involvement are utilized in helping with homework.

Walker (2017), in a study examining parents' and teachers' views on parental involvement with a sample of 250 parents and 28 teachers, found that over 70 per cent of the parents considered it important for them to check their children's homework. Checking students' homework suggests that students have some autonomy in completing homework. Parental involvement in homework seems to be most effective when it supports the child's autonomy and provides structure in the form of clear and consistent guidelines about homework (Pomerantz, Grolnick, & Price, 2005). If autonomy is positively correlated with effectiveness of parental involvement in homework, it suggests that too much direct involvement by parents in completion of homework can have adverse effects on student achievement. According to Cooper, Lindsay and Nye (2000), parents with students in higher grade levels reported giving students more homework autonomy. This autonomy is a good thing because if parental involvement in homework is characterized by high levels of control by the parent, it will have little impact (or possibly a negative impact) on children's motivation and achievement (Patall, Cooper, & Robinson, 2008). The increased autonomy that students at the secondary level experience may also be due in part to the varied factors affecting parental involvement at this level.

Factors Affecting Parental Involvement

The types of parental involvement that have been noted in the extant literature as having positive influence on students' academic success are also connected to several parent-related factors such as parents' academic background, parent self-efficacy, socio-economic status and parents' value systems (Benner, Boyle, and Sadler, 2016; Costa & Faria, 2017; Dauber & Epstein, 1993; Hill & Tyson, 2009). Dauber and Epstein (1993) explain that many parents feel less able to assist with homework or provide activities and experiences that increase their adolescents' knowledge or achievement at this level, which results in a decline in their involvement. This suggests that if parents do not feel competent to assist with their children's academic work, they may become less involved at the secondary level. This is also supported by Hoover-Dempsey and Sandler (1995) who contend that homework involvement is consistently based on parents' abilities, which is supported by the reports of many parents of having inadequate skills, knowledge and information for offering effective help. These studies suggest that parents' involvement in homework as their children progress to higher grade levels provides children with more autonomy. Likewise, Murphy (2002), in her study conducted in Jamaica, found significant differences in parents' attitude, level of involvement and assistance with homework based on their level of education. Seginer (2006) also found that at the secondary level parental involvement changed from assisting in the classroom to attendance at school activities, which according to Hill and Tyson (2009) is less likely to have a significant impact on students' academic achievement. This change in the type of involvement is potentially due to parents' belief that they are not competent enough to continue their involvement in classroom activities.

Parents' low efficacy beliefs may also affect the academic expectations they have for their children. Yamamoto and Holloway (2010) concluded that parents who do not consider themselves academically efficacious may develop low academic expectations for their children, even when the children's previous school performance is relatively high. In fact, they may worry that as parents they will not be able to provide support in the future due to a lack of intellectual capacity (Yamamoto & Holloway, 2010). Likewise, Wilder (2014) concluded that

> parental expectations reflect parents' beliefs and attitudes toward school, teachers, subjects, and education in general ... children are likely to harbour similar attitudes and beliefs as their parents ... [that is] having high parental expectations appears vital for academic achievement of children. (p. 392)

The importance of parent-related factors is also supported in the findings of a study conducted in Jamaica by Cook and Jennings (2016), which revealed that the value attached to education by Jamaican parents and their children attending secondary school were similar. This similarity is likely to affect both the level of parental involvement and the extent to which students are successful. Parental involvement may decline or change, especially during the latter years in high school when the work becomes more complex. As Costa and Faria (2017) concluded, parental involvement changes throughout high school for several reasons, including the demands of the level of education, the lack of time, adolescents' autonomy and teachers' communication style.

Parents' Satisfaction with Parental Involvement

Concerning parents' assessment of their satisfaction with parental involvement, the literature is sparse, especially in the Jamaican context. Relating to parents' satisfaction with their level of parental involvement, no studies were identified with this specific focus. A review of the literature available internationally revealed a similar gap, those studies identified that addressed satisfaction and parental involvement focussed on other issues such as parents' satisfaction with children's schooling (Gibbons & Silva, 2011; Meier & Lemmer, 2019) and students' satisfaction with their life as a consequence of parental involvement (OECD, 2017). This dearth of information on parents' satisfaction with their own level of parental involvement further substantiates the significance of the present study's contribution to the extant literature on parental involvement.

When a more general search of the literature was conducted, studies addressing parents' views on parental involvement were identified. However, those focussed on the Jamaican context were limited. The few studies related to the Jamaican context included a qualitative study conducted by Troupe (2017) with sixteen parents in Jamaica exploring their views on parental involvement across four schools. This study revealed that all parents felt that school communities should endeavour to have as many activities as possible to foster the various types of parental involvement, specifically communicating, parenting, volunteering and decision making (Troupe, 2017). The other study conducted locally suggested that parents might not be satisfied with opportunities provided by the schools for them to be involved. According to Watson-Williams (2011), low level of parental involvement in the Jamaican context is a result of the education system in Jamaica that "has created little social space for the participation of the parents … thereby limiting the scope for parents to actively bring about real change for their children" (p. 2). This argument suggests that schools might not be doing enough to involve parents. A similar idea was reported in a study conducted in the United States by Walker (2017), which revealed that 48 per cent of the 250 parents surveyed indicated that they did not believe the school considered them important partners, and 28 per cent were not convinced that the school had a climate conducive to parent participation. The findings of the studies conducted locally and internationally suggest that parents recognize that their involvement is critical to students' success, and that parents would welcome more opportunities provided by the school to facilitate their involvement.

The findings from local and international literature suggest that all types of parental involvement activities are prevalent; however, academic socialization which involves communicating parental expectations to children is the most important type of parental involvement at the secondary level in determining students' academic success. The analysis of the literature also indicates that parental involvement in homework can have a positive impact and seems more significant when students are given some autonomy over the process. However, the level of complexity of the assignments and parents' academic competence are factors that can result in a decline or change in the ways that parents become involved in homework.

Concerning parents' satisfaction with parental involvement, the few studies available suggest that parents are aware that they play a critical role in their children's academic success; however they are not necessarily satisfied with how the schools facilitate their involvement. The review also highlights that a dearth of research exists in the Jamaican context on parental involvement. Relating to parents' assessment of their satisfaction with their involvement, the review reveals a paucity both locally and internationally. These gaps substantiate the need for the present study and support the types of questions and methodology used to explore the scope and prevalence of parental involvement.

Methodology

Research Design

This study was designed as a descriptive survey exploring the prevalence of different types of parental involvement, parents' satisfaction with parental involvement and reported factors influencing their involvement. Gay, Mills and Airasian (2006) explained that "descriptive research or survey research determines and describes the way things are. It involves collecting data to test hypotheses or to answer questions about people's opinions on some topic or issue" (p. 175). Given the focus of this research, a descriptive design is suitable in examining the state of parental involvement in this rural high school in Jamaica.

Data Collection and Analysis

A cross-sectional survey was used to collect the data for this research. Epstein's (1995) and Hoover-Dempsey and Sandler's (1995) models of parental involvement seem to resonate across all borders and have been used as guides in developing parent surveys in various studies. This present study adapted one such parent survey designed by Wright (2015) in collecting data from parents using a descriptive survey design. The instrument developed by Wright (2015) was used in the Jamaican context; however, minor modifications were made, and the instrument was tested for reliability and validity in the present study. The Parent Survey instrument consists of ten demographic items and forty-four Likert scale response items. Demographic information included data on parents' gender, age, family type and level of educational attainment. The Likert scale items captured a series of statements related to Epstein's subscales of parental involvement and items related to Hoover-Dempsey and Sandler's (1995) model focusing on the factors influencing parental involvement. This Parent Survey was piloted and was found to be both reliable and valid with Cronbach Alpha results above 0.8 (see Bryman and Cramer, 2011).

As table 8.1 illustrates, the instrument remains reliable after piloting with the minor adjustments to Wright's (2015) instrument.

Sampling

The high school used in this study was an upgraded co-educational, government-owned high school located in St. Mary, Jamaica. The participants were selected from parents of the grade 11 cohort which comprised 260 ($n=260$) students; by extension this meant there were at least 260 parents in the population. The sample size was determined

Table 8.1 Participants' Response Rate and Reliability Coefficient of Parent Survey

	Current Study		Wright (2015)	
			Actual Study	
Participants	Response Rates	Reliability Coefficient	Response Rates	Reliability Coefficient
Parents/Guardians	76%	$\alpha = .834$	54%	$\alpha = .887$

using the Survey System Online Sample Size Calculator (Creative Research Systems, 2018). A confidence level of 95 per cent, a margin of error of 5.66 per cent and the population of 260 were inputted in the online sample size calculator for the sample size to be determined (Creative Research Systems, 2018). The confidence interval and sampling error inputted into the sample size calculator were in keeping with recommendations by Creswell (2014) for a rigorous standard for sample size estimation in educational research. The output from this calculation online determined the sample size to be 119 (Creative Research Systems, 2018).

In selecting the 119 parents to be included in the survey, a simple random sampling technique was employed. This method is based on a subset of a statistical population in which each member of the subset has an equal probability of being chosen (Creswell, 2014). The names of the grade 11 cohort were typed in Microsoft Excel and each student assigned a number from 1 to 260. This data set was then imported to SPSS and the data was used to generate a random sample of 119 participants. By employing a simple random sampling technique, "an unbiased representation" of the group was provided (Gay, Mills, & Airasian, 2006, p. 101). Oversampling (156 participants) was done to increase the likelihood of obtaining 119 completed questionnaires (Gay, Mills, & Airasian, 2006). The randomly selected numbers were assigned to the Parent Survey instrument that was used to collect the data.

Recruitment Procedures

In collecting the data for this study, all four major ethical issues identified by Leedy and Ormrod (2001) were observed. Additionally, this study adhered to the ethical guidelines as stipulated by the University of the West Indies, Faculty of Medical Science Ethics Committee. Permission was sought from the principal to administer surveys to parents of the grade 11 students. After permission was granted by the principal, the randomly selected numbers that were generated by SPSS were written on the 156 parent surveys, and these were placed in envelopes. Included in the envelopes were a letter explaining the purpose and benefits of the study and a request for parents' voluntary participation in completing the Parent Survey. Students were asked to deliver envelopes to their parents and return the completed instrument to their form teachers. The completed parent surveys were later collected from the form teachers and cross-referenced with the random numbers assigned. Of the 156 parent surveys that were issued, a total of 119 were completed and returned.

Data Analysis Procedures

The data obtained from the Parent Survey was coded and entered into the Statistical Software Program for Social Sciences (SPSS). The data were analysed using descriptive and inferential statistics. Sub-questions one to four were analysed using descriptive tables, graphs and box plots. The analysis involved the use of percentages, means and modes. Sub-question five was analysed using inferential statistics exploring whether significant differences existed in responses based on factors such as age, gender, educational attainment and type of employment.

Results

To begin this section, an overview of the results of the analysis of the demographic information collected from the sample was conducted. The analysis revealed that among the cohort of grade 11 students there were different persons playing the role of parent. In addition to those students living with biological parents, students lived with step-parents, aunts, uncles, siblings, grandparents and legal guardians who played the role of parents. The absence of biological parents in some cases in this rural community might be due to employment overseas as discussed previously in the background section. A little more than half (51.3 per cent) of the respondents were mothers. The analysis also revealed that for the majority of the respondents (66.4 per cent) the highest level of education attained was secondary level education. The analysis also revealed that most parents (78.2 per cent) live in St. Mary, and a total of 63 per cent of the respondents were employed. Appendix shows detailed characteristics of the respondents, and the following section presents the data for each research question.

RQ 1. What are the ways in which parents are involved in their children's education in grade 11 in a rural high school in Jamaica?

The construct of parental involvement using five of Epstein's (1995) Parental Involvement subscales – communicating, learning at home, volunteering, parenting and decision making – revealed that all five types were prevalent in varying degrees among parents at this rural high school. Learning at home was the most prevalent type of parental involvement. The learning at home subscale had the highest mean score ($m = 3.78$; SD $= .67$), while decision making had the lowest score ($m = 2.7283$). Further analysis of parents' overall level of involvement based on the reported levels for all five subscales revealed that there was a generally moderate level of parental involvement among respondents from this rural high school in Jamaica. Parents' involvement varied within the range of scores (169 to 186) identified as moderate level of involvement based on cut points calculated in SPSS.

An analysis of items related to academic socialization (parents' communication with children about academic expectations and future plans) as identified by Hill and Tyson (2009) revealed that most parents reported that they engaged their children in discussions about school. A total of 83 per cent of the parents reported that they talked about the importance of school often with their children. Additionally, 75 per cent of the parents reported that they talked to their children about future plans for college. These results suggest that parents are involved in various ways in their children's academic life – capturing home-based activities, school-based activities and academic socialization.

RQ 2. How prevalent is parental involvement in homework among the grade 11 parents?

In analysing the extent that parents were involved in homework, they were asked to report on the frequency with which they were involved in providing students with information to help with homework and other school projects. A total of 89 per cent of the parents reported that they provided information to help with homework, while 5 per cent reported that they rarely helped their children with homework and 5 per cent reported that they never helped with homework. Another aspect of parental involvement in homework that was explored related to parents' involvement in conversations with their children about homework. That analysis revealed that 78 per cent of respondents reported that they often talked to their children about homework. The mean score ($m = 4.13$) indicated that overall parents were involved in conversations with their children about homework. The findings also revealed that 37 per cent of the parents reported that the school provided adequate information on how to monitor and discuss schoolwork at home, while 32 per cent felt that the school did not provide adequate information. This indicates that parents were not completely satisfied with the support they received from the school.

RQ 3. What proportion of parents are satisfied with their parental involvement in the academic life of their children?

Parents were asked to assess the extent of satisfaction with their overall level of parental involvement. The analysis revealed that 86 per cent of the respondents reported some level of satisfaction with their overall involvement in their children's academic life in grade 11. This was supported by the results presented indicating the prevalence of parents' involvement in various home-based activities. On the other hand, this level of satisfaction was not supported by parents' reported participation in school-based activities, where 25 per cent of the parents reported that they had never volunteered to be a part of any school activity, and 53 per cent reported that they seldom volunteered for school activities. Additionally, 24 per cent indicated that they did not attend PTA meetings often, while 23 per cent reported some attendance. However, 71 per cent reported some agreement with the statement that school events are scheduled at different times to facilitate parents' attendance. The results also indicated that 98.3 per cent of the respondents thought that school-parent partnership was important to their children's academic success. These results suggest that although parents were satisfied with their level of parental involvement and acknowledged the importance of partnering with the school, their participation in school-based activities was relatively low. When data were analysed further to explore whether there were differences in overall levels of satisfaction based on factors such as age, gender and relationship to student, the results revealed that there were significant differences in parents' satisfaction with their involvement based on relationship to student ($p = 0.02$). Guardians, aunts and uncles were the least satisfied with their level of parental involvement, while mothers, fathers and grandparents were among the most satisfied.

RQ4. What are the reported factors affecting parents' level of involvement?

In examining the reported factors that affected parental involvement, parents were asked to indicate the frequency with which factors such as competing responsibilities at home and work and transportation costs regularly affected their ability to participate in school-based activities. The results revealed that competing responsibilities at home and work frequently affected parents' involvement in school-based activities. Table 8.2 provides a summary of the responses.

As illustrated in table 8.2, being needed at home ($m = 3.13$) was the main factor that affected parents' ability to participate in school-based activities: 20 per cent of the parents indicated that this factor always affected their attendance at school-based activities and 13 per cent considered it a factor

Table 8.2 Factors Affecting Parental Involvement in School-based Activities

	Mean	Frequency %		
		Always	Regularly	Never
(i) Needed at home	3.13	20	13.4	13.4
(ii) Availability of transportation	2.25	6.7	9.2	34.5
(iii) Transportation cost	2.52	15	11	35
(iv) Distance from school	2.24	9.2	6.7	36.1
(v) Unable to leave work	2.65	13.4	13.4	31.1
(vi) School staff unfriendly	1.69	3.4	1.7	52.1
(vii) My child does not want me at school	1.63	5.0	2.5	62.2
(viii) Not receiving announcements in a timely manner	2.34	9.2	6.7	28.6

that regularly affected their involvement. Transportation cost ($m = 2.5$) and being unable to leave work ($m = 2.6$) were also factors that frequently posed a challenge to parents' involvement.

In addition to exploring those factors affecting participation in school-based activities, parent factors were analysed using Analysis of Variance (ANOVA). These analyses explored whether there were significant differences in parents' level of involvement based on relationship to student, age, educational attainment and employment. The results of this analysis revealed that at the $p < .05$ level there were no significant differences in levels of parental involvement based on employment status [$F(3, 84) = 0.682, p = .56$], highest level of education attained [$F(4, 100) = 0.792, p = .53$], SES (Profession) [$F(8, 87) = 0.703, p = .70$], age [$F(4, 98) = 1.874, p = .121$] or relation to student [$F(7, 97) = 1.991, p = .064$].

Discussion

The findings of this study confirmed that, as proposed by Epstein (1995), parental involvement in this rural high school takes many forms – ranging from parenting, communicating, learning at home and volunteering to decision making. The most prevalent type of parental involvement at the Valley High School in Jamaica was "learning at home". At grade 11 in Jamaican high schools, parental involvement in home-based activities is particularly important and often connected to the SBA component of the CXC examinations. Parents' involvement in learning at home (especially with grade 11 children at this rural high school) has likely contributed positively to the academic performance of students in their CXC exams. As stated by Hoover-Dempsey et al. (2001), "parents' homework involvement activities give children multiple opportunities to observe and learn from their parents' modelling, to receive reinforcement and feedback on personal performance and capability, and to engage in instructional interactions related to homework content and learning processes" (p. 203).

According to the framework of Hoover-Dempsey and Sandler (1995), the prevalence of this type of involvement is tied to parental-role construction, which is critical for parents' involvement in children's education. Parents' decisions to be involved at home are undergirded by an understanding of their role "which reflects parents' expectations and beliefs about what they should do in relation to children's schooling. ... [It] appears to define the range of activities that parents believe important, necessary, and permissible for their own engagement in children's schooling" (Hoover-Dempsey et al., 2001, p. 201). This suggests that the range of activities that were common among the parents at this rural high school reflected their understanding of their role as parents.

The present study revealed that engaging with conversations about the importance of homework and providing information to help their children to complete homework were the most prevalent learning at home activities among parents. This suggests that parents in this study considered factors such as talking to their children about completing homework, helping and monitoring their children to ensure that their homework is completed as important to their role. It also suggests that parents from this rural community placed value on education, which in turn could positively influence students' views on the importance of education. In accordance with the conclusions of the study conducted by Cook and Jennings (2016) in Jamaica, the value systems of parents and students with regard to education are often similar. Therefore, parents' involvement in homework provides students with positive messages about the importance of education and is a form of involvement likely to have long-lasting positive effects. These conversations are considered part of academic socialization, which has been noted in the literature as being of significance in improving academic achievement (Benner, Boyle, and Sadler, 2016; Castro et al., 2015).

The high level of parental involvement at home in this study is a significant result, considering that the completion of secondary level is the highest educational level attained by most of the parents of the students from the Valley High School. Less than 10 per cent of the parents in this sample had attained a college degree. However, factors such as educational attainment, age and employment revealed no significant differences in parents' level of involvement. The literature also suggests that involvement in homework often wanes as the student progresses to higher grade levels in high school due to levels of complexity involved in homework and parents' knowledge and competence (Hoover-Dempsey et al., 2001). However, this was not the case at the Valley High School. The majority of the parents of the grade 11 students at this rural high school reported that they regularly provided information to their children to assist with homework. While this is encouraging, a large portion of the parents also reported that they did not believe that the school provided adequate information on how to monitor and discuss schoolwork at home. This is an indication that more guidance from the school is needed so that parents can help their children with homework. In tandem with Epstein (2002), "families need good information about middle and high school curricula, teachers' instructional approaches, and assessments in order to be able to discuss important academic topics with their children at home" (p. 252).

Although the parents of the Valley High School were not satisfied with the support received from school as they supported their children's learning at home, the results of this study showed that most of the parents felt satisfied with their level of involvement in their children's academic lives. However, the results revealed that guardians, aunts and uncles were the least satisfied with their level of parental involvement, indicating that relationship to the students is an important consideration in examining parental involvement. Furthermore, considering that home-based involvement was most prevalent, it is possible that parents' assessment of their satisfaction was based predominantly on their involvement with home-based activities and not based on their overall involvement in all types of parental involvement. At this rural high school, half of the parents indicated that they seldom volunteered to participate in school-based activities, and some had never attended a PTA meeting. Likewise, parents' involvement in decision making at school was found to be the least prevalent. These results indicate that there is some weakness in the home-school partnership at the Valley High School.

Several factors potentially account for this weakness. The findings of the study revealed that competing responsibilities at home and difficulty getting time off from work frequently affected parents' involvement in school-based activities. This is in keeping with the postulations of Epstein (2002) who noted that on average single parents, parents who are employed outside the home, parents who live far from the school and fathers are less involved in their children's education. The findings of this present study found no significant differences in parents' level of involvement based on age, educational attainment and job status. However, considering that in the present study most of the respondents were mothers and most were employed in low wage earning jobs, these demographics are potentially connected to the factors that were reported as most frequently having an effect on parents' participation in school-based activities at this rural high school.

As explained by Nelson (2018) in the Jamaican Gleaner, low wage earners often cannot attend school-based activities because time off from work means loss of salary. This is also supported by Munroe (2009) and Watson-Williams (2011) who argue that the state of parental involvement in education in Jamaica is not owing to a lack of parental interest; rather it is the result of a range of factors related to the social context, driven by issues such as poverty and social status. This seems to be applicable to this study because parents at the Valley High School were involved in home-based activities, indicating their interest in their children's academic life, but they were not as involved in school-based activities such as PTA and decision making. Also important is the dissatisfaction with the school's support reported by some parents who indicated that the school did not provide adequate assistance for monitoring homework. In agreement with Epstein (2002), the initial enthusiasm and decisions for parental involvement must be followed by actions that sustain productive collaborations over the long term. Therefore, the Valley High School must take action to sustain parental involvement at home and forge better parent-school relationships.

Conclusions, Implications and Recommendations

This research has provided a snapshot of the scope, prevalence and level of parental involvement in a rural high school in Jamaica. Based on the findings, one can reasonably conclude that parents at the Valley High School are involved in adolescents' academic life. However, the findings also suggest that schools can do more to support parental involvement, because six in ten parents did not feel that they received adequate support from the school as they tried to assist their children at home. This has implications for the approach to be taken in strengthening parental involvement. Since parental involvement at home is most prevalent at this rural high school and parents are not satisfied with the support received from the school, emphasis should be placed on providing adequate support to parents. Grade 11 is a critical year in students' academic life and parents are aware of this, but their attempts to assist their children at home are potentially hampered by a lack of information from the school. One recommendation based on this finding is that the school could ensure that they plan workshops and other activities to provide parents with information on how to assist their children with completion of the SBA component of their CXC exams. Text messages, emails and phone calls could be done at various points during the process of completion of the SBA to ensure that parents are receiving adequate information to support monitoring of homework. School administrators must see this effort as an ongoing priority that will improve outcomes for all stakeholders. The prevalence of learning at home in the present study also has implications for future research, as other researchers could explore the significance of learning at home on students' performance in the SBA component and overall academic performance.

Another important finding from this study was that parents were satisfied with their level of involvement even though they were not very involved in decision making at school or in school-based activities such as PTA. This suggests that parents do not necessarily associate their level of satisfaction with their overall involvement in all types of their parenting activities. Further studies are needed to explore the relationship between parents' assessment of their satisfaction with their involvement and its relationship to the types of activities. There is a dearth of information both locally and internationally pertaining to parents' assessment of their satisfaction with their level of involvement. Therefore, studies could examine parents' satisfaction with their involvement and how this relates to the types of involvement. This finding is also an indication that schools need to make explicit the importance of parental involvement in school in activities such as decision making.

The findings that the majority of the parents reported being satisfied with their involvement even though they seldom attended PTA, volunteered for school activities or participated in decision making at school suggest that these are not necessarily considered equally important types of involvement among parents at the Valley High School, and that the school may need to do more to involve parents in school-based activities. In planning for increased involvement in school-based activities, this rural high school should also consider the mitigating factors reported as frequently affecting parents' ability to participate in school-based activities and how best to reduce their impact. One recommendation for addressing the competing responsibilities at home and work is to have online meetings that parents can join from home; these meetings could be recorded and made available to parents, and opportunities could be provided for parents to submit their comments and concerns after watching the recordings. That way parents can become more involved through remote means in school-based activities. Decision makers at school could also increase parents' involvement by sending out suggested plans of action for feedback before making a final decision. This information could be circulated via WhatsApp and memos, with forms attached for comments to be returned to the school.

One of the limitations of this study was that it was conducted in one rural high school; therefore the findings and implications are not readily generalizable to other rural high schools in the Jamaican context. Researchers could conduct further studies on the topic with a larger population of schools to assess the scope and prevalence of parental involvement across Jamaica. Additionally, future studies could expand the scope of the study by examining the extent that factors such as parents' role, level of educational attainment, job and family demands account for variance in parental involvement. Additionally, other research designs such as qualitative designs and mixed method approaches could provide a deeper, more comprehensive understanding of this phenomenon. Future studies could also consider employing a longitudinal research design to assess whether there is decrease in parental involvement over time.

References

Anfara, V.A., Jr. & Mertens, S.B. (2008). Varieties of parent involvement in schooling. *Middle School Journal*, 39(3), 58–64. https://www.researchgate.net/profile/Steven_Mertens/publication/284576545_Varieties_of_Parent_Involvement_in_Schooling/links/56dd7f8f08ae628f2d249961.pdf

Aries, R. & Cabus, S. (2015). Parental homework involvement improves test scores? A review of the literature. *Review of Education*, 3(2), 179–99. doi: 10.1002/rev3.3055

Benner, A., Boyle, A., & Sadler, S. (2016). Parental involvement and adolescents' educational success: The roles of prior achievement and socioeconomic status. *Journal of Youth and Adolescence*, 45, 1053–64. doi: 10.1007/s10964016-0431-4

Berk, L. (2001). *Development through the lifespan*. Pearson Education India. https://www.pearsonhighered.com/assets/preface/0/2/0/5/0205968988.pdf

Bronfenbrenner, U. (1979). *The ecology of human development*. Harvard University Press.

Brown, D. & Grinter, R.E. (2012, September). Takes a transnational network to raise a child: The case of migrant parents and left-behind Jamaican teens. *UbiComp '12: Proceedings of the 2012 ACM Conference on Ubiquitous Computing*, USA, 123–32.

Bryman, A. & Cramer, D. (2011). *Quantitative data analysis with IBM SPSS 17, 18 and 19: A guide for social scientists*. Routledge-Cavendish/Taylor & Francis.

Castro, M., Exposito-Casas, E., Lopez-Martin, E., Lizasoain, L., Navarro-Asencio, E., & Gaviraria, J. (2015). Parental involvement on student academic achievement: A meta-analysis. *Educational Research Review, 14*, 33–46. https://doi.org/10.1016/j.edurev.2015.01.002

Catsambis, S. (1998). *Expanding the knowledge of parental involvement in secondary education: Effects on high school academic success* (Report No. 27). http://files.eric.ed.gov/fulltext/ED426174.pdf

Catsambis, S. & Garland, J.E. (1997). *Parental involvement in students' education during middle school and high school* (Report No. 18). http://files.eric.ed.gov/fulltext/ED423328.pdf

Cook, L.D. & Jennings, Z. (2016). Perspectives of Jamaican parents and their secondary school children on the value of education: Effects of selected variables on parents' perspectives. *International Journal of Educational Development, 50*, 90–99.

Cooper, H., Lindsay, J.J., & Nye, B. (2000). Homework in the home: How student, family, and parenting-style differences relate to the homework process. *Contemporary Educational Psychology, 25*(4), 464–87.

Costa, M.P. & Faria, L. (2017). Parenting and parental Involvement in secondary school: Focus groups with adolescents' parents. *Paidéia (Ribeirão Preto), 27*(67), 28–36. doi: 10.1590/1982-43272767201704

Creative Research Systems. (2018). Sample Size calculator [Online software]. http://www.surveysystem.com/sscalc.htm

———. (2014). *Research design: Qualitative, quantitative and mixed methods approaches* (4th ed.). Sage Publications.

Dauber, S.L. & Epstein, J.L. (1993). Parents' attitudes and practices of involvement in inner-city elementary and middle schools. In N. Chavkin (Ed.), *Families and schools in a pluralistic society* (pp. 53–72). State University of New York Press.

Eccles, J. & Harold, R. (1993). Parent-school involvement during the early adolescent years. *The Teachers College Record, 94*(3), 568–87. https://eric.ed.gov/?id=EJ463351

———. (1996). Family involvement in children's and adolescents' schooling. In A. Booth & J.F. Dunn (Eds.), *Family-school links: How do they affect educational outcomes?* (pp. 3–34). Erlbaum.

Epstein, J.L. (1992). *School and Family Partnerships* (Report No. 6). http://files.eric.ed.gov/fulltext/ED343715.pdf

———. (1995). School-Family-Community Partnerships: Caring for the children we share. *Phi Delta Kappan, 76*, 701–12.

———. (2002). A comprehensive framework. In J. Epstein, M. Sanders, B. Simon, K. Salinas, N. Jansorn, & F. Van Voorhis (eds.), *School, family, and community partnerships: Your handbook for action* (pp. 5–40, 2nd ed.) Corwin Press.

———. (2007). Improving family and community involvement in secondary schools. *Principal leadership, 8*(2), 16–22.

Epstein, J.L. & Connors, L.J. (1995). School and family partnerships in the middle grades. In B. Rutherford (Ed.), *Creating school/family partnerships* (pp. 137–66).

National Middle School Association. http://files.eric.ed.gov/fulltext/ED401361.pdf#page=137

Epstein, J.L. & Salinas, K. (2004). Partnering with families and communities. *Educational Leadership*, 61(8), 12–18. http://www.ascd.org/ASCD/pdf/journals/ed_lead/el200405_epstein.pdf

Fan, X. & Chen, M. (2001). Parental involvement and students' academic achievement: A meta-analysis. *Educational Psychology Review*, 13(1), 1–22. http://files.eric.ed.gov/fulltext/ED430048.pdf

Francis, J. (2014, June 9). Schools failing, another report shows. *The Gleaner*. http://jamaicagleaner.com/gleaner/20140609/lead/lead5.html

Gay, L.R., Mills, G.E., & Airasian, P. (2006). *Educational research competencies for analysis and applications*. Pearson Education.

Gibbons, S. & Silva, O. (2011). School quality, child wellbeing and parents' satisfaction. *Economics of Education Review*, 30(2), 312–31. https://www.researchgate.net/publication/48910175_School_Quality_Child_Wellbeing_and_Parents'_Satisfaction

Griffith, S. (2015). *School-based assessment in a Caribbean public examination*. University of the West Indies Press.

Hagiwara, S. & Davis, D. (2018). In our family education is our culture: A Jamaican mom's effort to connect home and school. In A. Esmail, A. Pitre, D. Lund, H. Baptiste, & G. Duhon-Owens (Eds.), *Research studies on educating for diversity and social justice* (pp. 17–30). Rowman & Littlefield.

Hattie, J. (2008). *Visible learning: A synthesis of over 800 meta-analyses relating to achievement*. Taylor & Francis.

Henderson, A.T. & Mapp, K.L. (2002). *A new wave of evidence: The impact of school, family, and community connections on student achievement*. Annual Synthesis 2002. National Center for Family and Community Connections with Schools.

Hill, National. (2001). Parenting and academic socialization as they relate to school readiness: The roles of ethnicity and family income. *Journal of Educational Psychology*, 93, 686–97. https://doi.org/10.1037/0022-0663.93.4.686

Hill, N.E. & Taylor, L.C. (2004). Parental school involvement and children's academic achievement: Pragmatics and issues. *Current Directions in Psychological Science*, 13(4), 161–64.

Hill, N.E. & Tyson, D.F. (2009). Parental involvement in middle school: A meta-analytic assessment of the strategies that promote achievement. *Developmental Psychology*, 45(3), 740.

Hoover-Dempsey, K. & Sandler, H. (1995). Parental involvement in children's education: Why does it make a difference? *Teachers College Record*, 97(2), 310–31.

Hoover-Dempsey, K.V., Battiato, A.C., Walker, J.M., Reed, R.P., DeJong, J.M., & Jones, K.P. (2001). Parental involvement in homework. *Educational psychologist*, 36(3), 195–209.

Jamaica Information Service. (2008, March). *Greater parental involvement in education stressed*. https://jis.gov.jm/greater-parental-involvement-in-education-stressed/

Jamaica Observer. (2011, October 2). Many primary-level students lack parental support at school. https://www.jamaicaobserver.com/magazines/career/Many-primary-level-students-lack-parental--support-at-school_9813152

Jeynes, W.H. (2005). A meta-analysis of the relation of parental involvement to urban elementary school student academic achievement. *Urban Education, 40*(3), 237–69. https://doi.org/10.1177/0042085905274540

Johnson, E.J. & Descartes, C. (2017). Parental influence on academic achievement among the primary school students in Trinidad. *Early Child Development and Care, 187*(7), 1221–27. https://doi.org/10.1080/03004430.2016.1163549

Khajehpour, M. & Ghazvini, S. (2011). The role of parental involvement affect in children's academic performance. *Procedia Social and Behavioral Sciences, 15,* 1204–08.

Krane, V. & Klevan, T. (2019). There are three of us: Parents' experiences of the importance of teacher-student relationships and parental involvement in upper secondary school. *International Journal of Adolescence and Youth, 24*(1), 74–84. https://www.tandfonline.com/doi/full/10.1080/02673843.2018.1464482

Leedy, P.D. & Ormod, J.E. (2001). *Practical research: Planning and design.* Pearson Education.

Mahuro, M.G., Hungi, N., & Lamb, S. (2016). Parental participation improves student academic achievement: A case of Iganga and Mayuge districts in Uganda. *Cogent Education, 3*(1). https://doi.org/10.1080/2331186X.2016.1264170

Marshall, I., Browne, D., & Fongkong-Mungal, C. (2014). Investigating the relationship between parental involvement and student academic achievement in Barbados. *Caribbean Educational Research Journal, 2*(2), 3–13.

Meier, C. & Lemmer, E. (2019). Parents as consumers: A case study of parent satisfaction with the quality of schooling, *Educational Review, 71*(5), 617–30. https://doi.org/10.1080/00131911.2018.1465395

Mills, K., Lawlor, J., McAlindon, K., Watling Neal, J., & Neal, Z. (2018). Beyond report cards and conferences? The salience of types of parent engagement to educators. *Michigan State University AGEP Science Today Bulletin,* 35–40. https://grad.msu.edu/sites/default/files/content/AGEP/2018%20AGEP%20Science%20Today%20Bulletin%20Final.pdf

Muhammad, H., Rafiq, W., Fatima, T., Sohail, M.M., Saleem, M., & Khan, M.A. (2013). Parental involvement and academic achievement: A study on secondary school students of Lahore, Pakistan. *International Journal of Humanities and Social Science, 3*(8), 209–23.

Munroe, G. (2009). *Parental involvement in education in Jamaica.* [Unpublished mimeo]. Policy Research Unit, Planning Institute of Jamaica.

Murphy, S. (2002). *The attitudes of Jamaican parents towards parental involvement in high school education.* [Unpublished master's thesis]. University of Wisconsin-Stout.

Nelson, J. (2018, August 5). Parental involvement is a luxury. *The Gleaner.* http://jamaica-gleaner.com/article/commentary/20180805/jaevion-nelson-parental-involvement-luxury

OECD. (2017). *PISA 2015 Results (Volume III): Students' Well-Being.* Paris: PISA, OECD Publishing. http://dx.doi.org/10.1787/9789264273856-en

Park, H., Byun, S., & Kim, K. (2011). Parental involvement and students' cognitive outcomes in Korea: Focusing on private tutoring. *Sociology of Education, 84*(1), 3–22. https://doi.org/10.1177/0038040710392719

Patall, E.A., Cooper, H., & Robinson, J.C. (2008). Parent involvement in homework: A research synthesis. *Review of Educational Research, 78*(4), 1039–101. https://doi.org/10.3102/0034654308325185

Pomerantz, E.M., Grolnick, W.S., & Price, C.E. (2005). The role of parents in how children approach achievement: A dynamic process perspective. In A.J. Elliot & C.S. Dweck (Eds.), *Handbook of competence and motivation* (pp. 229–78). Guilford Publications.

Robinson, K. & Harris, A.L. (2014). *The broken compass: Parental involvement with children's education.* Harvard University Press. https://doi.org/10.4159/harvard.9780674726291

Seginer, R. (2006). Parents' educational involvement: A developmental ecological perspective. *Parenting: Science and Practice, 6,* 1–48.

Sheldon, S.B. & Epstein, J.L. (2005). Involvement counts: Family and community partnerships and mathematics achievement. *The Journal of Educational Research, 98*(4), 196–207.

Troupe, K. (2017). *Motivations influencing home support engagements in Jamaican high schools* [Doctoral dissertation, Walden University]. https://scholarworks.waldenu.edu/cgi/viewcontent.cgi?article=5509&context=dissertations

Walker, C. (2017). *Parents' and teachers' perspectives regarding parental involvement and student achievement* [Doctoral thesis]. https://scholarworks.waldenu.edu/cgi/viewcontent.cgi?article=5441&context=dissertations

Walker, J.M.T., Hoover-Dempsey, K.V., Whetsel, D.R., & Green, C.L. (2004). *Parental involvement in homework: A review of current research and its implications for teachers, after school program staff, and parent leaders.* Harvard Family Research Project; Harvard Graduate School of Education. http://citeseerx.ist.psu.edu/viewdoc/download?doi=10.1.1.869.717&rep=rep1&type=pdf

Wang, M., Hill, N., & Hofkens, T. (2014). Parental involvement and African American and European American adolescents' academic, behavioral, and emotional development in secondary school. *Child Development, 85*(6), 2151–68.

Wang, M.T. & Sheikh-Khalil, S. (2014). Does parental involvement matter for student achievement and mental health in high school? *Child development, 85*(2), 610–25.

Watson-Williams, C. (2011). Challenges to achieving generational transformation in Jamaica through parental involvement in children's education: The role of schools. *Caribbean Journal of Education, 3*(1), 61–78. https://www.mona.uwi.edu/soe/publications/cje/article/117

Wei, J., Pomerantz, E.M., Ng, F.F.Y., Yu, Y., Wang, M., & Wang, Q. (2019). Why does parents' involvement in youth's learning vary across elementary, middle, and high school?. *Contemporary Educational Psychology, 56*, 262–74.

Wilder, S. (2014). Effects of parental involvement on academic achievement: A metasynthesis, *Educational Review, 66* (3), 377–97. https://www.tandfonline.com/doi/abs/10.1080/00131911.2013.780009

Wright, N. (2015). *The extent to which parental involvement impacts the academic performance of tenth grade students.* [Unpublished master's thesis]. The University of the West Indies, Mona.

Xu, M., Kushner Benson, S.N., Mudrey-Camino, R., & Steiner, R.P. (2010). The relationship between parental involvement, self-regulated learning, and reading achievement of fifth graders: A path analysis using the ECLS-K database. *Social Psychology of Education, 13*(2), 237–69.

Yamamoto, Y. & Holloway, S. (2010). Parental expectations and children's academic performance in sociocultural context. *Educational Psychology Review, 22*, 89–214. https://doi.org/10.1007/s10648-010-9121-z

Yulianti, K., Denessen, E., & Droop, M. (2018). The effects of parental involvement on children's education: A study in elementary schools in Indonesia. *International Journal about Parents in Education, 10*(1), 14–32.

Appendix Participant Demographics

High school caregivers		n	% of sample
Relations	Mother	61	51.3
	Father	18	15.1
	Aunt	6	5.0
	Uncle	2	1.7
	Stepmother	7	5.9
	Grandparent	15	12.6
	Guardian	5	4.2
	Sibling	5	4.2
Age Range			
	21 or Below	8	6.7
	21–30	12	10.1
	31–40	31	26.1
	41–50	28	23.5
	51–60	40	33.6
Marital Status			
	Married	46	38.7
	Single	31	26.1
	Divorced	5	4.2
	Widowed	4	3.4
	Separated	30	25.2
	No response	3	2.5
Family structure			
	Single Parent	25	21.0
	Nuclear	46	38.7
	Extended	46	38.7
	Siblings	2	1.7
Parish			
	St. Mary	93	78.2
	St. Ann	17	14.3
	St. Catherine	5	4.2
	Portland	4	3.4

(Continued)

(Continued)

High school caregivers		n	% of sample
Employment Status			
	Yes	75	64
	No	44	37
Education			
	Primary	2	1.7
	High School / Secondary School	79	66.4
	Vocational or Training School	29	24.4
	College	7	5.9
	University	2	1.7

Characteristics of respondents (*n* = 119).

Chapter 9

School Violence in Jamaica

The Impact of Parental Involvement

CLAUDINE MIGHTY AND THERESE FERGUSON

Introduction

One of the most critical and worrying issues for the countries of the Caribbean region is that of violence, as this has increased in the past decades and is recognized as a serious problem that can impact social and economic development (Anderson, 2004/5; Moser & van Bronkhurst, 1999; Rodgers, 1999). According to a 2007 report of the United Nations Office of Drugs and Crime (UNODC) and the Latin America and the Caribbean Region of the World Bank, murder rates in the Caribbean region are high and have been rising for a number of countries in the region (UNODC & World Bank, 2007). More recently, a 2012 report of the United Nations Development Programme (UNDP) also stated that violent crimes in the region have been on the increase. In various parts of the world, the phenomena of youth violence is a worrying issue (Moestue, Moestue, & Muggah, 2013; UNDP, 2012). While various reasons can be identified for violence in the region, the overall result is the same: "the increase in criminal violence across the region threatens the post-independence development trajectory of most nations" (UNDP, 2012, p. 20). As stated in a UNODC report:

> One reason for the concentration of violent crime has to do with the characteristics of the places in which it occurs. If the social ties within a community or neighbourhood are too weak to influence how local people behave, criminality, in particular juvenile crime, is more likely. (UNODC, 2019, p. 28)

Indeed, both the direct and indirect costs of violence, such as loss of life and loss of foreign investment opportunities respectively, are troubling considerations for the region (Moser & van Bronkhurst, 1999).

Jamaica, the largest English-speaking island in the region, is not immune from this issue of violence. According to the UNDP, Jamaica has consistently exhibited high levels of violent crime in the post-independence period and is classed as one of the most violent countries in the world (UNDP, 2012). Over the past six decades, Jamaica has recorded increase in interpersonal violence (UNODC, 2019). Violence among the youth population has also increased (Cole & Anderson, 2016). As might be expected, some students in schools copy the violence they see around them in the wider society. Campbell-Livingston (2017), writing in the *Gleaner*, reported that conflicts and violence that were once in the community are now carried into the schools. A number of media reports highlight incidents of violence in schools. Dunkley (2013), writing in the *Jamaica Observer*, reported on the number of violent incidents in schools, which accounted for 3 murders, 915 fights and 160 robberies in the academic year 2012. In a report written by Angus (2016) and published by the Jamaica Information Service (JIS), it was noted that there was a reduction in the number of fights reported, from 915 in 2012–13 to 786 in 2014–15. Patterson (2017), also of the JIS, reported from the then minister of education, youth and information that there was a decrease in school violence in recent years, sharing figures of 165 reported fights, 8 robberies, 1 murder, 30 thefts, 32 woundings for 2015 as against 2016 where figures show that there were 16 reported fights, 14 robberies, 0 murders, 45 thefts, 16 woundings (Patterson, 2017). For 2017, Patterson (2017) shared that between January and April there were only seven school violence incidents, but no breakdowns were provided. Although the data suggest that there may be a decrease in school violence (Patterson, 2017), the phenomenon is still a worrying concern for the nation and for the education sector, as instances of school violence can disrupt learning opportunities and affect educational outcomes.

There are also concerns about what could be fuelling these violent incidents. The National Children's Registry (NCR) (2017) reported an increase in the number of reports received of children exhibiting behavioural problems over a 10-year period; in 2007, 66 reports were received, increasing to 5,534 in 2017. In addition, forms of abuse against children accounted for a total of 96,364 cases over the 10-year period (2007–17). This chapter offers insights into other factors that may be responsible for students in schools becoming more violent, such as ongoing exposure to corporal punishment in the school system and in the home. A range of programmes and initiatives have been instituted in an attempt to address the problem of school violence. These include teacher-led interventions, school policies and communication campaigns (Moestue, Moestue, & Muggah, 2013). A number of researchers have suggested that parental involvement and family-oriented strategies are also significant (e.g., Murray et al., 1998; Brubaker, Brubaker, & Link, 2001; Edwards-Kerr,

2017). With this in mind, this chapter shares the findings of a descriptive research study which sought to examine the relationship between parental involvement and the level of school fights (as one aspect of school violence) among a population of grade 11 students at a co-educational high school in Central Clarendon, Jamaica. In particular, the following research questions were at the forefront of the study:

1. What are parents' attitudes towards school-parent partnerships?
2. How involved do parents think they need to be with respect to monitoring their children's behaviour?
3. What per cent of students get involved in fights?
4. What are parents' responses to their children's involvement in fights?

Theoretical Framework

The study draws on two theories: Epstein's Six Types of Parental Involvement Model and Bandura's Social Learning Theory. Epstein's model focuses on parents while Bandura's theory focuses on students' behaviour.

Parental Involvement

Epstein identified six types of parental involvement in creating school and family partnership programmes and postulated that "the main reason to create such partnerships is to help all youngsters succeed in school and in later life" (Epstein et al., 2002, p. 7). These six types of parental involvement include

1) Parenting: Helping families to build supportive home environments that facilitate children's development and learning;
2) Communicating: Designing and ensuring effective two-way communication between school and home about school programmes and children's progress;
3) Volunteering: Recruiting and organizing parental help and support;
4) Learning at home: Sharing information with families as to how they can support students at home with curriculum activities, including homework;
5) Decision making: Including families in school decision making, and developing parents for leadership and other representative roles; and
6) Collaborating with the community: Fostering collaboration with the community in order to mobilize resources and services for families,

students and the school and providing services to the community in turn (Epstein & Salinas, 2004).

These six elements developed by Epstein are critical components of an individual's day-to-day development. The theory of overlapping spheres of influence highlights collaboration among family (inclusive of parents), school and the community to ensure student outcomes. Within this study, the parenting, communicating and volunteering components are analysed. These steps impact children the most and greatly influence children's behaviour patterns.

Social Learning Theory

The Social Learning Theory proposed by Albert Bandura proposes that "new patterns of behaviour can be acquired through direct experience or by observing the behaviour of others" (Bandura, 1971, p. 3). The models in children and adolescents' lives are likely to influence their behaviour based on what they observe. In social learning theory, behaviours are learned through four phases – attention, retention, reproduction and motivation (Slavin, 2012). The attention is focussed on the model's behaviour. A model that is considered to be important or popular to the individual is more likely to contribute to retention and reproduction of the behaviour. If the reproduced behaviour is reinforced, there will be motivation to repeat it in the future. This therefore suggests that reinforced behaviours are more likely to be repeated (Bandura, 1971). Bandura and Ross's Bobo Doll Experiment investigated that children can acquire aggressive behaviour through observation and imitation (Bandura, Ross, & and Ross, 1961). Based on the experiment, children who observed the models being aggressive were more likely to imitate the aggressive behaviour towards the Bobo Dolls than those who did not witness the models hitting the Bobo Dolls. Bandura suggested that the imitation and modelling of "most of the behaviours that people display are learned, either deliberately or inadvertently, through the influence of example" (Bandura, 1971, p. 5). In addition, it can be argued that it is difficult to conceive of the socialization process without culture and language, which are learned from models "who exemplify the cultural patterns in their own behaviour" (Bandura, 1971, p. 4). This is consistent with aspects of Epstein's overlapping spheres of influence where communication among families, schools and communities influence a child's behaviour. The type of parenting a child is exposed to is a significant factor in determining their upbringing. Cole and Anderson (2016) reported that some adolescents felt they were not understood by parents – as evidenced by the lack of communication which is critical between both parents and children.

It is important to note that children who are involved in school violence may not necessarily learn these behaviours at home. They may be influenced by peers, popular media or the internet. This can also be transmitted through "modelling", a term used by Bandura to explain how humans can swiftly learn explicit acts of aggression and integrate them into their behaviour patterns. Additionally, Bandura maintains that vicarious learning is also significant, in that individuals learn not only from direct experience but from the experiences of others, that is, the occasions and events for which other individuals might be rewarded, ignored or punished (Bandura, 1971, p. 24).

This theory is useful in order to get a clearer understanding of violence in schools. Observation and imitation of behaviour are key elements that can determine students' behavioural outcomes, and as such, these theories are central to the research.

Literature Review

Violence among Youths in Schools

Violence encompasses "all forms of physical or mental violence, injury or abuse, neglect or negligent treatment, maltreatment or exploitation, including sexual abuse" (UN, 2011). The World Health Organization (WHO) has characterized violence among young people as "one of the most visible forms of violence in society" (Krug et al., 2002, p. 25). The WHO has also found physical fighting to be a common occurrence among school-age children globally and bullying to be prevalent among school-age children (Krug et al., 2002). Researchers in various parts of the world (such as the Caribbean, Taiwan and America) have also engaged with the issue of school violence (e.g., Brubaker, Brubaker, & Link, 2001; Chen & Astor, 2010; Gentle-Genitty et al., 2017).

According to the UNDP, there are six patterns characterizing violence among youth in the Caribbean region. Two of these are particularly relevant to this discussion. The first is that citizens are increasingly concerned about violence among pre-adolescents: "Although rare, primary school children as young as 11 years of age have begun using violence at home or at school" (UNDP, 2012, p. 48). The second pattern is that school violence in the Caribbean has increased. Thus, it is a very real issue for countries in the region. Violence within schools can disrupt schooling and educational opportunities for students and impact educational outcomes (Gentle-Genitty et al., 2017; Moser & van Bronkhurst, 1999).

School violence has been defined as encompassing various behaviours which can run the gamut from disrespectful behaviour to physical assault (Alexander & Curtis, as cited in Brubaker, Brubaker, & Link, 2001). Drawing on reports and data, Gentle-Genitty et al. (2017) indicate that violence within the Caribbean region includes acts such as vandalism, bullying, fights and homicide. They point out that these violent acts occur between groups, including student/student, student/teacher and teacher/parent groups.

King (2002) suggested that the use of violence as a conflict resolution method has become the norm within schools at the global and national levels. With reference to the Jamaican context, she notes that there have been various forms of physical and verbal violence taking place within these institutions, targeted at staff and students. Anderson (2004/05) reported that "violence and aggression have become an endemic problem in Jamaica" (p. 97). With reference to violence within Jamaican schools, a number of researchers, as well as international and national bodies, have drawn attention to the existence of violence in the nation's schools and its growing and troubling presence and impact (e.g., Edwards-Kerr, 2017, 2018; Evans, 2001; Gentle-Genitty et al., 2017; King, 2002; Ministry of Education, 2012; Pottinger, 2012). Anderson, referring specifically to violence within schools, posits that "the increasing incidences of aggressive behaviour in our schools and classrooms have underscored the urgency for educators, concerned citizens, and indeed the government to take action to curb, if not to eliminate such acts" (2004/5, p. 98). Miller (2016) believes that violence in schools has a devastating effect on the educational outcomes of many Jamaican students. Poyser (2016) reported that "children, including boys and girls, living in communities with high percentages of violence, is a special issue that needs to be taken up because the brutality of those circumstances seems to have a tremendous effect on them and sometimes they develop a short view of their life span" (para. 2).

Several researchers focussed on the issue of violence in Jamaica, with their findings giving insight into the nature and scope of the problem (Bailey, 2011; Fernald & Meeks-Gardner, 2003, Pottinger, 2012). Fernald and Meeks-Gardner (2003), as part of a larger study on nutrition, growth and stress, interviewed 123 children aged 8–10 years. When asked what happens at school, almost half of the children reported incidents related to violence, aggression, punishment, shooting or killing within these environments (Fernald & Meeks-Gardner, 2003). In a series of three unrelated qualitative studies which focussed on in-school and out-of-school teenagers in urban and rural areas of Jamaica from 2005 to 2009, adolescents shared their experiences witnessing and experiencing violence in their environments, including their school environments (Bailey, 2011). They highlighted incidents of fights, with one student even pointing to incidents involving security guards and students (Bailey, 2011). In her overview of research on children's exposure to violence, Pottinger (2012) highlights one study of 3,124 students in which 61 per cent had witnessed violence in their schools. She also highlights another study of seventy-four teachers from public and primary schools in which 29 per cent admitted to pinching or thumping students and 70 per cent to verbally humiliating students (Pottinger, 2012). More recently, in a survey carried out at 6 primary and high schools, 105 individuals (principals, vice-principals, guidance counsellors and teachers) reported manifestations of antisocial behaviour including fighting, aggression, bullying and threatening (Ferguson, 2019a).

Researchers have also explored the possibility of addressing the phenomenon of violence. Research, for instance, has focussed on various facets of the Change from Within programme in Jamaica, a programme that utilizes an eight-pillared approach to address the issue by enhancing the agency and facilitating the participation of various school stakeholders (Down, Lambert, & McPherson-Kerr, 2005; Ferguson, 2019b). Down (2015) points to the need to totally reculture schools towards sustainability and to get them to address the problem of violence in schools. Based on the body of research, it is noted that violence in schools is a multifaceted phenomenon that necessitates a multi-pronged approach, including, as is the focus of this chapter, parental involvement.

Fighting

In this study, the focus is on fights, which are defined by Meador (2016), as "a physical altercation occurring between two or more students" (para. 4). According to the non-profit research organization Child Trends Databank (2017), "about 1 in every 4 high school students report having been in a physical fight in the past year" (para. 1). They also reported that the percentage of students in grades 9–12 who have been involved in at least one physical fight has lessened from 43 per cent in 1991 to 25 per cent in 2013. Perhaps unsurprisingly, they reported that male high school students are more likely to be involved in fights than female high school students. In 2013, 30 per cent of male students were reported to have been in a physical fight, compared to 19 per cent of female students (Child Trends Databank, 2017).

The report also shows that the number of incidents declined as students got older.

> Among females in 2013, ninth- and tenth-grade students were more likely to report being in a physical fight in the past year than eleventh- and twelfth-grade students: 23 and 22 percent, versus 17 and 14 percent, respectively. Among males in the same year, twelfth-grade students were less likely than their peers to report physically fighting: 24 percent, compared with 33 percent among ninth-graders, 31 percent among tenth-graders, and 32 percent among eleventh-graders. (Child Trends Databank, 2017, para. 7)

Parental Involvement

Various writers have interpreted parental involvement in different ways. LaBahn (1995) defines parental involvement as "a combination of commitment and active participation on the part of the parent to the school and to the student" (line 1). Rafiq et al. (2013) say that parental involvement can include activities such as "helping children in reading, encouraging them to do their homework independently, monitoring their activities inside the house and outside the four walls of their house, and providing coaching services for improving their learning in different subjects" (p. 210).

Parents are the most significant influence in the lives of their children (Pennsylvania PTA, n. d.). The Pennsylvania Parent Teacher's Association underscores the different forms parental involvement can take. These include the following: dialogue between parents and schools, parents' role as children's primary educators which is fundamental to their education, volunteerism, decision making about children's education, children's health and welfare and partnerships with community organizations that reflect schools' aspirations for all children.

Henderson and Mapp (as cited in Rafiq et al., 2013) indicate that "parental involvement is associated with children's higher achievements in language and mathematics, enrolment in more challenging programs, greater academic persistence, better behaviour, better social skills and adaptation to school, better attendance and lower drop-out rates" (p. 210). The role of parenting in education is therefore an important one.

Importance of Communication in Parent Involvement

Epstein et al. (2002) posit that "communicating activities include school-to-home and home-to-school communications about school and classroom programmes and children's progress" (p. 47). They further noted that dialogue with educators and parents augments the understanding and support between school and home. In order to have a good relationship between parents and teachers, there must be an effective communication strategy that can foster school-family partnerships (American Federation of Teachers, n.d.). All other types of family involvement in education build on this foundation. This is supported by Davis (2000) as she posits that the more parents and teachers share relevant information with each other about students, the better able they will be to aid in the success of the child. In the long run, it will benefit the parents as they become knowledgeable about the school's activities; they will also know how to help support their children. According to Wheelock College's Professor of Education Dr. Diane Levin (as cited in PBS Parents, n. d.), a positive parent-teacher partnership supports children's success in school. Dunham (2016) argues that it gives the child confidence in knowing that his or her role model has their interest at heart, and so, while teachers are experts in teaching, parents are the experts on their children. They know what motivates, bores and interest them, what they are good at and what they struggle with.

Volunteering

Epstein et al. (2002) postulate that volunteering, one of the parental involvement subscales, provides opportunities which enable parents to contribute their time and talents to assist the school, teachers and students. With this in mind, Kids Health (n. d.) stated that "volunteering by parents offer a huge resource and support base for the school community while showing their kids the importance of participating in the community" (para. 3). Various strategies, according to Epstein et al. (2002), may be used to enlist and train volunteers. They continue by suggesting that it is the role of the school to schedule opportunities so that parents can volunteer. Five tips were suggested by Bantuveris (2013) to facilitate this, including opening communication channels, clearly outlining where assistance is needed, engaging working parents, planning for parent volunteers and expressing appreciation.

Parenting

Parenting is important to a child's development. Epstein and Salinas (2004) posit that parenting is assisting with requisite parenting skills and the necessary family support needed to understand the child's development, in addition to the home environment which facilitates learning. In this case, the learning that is being referred to is modelling appropriate behaviour.

Additionally, parenting will assist schools in understanding families and goals for the students.

When families are involved in their children's lives, there is improvement in self-concept (Christenson & Conoley, 1992; Henderson, 1989; Sanders & Herting, 2000, as cited in Haack, 2007), and there are "fewer suspensions and conduct problems" (Comer & Haynes, 1991; Fantuzzo et al., 2004, as cited in Haack, 2007, p. 2). Grover (2016) posits that good parenting is not natural; it takes years of hard work. He argues that it takes a toll on one's physical, mental, emotional and spiritual well-being. This being the case, the strategies suggested by Epstein et al. (2002) may assist in improving parenting, for example, workshops, parent education and other types of courses, and home visits.

Parenting and Violence

Parenting is one of the central factors associated with violence among children and young people, ages 13–17, as the use of physical punishment and inconsistent monitoring of behaviour are said to be strong predictors of violent tendencies in adolescence and adulthood (Krug et al., 2002). Other authors have posited that poor parenting techniques, including harsh physical punishment, inconsistent punishment and lack of behaviour monitoring, can lead to children adopting violence as an unhealthy means of conflict resolution and involvement in other types of antisocial behaviour (e.g., Moser & Bronkhurst, 1999; Murray et al., 1998; Steinberg, 2000). Cole and Anderson (2016) point out that the family unit is a child's first unit of socialization, and, as a consequence, if there is violence and aggression in the home, that child can be socialized towards violent and aggressive behaviours and tendencies. Steinberg (2000) suggests that the family is the strongest influence on the development of antisocial behaviour in youth.

According to Bandura (n. d.), "if a person believes that they are capable of carrying out the behaviour which they have observed and that they are likely to achieve the desired result, then the aggressive act is more likely to be imitated" (para. 3). One such factor is exposure to violence at home. This therefore is connected to Bandura's claim that behaviour observed is more likely to be imitated, resulting in this behaviour being exhibited in school. That is why Epstein's parental involvement subscales of parenting and communicating are so important, as healthy communication between teachers and parents may be what is needed to deter such aggressive behaviour among students.

Inadequate parental supervision and involvement is one of the reasons for violence within schools. The APA recommends a holistic approach to the prevention of violence which includes interventions targeting and including parents (Murray et al., 1998). Brubaker, Brubaker and Link (2001) point out that in dealing with school violence, schools need to reorganize their educational structure, taking into account the role of the family and implementing more effective interventions that involve partnerships with families. These authors propose that families can offer insights into the nature of their children and strategies that work or do not work with their children. Additionally, their involvement in helping to create strategies to address violence communicates to their children a clear anti-violence message and helps to foster a "non-violent atmosphere" (p. 4). Steinberg (2000) proposes that parental engagement is perhaps the most important factor in the healthy psychological development of children and states that children (specifically adolescents whose parents are not involved in their lives) are "more likely to get in trouble than other youngsters" (p. 36). Murray et al. (1998) describe the process of developing an intervention to increase parental monitoring as part of a wider school-based prevention project among Hispanic students in America, noting that students with high parental monitoring tend to have less aggression than those with low parental monitoring.

Among the findings of their research involving fifty-four children in Russia, which tested the effectiveness of a programme called "Together With My Mom", Valeeva and Kalimullin (2016) found that schoolchildren's adoption of a position of non-violence was effectively formed if parents (particularly mothers) "organize the life of children on the basis of non-violent and personal models of interaction with them" (p. 6183). Thus, the parent-child relationship was seen as an important factor in children exhibiting non-violence. Edwards-Kerr (2017) suggests that, based on the findings of various research studies, relationship-based interventions such as mentoring and the inclusion of parents "can have a powerful and positive impact on [children and young people's] life chances" (p. 130).

Anderson (2004/5), writing in the Jamaican context, states that "parents need to take an interest not only in their children's welfare on the home-front but should be involved in what goes on at school. They should also be held accountable" (p. 109). Anderson identifies activities such as parent/teachers' meetings, parents' days, school visits and observation of children's behavioural patterns, as some activities that parents can undertake in this area. Of significance is the following sentiment expressed by a participant in research carried out by Cole and Anderson (2016), which focussed on aggression in the family and the development of aggression in adolescents: one student reported that his mother was too tired and busy to be involved in what was happening at school. This indicates that some parents may not be as involved as they should be, because of competing demands on their time and energy.

Methodology

Research Design

A cross-sectional descriptive research design was used to examine the level of parental involvement and school violence (fights) among high school students, particularly in grade 11. In a cross-sectional design, the data were collected at one point from the participants. While a descriptive design "presents information that helps a researcher describe responses to each question in the database as well as determine overall trends and the distribution of the data" (Creswell, 2008, p. 638), this cross-sectional design allowed for the needed data to be captured, hence meeting the specified purpose of the research.

Population and Sample

The research drew on a population of grade 11 students at a co-educational high school in Central Clarendon, Jamaica. The enrolment at the time of the research was 263, with girls totalling 144 and boys 119. Students were randomly selected using simple random sampling and matched with one parent. A total of eighty-eight parents and students were selected to participate in the research.

Using simple random sampling provided a representative sample of the population and, as such, generalization can be used in relation to the population. Simple random sampling ensures that each participant has equal probability of being selected for the sample (Creswell, 2008).

Instrumentation

Data collection methods included questionnaires and secondary data. A standard questionnaire for parents (consisting of forty-eight closed-ended items) was used as a method of data collection. This instrument was adapted with permission from Wright (2015, see Chapter 7) to assist in ascertaining information from parents about the level at which parental involvement affects students' behaviour – that is, how often they get involved in school fights. The questionnaire had items focussed on the participants' demography in addition to items written based on the research questions to be answered. Items were set using the Likert scale, with a response format of strongly agree to strongly disagree. There were also seventeen multiple-choice questions. The secondary data were collected from the Dean of Discipline's incidence records log, which provided information about the number of fights.

Reliability

Reliability is consistency over time and means that "scores should nearly be the same when researchers administer the instrument multiple times at different times" (Creswell, 2012, p. 159). Internal consistency was used to measure the reliability of the survey using Cronbach or coefficient alpha (Creswell, 2012). Table 9.1 highlights the Cronbach alpha reliability coefficient of 0.846 which was run and documented by Wright (2015) and reflected in Chapter 7 of this book. Table 9.2 shows a Cronbach alpha of 0.844. The minimum acceptable value is 0.7 and the maximum is 0.9; the preferred range is usually between 0.8 and 0.9. Therefore, having a Cronbach alpha reliability coefficient of 0.844 means that it is acceptable and reliable.

Data Analysis Procedures

According to Creswell (2008), there are three main steps to be followed when analysing research questionnaires and secondary data. First, the researcher identifies the response rate and bias by creating a table of specification. Second, the researcher prepares a codebook to aid in preparing and

Table 9.1 Participants' Response Rate and Reliability Coefficient of Surveys (Wright, 2015)

Participants	Pilot Study		Actual Study	
	Response Rate	Reliability Coefficient	Response Rate	Reliability Coefficient
Students	100%	.742	100%	.853
Parents/Guardians	83%	.846	54%	.887

Table 9.2 Participants' Response Rate and Reliability Coefficient of Survey

Actual Study	
Participants Reliability Coefficient	Response Rate
Parents/Guardians .844	82%

organizing data for analysis. A codebook is a "list of variables or questions that indicate how the researcher will code or how values will be assigned to each response for each item in the questionnaire" (Creswell, 2008, p. 184). Numeric codes were assigned to each response for each item in the questionnaire. Third, the data were entered into the Statistical Package for the Social Sciences (SPSS programme, version 24), after coding the data. Descriptive statistics were used to present data from the questionnaires and information related to the percentage of fights in which students were involved.

Ethical Considerations

According to Hesse-Bieber and Leavy, "ethics should, at all times, be at the forefront of the researcher's agenda" (as cited in Creswell, 2008, p. 13). In order to carry out this research, an official letter from the School of Education at the University of the West Indies (Mona Campus) was prepared, outlining the purpose of the research, methodology and ethical issues. This letter was shared with the principal of the school to seek permission to undertake the study. After receiving permission, a letter was prepared and shared with the research participants (the parents), seeking their permission to conduct the research. In the letter to the parents, the purpose of the study was outlined, along with the affirmation that confidentiality and anonymity would be maintained. Participation in the study was therefore voluntary and they can withdraw if they wish. The participants gave consent to participate in the study.

Limitations

There are several limitations to the study which must be outlined. One is the refusal of some participants to complete the survey after initially agreeing to take part. This affected the process, as other participants had to be selected so as not to greatly affect the sample size. Another limitation was that some of the items were unanswered. Additionally, not all of the questionnaires were returned and so twenty-five more questionnaires had to be redistributed. Giving consideration to ethical issues, the parents of students who were constantly involved in fights were not targeted, so as to avoid the students being stigmatized or labelled in a negative manner. Consequently, parents were selected randomly. Some parents may also not have responded truthfully to some items, hence this could affect the outcome of the results. To ensure that the parents were truthful with their responses, it was impressed upon them and guaranteed that the information shared would be confidential and that they would remain anonymous, as they were not required to write their names nor the names of their children.

Findings

In presenting these findings, descriptive statistics will offer an overview of the demographic details of the respondents, including elements such as their attitudes towards parent-school partnerships, communication with their children about incidents of fights and behaviour and responses to their children's involvement in fights.

Demographic Data for Parents' Questionnaires

The parents' demographic data revealed that of all the family members and guardians, mothers were mostly involved in their children's lives, as they accounted for 67 per cent of the eighty-eight participants who responded to this item. Fathers followed with 18.2 per cent. The majority of the persons who completed the survey were in the 41–50 age group (39.8 per cent, $n = 88$). The data revealed that 44.3 per cent of participants were in common-law relationships, while 42 per cent were legally married (42 per cent). Approximately 61 per cent were employed, with approximately 88 per cent living in the parish of Clarendon. It was also revealed that most of the participants completed high school – which accounted for approximately 27 per cent, while approximately 23 per cent had vocational training, and approximately 40 per cent completed tertiary level education.

Parents' Attitudes towards School-Parent Partnerships

The majority of the parents (97.7 per cent) indicated that they felt that the partnership between school and parents was necessary (see figure 9.1).

Approximately 16 per cent of the parents strongly agreed that they attended PTA meetings often and 25 per cent agreed that they attended these meetings. Twenty-two per cent strongly disagreed, suggesting that they did not attend PTA meetings on a regular basis. However, through this partnership, approximately 28 per cent and 41 per cent strongly agreed and agreed respectively that the school has helped them with their child's conduct by providing them with the relevant information.

Approximately 41 per cent of the parents strongly agreed that they were involved in the disciplinary making process involving their children. With respect to volunteerism in the schools, however, approximately 39 per cent of them reported that they had never volunteered, and approximately 31 per cent reported that they did not volunteer often enough in school activities.

In response to parents' communication with their children about their behaviour, a majority of parents (68.2 per cent) seemed to recognize the importance of communicating with their children about their behaviour, as

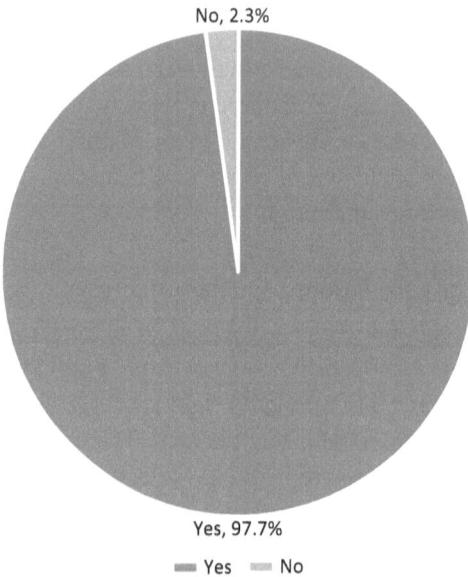

Figure 9.1 Pie chart showing responses to school-parent partnership.

they strongly agreed that they talked to their children about their behaviour. In addition, 47 per cent of the parents strongly agreed, while approximately 35 per cent agreed that they also talked to their children about conflict resolution (see figure 9.2). This happened after ensuring that they listened to their children if there was an issue with other students (as signalled by their responses), with approximately 60 per cent of respondents indicating that they strongly agreed with the statement that they listened to their children when they shared about a conflict or issue that they had with other children; and approximately 32 per cent of respondents indicated that they agreed with this statement. Also highlighted was the importance of communication at all times from school to home, as well as from home to school, with school reporting that approximately 26 per cent of the parents agreed that the school provides ongoing information to educate them on how to assist their child with behaviour management.

On the other hand, approximately 26 per cent of the parents also disagreed that the school provided ongoing information to educate them about behaviour management. Additionally, approximately 30 per cent disagreed that the school provides information on how to monitor behaviour at home. Furthermore, approximately 31 per cent (the higher percentage) of the parents disagreed that teachers help them to set behavioural goals for their child.

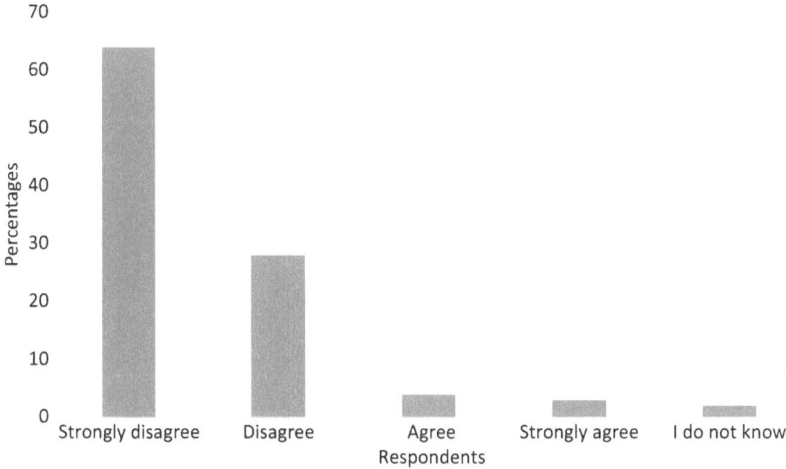

Figure 9.2 Parents' responses about talking to their child about behaviour.

Parents' Communication with their Children about their Behaviour

The percentages of fights involving students over a two-year academic period (2015/16 and 2016/17) revealed that in the academic year 2015/16, males accounted for 70 per cent of the fights that occurred, with the remaining 30 per cent involving females. Contrary to the previous year, 2016/17 showed an increase in the number of fights by females, who accounted for approximately 48 per cent (an increase of 18 per cent), but saw a reduction in the percentage of males, who accounted for approximately 52 per cent (see figure 9.3).

Percentages of Students Involved in Fights

Approximately 41 per cent of the parents reported that their children have been involved in a fight at least one or two times. With regard to receiving notification about their children being involved in fights, 45 per cent of the parents strongly agreed and 26.1 per cent agreed that they were notified by the school if their child was involved in a fight (see figure 9.4). As a consequence, 28 per cent of the parents agreed and 25 per cent strongly agreed that they followed up on their child's behaviour. After consultation, it was revealed that 28.4 per cent of the students got into a fight in self-defence; 38.6 per cent because they were provoked; and 21 per cent reported that the fight was started by another student.

In order to help their children when they were involved in fights, the majority, accounting for 75 per cent of the parents, strongly agreed that they sought action or assistance. The punishment rendered ranged from

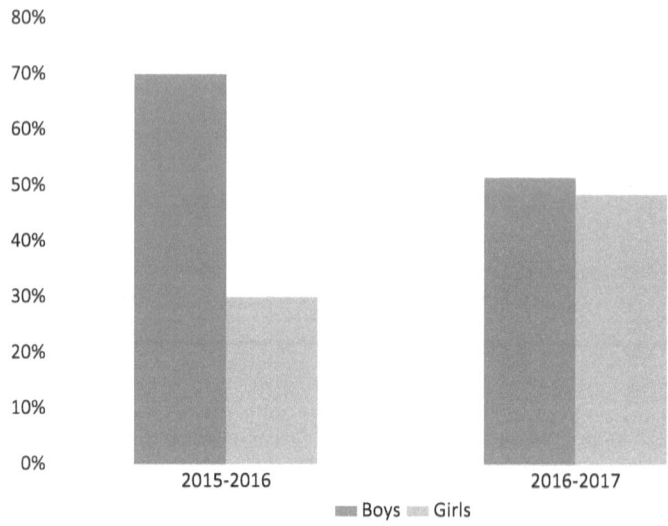

Figure 9.3 Percentage of fights over a two-year period.

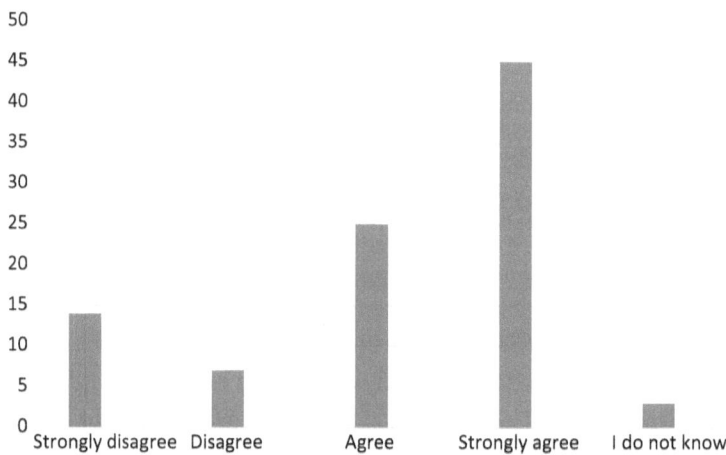

Figure 9.4 Parents' responses to being notified by the school.

suspension (44.3 per cent) to detention (33 per cent), and community service (21.6 per cent). A number of the parents (61.4 per cent) sought counselling for their children. In addition, parents reported that they were disappointed (50 per cent) and surprised (37.5 per cent) when their children got into fights.

Discussion

The majority of the parents reported that they believed it was important to be in partnership with their children's school. This is in keeping with the suggestion of Epstein et al. (2002) that home-school and school-home communication is important to a child's progress. The American Federation of Teachers (n.d.) also confirm the results as they too believe that this partnership is necessary. It was noted in *The Centre* (2005) by Salinas that one of the factors hindering this partnership is "parents believing they are not welcome" (para. 1), which could possibly be the reason some parents did not volunteer for school activities. Additionally, a high percentage of the parents strongly agreed that they spoke with their children about their behaviour, hence confirming their agreement that parental involvement is important to their child's behaviour.

With respect to the percentage of students who were involved in fights, the findings showed that over the two-year span, boys had the highest percentage of involvement in fights. Interestingly though, Child Trends Databank (2017) reported that as the students got older, they fought less. The data, however, showed that when the girls were in grade 10, they did not engage in many fights, as they accounted for 30 per cent of the fights that took place, but when they moved to grade 11, their percentage increased by 18.48 per cent, thus increasing their involvement in fights to 48.48 per cent. On the other hand, the data showed that the percentage for the boys declined. As a result, one could possibly deduce that when boys get older, they are less involved in fights, but when girls get older, their involvement in fights increases. This of course would have to be explored further across a much larger data set.

Epstein's parental involvement processes show that parenting is extremely important, hence Professor of Education Dr. Diane Levin's reason for advising that "a positive parent-teacher relationship helps your child ... to be successful in school" (PBS Parents, n.d., para. 3). This positive parent-teacher relationship contributes to positive student behaviour. The data presented showed that a high percentage of the parents indicated that they were notified by the school once their children were involved in a fight. Fifty per cent of the parents were disappointed and 37.5 per cent expressed surprise when they were informed about their children's involvement in fights, as they reported that they talked to their children about their conduct.

Bandura (n. d.) stated, "if a person believes that they are capable of carrying out a behaviour which they have observed and that they are likely to achieve the desired result, the aggressive act is more likely to be imitated" (para. 3). The findings from the research refute this, as the data show that parents were positively involved in their children's lives through exercising Epstein's subscales of parenting and communicating. This arguably tells us that positive behaviour is being practised by the parents, yet their children have been involved in fights at least one or two times.

The literature speaks to the likelihood of children getting fewer suspensions and having problems with their conduct if their parents are involved; however, the data presented showed that though the parents were involved 44.3 per cent of the time, students were suspended as a result of conduct problems, specifically fights. Though it is evident that Epstein's parental involvement subscales of parenting and communicating were being practised, the findings showed that they did not serve as a deterrent to students getting involved in fights. As was highlighted in Bailey's (2011) qualitative study, teenagers in and out of school had experienced and witnessed violence in their general environment and in school. Additionally, students indicated that there were incidents involving security guards and students (Bailey, 2011). Thus, socialization and student experiences outside of the home may also contribute towards school violence.

Some students may have developed aggressive tendencies as a result of how they were treated by persons in authority. This can be supported by Pottinger's (2012) review, for instance, in which she reported on a study about teachers in public and private schools who were physically and verbally abusive to students (Pottinger, 2012). Since students may have some respect for authority figures, this may account for violent behaviour being directed towards their classmates and schoolmates, possibly proving that Bandura's observing and imitating of behaviour from outside factors (and not the behaviour of their parents) is being practised.

Recommendations

Students are not necessarily responding to the guidance of their parents. In an attempt to reduce the number of fights (having obtained permission from the parents), the Guidance Department, in collaboration with the principal, can initiate a mentorship or Big Brother/Big Sister programme using persons who were deemed "at risk" when they were in school, but have become successful. It is the hope that students will see themselves in these mentors and aspire to change, making them productive citizens.

There are several recommendations emerging from this research. The current school policies governing fights should not only include detention and suspension but policies that will serve as a deterrent to fighting. School Resource Officers (SROs) have multiple responsibilities, two of which are: (1) to partner with the Deans of Discipline (DoD) and school administrators to promote and maintain discipline, as well as mediate disputes; and (2) to work with students who are deemed at risk (Reynolds-Baker, 2014). Given their first-hand interactions with the students and the school environments, SROs should therefore play a part in suggesting or developing these policies.

Following on from this, the findings signal that the school environment and other mentors, alongside parents, have to serve as agents of change for these students. All stakeholders therefore need to work collaboratively and be integrally involved in attaining the primary objective of fashioning productive young men and women. Home-school partnership is therefore extremely important.

Conclusion

School violence, as an extension of the wider violence in the Jamaican society, is a worrying issue that needs to be addressed. Within the country, various programmes and initiatives have been mounted to address the problem. Based on the existing body of research, parental involvement is one factor that has the potential to reduce violence and aggression among children and adolescents, particularly as the family is a primary unit of socialization for children. As a consequence, this research sought to examine the relationship between the level of parental involvement and school children's involvement in one manifestation of school violence – fights.

The research findings suggest that although parenting and communication (subscales of Epstein's parental involvement theory) were being practised by parents, this did not serve as a deterrent to students' engagement in fights. This finding does not diminish the important role that parenting has to play in addressing the phenomenon of school violence. Indeed, the literature supports the need for parental involvement. This suggests that other factors influence aggression and violence. Factors such as peers, authority and media influences on aggression and violence among children and youth need to be examined. Indeed, this highlights that parenting is perhaps only one of the elements needed in a wider systemic approach to a phenomenon – violence – that is caused by systemic issues. Thus, parental involvement in all its facets has to work alongside school-based initiatives and has to be embedded in wider school and cultural societal change, given that students may be using violence to resolve conflicts, mimicking what they see in the wider school and societal environments.

References

American Federation of Teachers. (n.d.). Building parent-teacher partnerships. http://ms.aft.org/files/ct-parent-teacherpartnerships_0.pdf

Anderson, S. (2004/5). Dealing with violence and aggression in the classroom: Some suggestions. *Journal of Education and Development in the Caribbean*, 8(1&2), 97–111.

Angus, G.L. (2016, June 15). Drop in school violence. Jamaica Information Service. http://jis.gov.jm/drop-school-violence/

Bailey, A. (2011). The Jamaican adolescent's perspective on violence and its effects. *West Indian Medical Journal*, 60(2), 165–71.

Bandura, A. (1971). *Social learning theory*. General Learning Press. http://www.asecib.ase.ro/mps/Bandura_SocialLearningTheory.pdf

――― (n.d.). Social learning theory and aggression: Learning by imitation of a role model. https://www.learning-theories.com/social-learning-theory-bandura.html#:~:text=Social%20Learning%20Theory%2C%20otheorized%20by,attention%2C%20memory%2C%20and%20motivation

Bandura, A., Ross, D., & and Ross, S.A. (1961). Transmission of aggression through imitation of aggressive models. *Journal of Abnormal and Social Psychology*, 63, 575–82.

Bantuveris, K. (2013). 5 tips for engaging parent volunteers in the classroom. https://www.edutopia.org/blog/strategies-for-engaging-parent-volunteers-karen-bantuveris

Brubaker, T.H., Brubaker, E., & Link, M. (2001). School violence: Partnerships with families for school reform. *Michigan Family Review*, 6(1), 1–11.

Campbell-Livingston, C. (2017). Violence spilling into schools - Principals say conflicts escalate to dangerous levels outside institutions' walls. *The Gleaner* (January 12). http://jamaica-gleaner.com/article/lead-stories/20170112/violence-spilling-schools-principals-say-conflicts-escalate-dangerous

Chen, J. & Astor, R.A. (2010). School violence in Taiwan: Examining how western risk factors predict school violence in an Asian culture. *Journal of Interpersonal Violence*, 25(8), 1388–410.

Child Trends Databank. (2017). Physical fighting by youth. https://www.childtrends.org/indicators/physical-fighting-by-youth/

Cole, S.M. & Anderson, S.R. (2016). Family interaction and the development of aggression in adolescents: The experiences of students and administrators. *American International Journal of Contemporary Research*, 6(4), 12–21.

Creswell, J.W. (2008). *Educational research: Planning, conducting, and evaluating quantitative and qualitative research* (3rd ed.). Pearson Merrill Prentice Hall.

――― (2012). *Research design: Qualitative, quantitative and mixed methods approaches* (4th ed). Sage Publications.

Davis, D. (Ed.). (2000). *Supporting parent, family and community involvement in your school*. Northwest Regional Educational Laboratory, Portland.

Down, L. (2015). Transforming school culture through education for sustainable development (ESD). *Journal of Eastern Caribbean Studies*, 40(3), 157–67.

Down, L., Lambert, C., & McPherson-Kerr, C. (2005). *Violence in schools and the change from within project*. Institute of Education.

Dunham, H. (2016). *The importance of parent-teacher communication*. http://au.mathletics.com/importance-parent-teacher-communication/

Dunkley A. (2013). *School violence focus: New roles for guidance counsellors, deans of discipline*. http://www.jamaicaobserver.com/news/School-violence-focus---Education-ministry-to-implement-measures-starting-summer

Edwards-Kerr, D. (2017). Violence in schools in Jamaica. In Z. Jennings & D. Edwards-Kerr (Eds.), *Re-imagining Education in the Commonwealth Caribbean* (pp. 123–33). Ian Randle Publishers.

——— (2018). Locating violence in urban inner-city schools in Jamaica. *Caribbean Journal of Education, 40*(1&2), 1–27.

Epstein, J.L. & Salinas, K.C. (2004). Partnering with families and communities: A well-organized program of family and community partnerships yields many benefits for school and their student. *Educational Leadership, 61*(8), 12–18. http://www.ascd.org/ASCD/pdf/journals/ed_lead/el200405_epstein.pdf

Epstein, J.L., Sanders, M.G., Simon, B.S., Salinas, K.C., Jansorn, N.R., & Van Voorhis, F.L. (2002). *School, family, and community partnerships: Your handbook for action* (2nd ed.). Corwin Press.

Evans, H. (2001). *Inside Jamaican schools*. University of the West Indies Press.

Ferguson, T. (2019a). Addressing anti-social behaviour and violence as barriers to learning: Lessons from Jamaica's change from within programme. In S. Blackman, D. Conrad, & L. Brown (Eds.), *Achieving inclusive education in the Caribbean and beyond: From philosophy to praxis*, 133–44. Springer.

——— (2019b). Reflection, dialogue, and transformation through participatory action research: Experiences of Jamaica's change from within programme. In S. Stewart (Ed.), *Decolonizing qualitative approaches for and by the Caribbean* (pp. 139–58). Information Age Publishing.

Fernald, L.C. & Meeks-Gardner, J. (2003). Jamaican children's reports of violence at school and home. *Social and Economic Studies, 52*(4), 121–40.

Gentle-Genitty, C., Kim, J., Yi, E.-H., Slater, D., Reynolds, B., & Bragg, N. (2017). Comprehensive assessment of youth violence in five Caribbean countries: Gender and age differences. *Journal of Human Behavior in the Social Environment, 27*(7), 745–59.

Grover, S. (2016). Top ten best parenting qualities. http://www.seangrover.com/top-ten-best-parenting-qualities

Haack, M.K. (2007). Parents' and teachers' beliefs about parental involvement in schooling [Doctoral dissertation, University of Nebraska]. http://digitalcommons.unl.edu/cgi/viewcontent.cgi?article=1011&context=cehsdiss

Kids Health. (n.d.). Reasons to get involved. http://kidshealth.org/en/parents/school.html

King, R. (2002). Violence and schools in Jamaica: Historical and comparative perspectives. *Institute of Education Annual 3*, 1–15.

Krug, E.G., Dahlberg, L.L., Mercy, J.A., Zwi, A.B., & Lozano, R. (Eds.). (2002). *World report on violence and health*. World Health Organization. https://apps.who.int/iris/bitstream/handle/10665/42495/9241545615_eng.pdf?sequence=1

LaBahn, J. (1995). Education and parental involvement in secondary schools: Problems, solutions, and effects. *Educational Psychology Interactive*. Valdosta State University. http://www.edpsycinteractive/files/parinvol.html

Meador, D. (2016). *Developing an effective policy to deter fighting in school*. https://www.thoughtco.com/developing-an-effective-policy-to-deter-fighting-in-school-3194512

Miller, E. (2016, March 16). Violence is greatest threat to student's educational outcomes. *The Gleaner*. http://jamaica-gleaner.com/article/news/20160307/violence-greatest-threat-students-educational-outcomes-miller

Ministry of Education. (2012). *National education strategic plan: 2011-2020*. Ministry of Education.

Moestue, H., Moestue, L., & Muggah, R. (2013). *Youth violence prevention in Latin America and the Caribbean: A scoping review of the evidence*. http://www.oas.org/en/asg/moas/high_schools/34_MOAS_HS/annotated_agenda/documents/youth_protection_and_empowerment/NOREF_evaluations_youth_violence_LAC.pdf

Moser, C. & van Bronkhorst, B. (1999). *Youth violence in Latin America and the Caribbean: Costs, causes, and interventions*. http://documents.worldbank.org/curated/en/430541468772467666/pdf/multi-page.pdf

Murray, N., Kelder, S., Parcel, G., & Orpinas, P. (1998). Development of an intervention map for a parent education intervention to prevent violence among Hispanic middle school students. *Journal of School Health, 68*(2), 46–52.

National Children Registry. (2017). *Statistics on the total number of reports received by the NCR by type, sex, month and year, 2007 to 2017*. http://www.ocr.gov.jm/index.php/statistics

Patterson, C. (2017). *School violence trending down*. Jamaica Information Service. https://jis.gov.jm/school-violence-trending/

PBS Parents. (n.d.). The parent-teacher partnership. http://www.pbs.org/parents/education/going-to-school/parent-involvement/parent-teacher-partnership/

Pennsylvania PTA. (n.d.). PTA and parent involvement-background information: Definition of parental involvement. http://www.papta.org/domain/73

Pottinger, A. (2012). Children's exposure to violence in Jamaica: Over a decade of research and interventions. *West Indian Medical Journal, 61*(4), 369–71.

Poyser, A. (2016, March 7). Violence greatest threat to students' educational outcomes. *The Gleaner*. http://jamaica-gleaner.com/article/news/20160307/violence-greatest-threat-students-educational-outcomes-miller

Rafiq, H.M.W., Fatima, T., Sohail, M.M., Saleem, M., & Khan, M.A. (2013). Parental involvement and academic achievement: A study on secondary school students of Lahore, Pakistan. *International Journal of Humanities and Social Science, 3*(8), 209–23.

Reynolds-Baker, A. (2014, February 18). Safe School Programme Having Positive Impact on Students. Jamaica Information Service. http://jis.gov.jm/safe-schools-programme-positive-impact-students/

Rodgers, D. (1999). *Youth gangs and violence in Latin America and the Caribbean: A literature survey.* http://documents.worldbank.org/curated/en/474291468770479198/pdf/multi-page.pdf

Slavin, R.E. (2012). *Educational psychology: Theory and practice* (10th ed.). Pearson.

Steinberg, L. (2000). Youth violence: Do parents and families make a difference? *National Institute of Justice Journal, 243,* 31–38.

United Nations. (UN). (2011). *General comment no. 13: The right of the child to freedom from all forms of violence.* https://www.refworld.org/publisher,CRC,GENERAL,,4e6da4922,0.html

United Nations Development Programme (UNDP). (2012). *Caribbean human development report 2012: Human development and the shift to better citizen security.* UNDP.

United Nations Office on Drugs and Crime (UNODC). (2019). *Global study on homicide: Homicide trends, patterns and criminal justice response.* UNODC, *Global Study on Homicide 2019* (Vienna, 2019). https://www.unodc.org/documents/data-and-analysis/gsh/Booklet2.pdf

United Nations Office on Drugs and Crime (UNODC) and the World Bank. (2007). *Crime, violence, and development: Trends, costs, and policy options in the Caribbean.* https://www.unodc.org/pdf/research/Cr_and_Vio_Car_E.pdf

Valeeva, R.A. & Kalimullin, A.M. (2016). Effects of parent-child relationship on the primary school children's non-violence position formation. *International Journal of Environmental and Science Education, 11*(13), 6178–84.

Wright, N. (2015). *The Extent to which Parental Involvement Impacts the Academic Performance of Tenth Grade Students.* [Unpublished master's thesis]. University of the West Indies, Mona.

Conclusion

SARAN STEWART, YEWANDE LEWIS-FOKUM, SHENHAYE FERGUSON
AND SHARLINE COLE

In this volume, we call attention to the importance of parental involvement and family engagement in Jamaica's education system. More specifically, we explore the relevance of more *Caribbeanized* epistemological frameworks to assess the scope, prevalence, experiences with, impact and effects of parental involvement and family engagement. Although "parental involvement" is the more popular term and is used throughout the book, Yewande Lewis-Fokum and Kayon Morgan in chapter 1 push for a broadening of the term from parental involvement to family engagement as this is a global trend. Further, "family engagement" fits well in Jamaica, since this is a more inclusive term, given the Jamaican family structure in which relatives/guardians, other than parents, also carry out the parent role. Notably, engagement moves beyond a school-directed approach for parents' involvement to an approach which facilitates collaboration and partnership between home and school and vice versa.

In section 1 of the book, there is a concerted effort to better conceptualize and theorize contextually relevant models to gain an understanding of the Jamaican challenges, postcolonial legacies and unique dynamics of familial structures and involvement in schooling in Jamaica. In section 2, the authors examine the impact of parental involvement and family engagement in early childhood, primary and special education. The final section hones in on the effects of parental involvement in secondary schooling including rural and non-traditional schools.

Throughout the book, most of the chapters use Joyce Epstein's Overlapping Spheres of Influence (1987) or Hoover-Dempsey and Sandler's (1995) models to provide theoretical framing for their studies. Both sets of frameworks were developed outside of the Jamaican context, and as such, the authors use these models as guides to build upon and develop new epistemologies and frameworks culturally relevant and better suited for the Jamaican education system. Each chapter provides new theoretical and conceptual frameworks and models to ground future research for the Jamaican context. At the onset of this book project, the authors set out to illustrate how parents and families were involved in their child/ children's school and academics. Across the chapters, we realize that the type of school and level of education influence the extent to which parents/guardians and family members engage with the school. For example, patterns in the data from chapters 4 to 6 suggest that there is a greater level of involvement for students in early childhood, primary and special education than in secondary schooling as mentioned in chapters 7 to 10. The level and rate of involvement are further complicated by three themes that emerged from the chapters in this volume. They are (1) the influence of parents, guardians and familial socio-economic status; (2) the relevance of home, yaad and community; and (3) the role of parents, especially mothers, in parental involvement and family engagement.

The Influence of Parents', Guardians' and Familial Socio-Economic Status

Many chapters in the book emphasized the influence of socio-economic status on parent/guardian engagement as a theme, whether it was the education level of the parents/guardians, the type of school the students attended or the locale of the schools. Patterns in the data suggested that parents/guardians believed family-school partnership is important yet only a small percentage from lower-socio-economic backgrounds attended PTA meetings often or communicated regularly with the school. As a result, the authors throughout the book recommended more creative ways of engaging parents and guardians, especially those from lower socio-economic backgrounds. Natrecia Whyte Lothian and Tashane Haynes-Brown in chapter 8 examine factors related to socio-economic status, such as poverty and underemployment, which made engagement for some parents difficult, for example, the authors noted that attending PTA meetings might mean a loss of income for some parents/guardians. The authors therefore call on the schools to be more creative in reaching parents, which is a theme shared in chapters 1 and 3. Also, in chapter 8, the authors' study focused on rural schools which were typically lower resourced where most students were from lower socio-economic backgrounds. Interestingly, most of the respondents (66.4 per cent) had as their highest level of education a secondary level education and talked to their children about the importance of school. Roncell Brooks and Carmel Roofe in chapter 2 focus on social class and students in non-traditional schools.[1]

---

[1] Non-traditional schools especially high schools are newly upgraded high schools that were once former junior high schools. They are commonly understood in Jamaica as schools that were built during post-independence by the government and not typically associated with a religious entity. These schools tend to be more under-resourced and the students are largely from lower-socio-economic families (see Stewart 2015).

They use a cultural capital lens that is strengths-based and address how in spite of social class parents have high aspirations for their children. Although conceptual in nature, their chapter synthesizes that more involved parents at the secondary level can encourage and influence students interested in post-secondary education, which again speaks to Morgan's model in chapter 1 of parental involvement from basic school to post-secondary and workforce readiness.

The Relevance of Home, Yaad and Community

The concepts of home and yaad in the Jamaican context seemingly connote similar meanings, that is, one being of formal English language (home) and the other Jamaican Creole or colloquial (yaad). However, the research revealed that for many these terms were ascribed different meanings. For some, home within the context of the chapters was seen as the place where children felt a deep sense of belonging to a familial unit, while yaad was closely linked to a more expansive form of the familial unit to the neighbourhood or larger community where they reside. This theme also calls for more community-based schooling similar to that of basic schools and some early childhood institutions, where there is more oversight and responsibility between parent/guardian engagement and schooling. Danielle Campbell and Zoyah Kinkead-Clark, in chapter 4, promote the concept of the "yaad" and community involvement in parenting especially given the fact that many basic schools (i.e., early childhood schools) are community owned in Jamaica. Parents interviewed in this study realized the importance of parental involvement and how it could impact their child's academic achievement and readiness for primary education. The focus of their study was on communication between the teacher and school, as well as extending the school into the home via homework, attending special school celebration functions (e.g. Jamaica Day) and the desire for parents to have targeted parenting workshops. Similarly, in chapter 3, Kadine Haynes and Lois George focus on strategies to transform negative parental perceptions about math to a mindset of positive academic socialization towards mathematics. The chapter emphasized two parts of Epstein's model with the use of the Jamaican Creole language in "Talk to di Teacha" category and "Help Di Chile a Yaad" and argued that both are culturally relevant and insightful methods of involvement at home. The focus on the emotions as it relates to mathematics is imperative if parents are going to help their children at home move beyond the negative attitudes towards the subject to a sense of mathematical self-efficacy. Concrete tips were given, for example, sending motivational quotes about math progress and reviewing students' math homework at home. However, in chapter 7, Natalia Wright, Shenhaye Ferguson and Saran Stewart noted that at the secondary level, there is a tension for parents and guardians between being greatly involved and allowing adolescents greater autonomy. More so, they found that a family involvement approach which was "more distal" was better for students' overall academic performance. The parent survey revealed that there is a significant relationship between two constructs tested – *communicating* and *learning at home* – and students' self-reported academic performance. Conversely, in chapter 9, Claudine Mighty and Therese Ferguson provide a hybrid framework of Bandura's Social Learning Theory (1971) and Joyce Epstein's model (2002) to theorize how children are imitators of behaviour in the home, whether good or bad. The authors illustrate how Epstein's parental involvement subscales of *parenting* and *communicating* are critical, as healthy communication between teachers and parents may be what is needed to deter such aggressive behaviour among students.

Role of Parents, Especially Mothers, in Parental Involvement and Family Engagement

The book's focus on parents/guardians and family engagement is central to the reciprocal role of partnership and collaboration between home and schools. However, as most authors found in their studies, the primary parent role was placed on the mother. In most of the studies, the mothers are either named or are the primary respondents between the home and the school. At all levels of schooling, the authors point out the importance of the mother's involvement, education level and socio-economic status. Danielle Campbell and Zoyah Kinkead-Clark in chapter 4 place an important focus on parental involvement at the early childhood level. Of significance was the fact that although many households comprised of single-parent households (90 per cent) in a study by Cole (2020), which was cited in the chapter, there was no difference in the level of parental involvement from either single or nuclear family structures. This suggests that regardless of family structure, parents (mainly mothers) reinforce the link between parental involvement and education. Similarly, Susan Anderson and Sharline Cole in chapter 5 explore the levels of parental involvement and suggest that mothers in particular described more engagement with their children with disabilities. Additionally, the authors found that the higher the level of education for the mother, the more likely she is to be involved in her child's education and development. The authors further suggest that "[t]he participation of parents in special education is critical because children with disabilities need even more parental support and advocacy than other children in general education" (chapter 5). Interestingly, as it relates to gender, Sharline Cole states in chapter 6, "teachers are least likely to invite parents to be involved when their children are performing according to the standard set by the school". She goes on to explain that parents of boys are more likely to be invited to school to discuss overall student outcomes and behaviour. The longitudinal study also found that parents who were more involved had students who performed better on the national standardized assessments in primary education and reported that "parental involvement, parent efficaciousness, and invitation to be involved are statistically significant predictors of students' academic outcomes throughout primary education".

In chapter 8, Natrecia Whyte Lothian and Tashane Haynes-Brown discussed the various familial structures in Jamaica and in particular how other family members played the role of parent or guardian. Although most of the respondents in their study were mothers (51.3 per cent), the remaining 48.7 per cent consisted of fathers, grandparents, aunts, uncles and other relatives. This is further evidence for expanding the term from "parental involvement" to "family engagement". Noteworthy too was that while mothers, fathers and grandparents were most satisfied with the level of their parental involvement, guardians, aunts and uncles were the least satisfied. Crudely put, this is an interesting finding because it begs the question about the type of parental involvement that "barrel"[2] children receive if they are being cared for by a relative other than their mother, father or grandparent.

To conclude, Lewis-Fokum and Morgan's chapter advances a new framework that links most of the key issues discussed throughout the book. For example, these issues are parent efficaciousness in chapters 3 and 6; parental involvement including advocacy as highlighted in chapter 5; life circumstances that impact parental involvement as discussed in chapter 8; and aspirations as a form of family engagement as discussed in chapter 2. Parent-initiated and school-initiated types of involvement hint at that broader

---

[2] In the twentieth century, Jamaican social workers described children separated from their parents due to migration as barrel children. This was in reference to the cardboard barrels used for shipping goods to family residing back home. For example, parents shipping food and clothing from the United States to children and family in the Caribbean (see Jokhan, 2017).

concept of engagement in which involvement incorporates collaboration and partnership. As previously stated in chapter 8, little research exists on parental involvement among Jamaicans, and while Jamaican parents' experiences and contributions may be subsumed in information about black parents in other countries such as the United States, there is a need for further research because the common values and beliefs shaping parental involvement are "rooted in and bounded by nationality" (Hagiwara & Davis, 2018, p. 20).

Finally, the value of parental involvement and engagement to improve children's learning has always been a topic of high importance within education in Jamaica. More than ever, due to the impact of the COVID-19 pandemic on school closures, Jamaica has to prioritize how children are learning from home. As of April 2020, an estimated 1.6 billion children and young people around the world were out of school due to the COVID-19 pandemic. In Latin America and the Caribbean, there was an estimated 95 per cent of enrolled children or over 150 million children who were temporarily out of school (Miks & McIlwaine, 2020). Arguably, in Jamaica, the inequality gap will widen as it pertains to advantaged and disadvantaged children and young persons. Some students have remained out of school for over one year and reside in unstable living conditions that make it difficult to learn or where caregivers are unable to provide the necessary assistance receiving and completing lessons and assignments. The implications from this book to policymakers, parents/guardians and schools will provide strategies and lessons learned on how best to engage parents/guardians and schools when more than any other time, the home has become the centre of learning.

References

Bandura, A. (1971). *Social learning theory*. General Learning Press. http://www.asecib.ase.ro/mps/Bandura_SocialLearningTheory.pdf

Cole, S.M. (2020). Contextualising parental involvement at the elementary level in Jamaica. *International Journal of Early Years Education*. doi:10.1080/09669760.2020.1777844; https://doi.org/10.1080/09669760.2020.1777844

Epstein, J.L. (1987). Toward a theory of family-school connections: Teacher practices and parental involvement. In K. Hurrelman, F. Kaufmann, & F. Losel (Eds.), *Social intervention: Potential and constraints* (pp. 121–36). DeGruyter.

Epstein, J.L., Sanders, M.G., Simon, B.S., Salinas, K.C., Jansorn, N.R., & Van Voorhis, F.L. (2002). *School, family, and community partnerships: Your handbook for action* (2nd ed.). Corwin Press.

Hagiwara, S. & Davis, D. (2018). In our family education is our culture: A Jamaican mom's effort to connect home and school. In A. Esmail, A. Pitre, D. Lund, H. Baptiste, & G. Duhon-Owens (Eds.), *Research studies on educating for diversity and social justice* (pp. 17–30). Rowman & Littlefield.

Hoover-Dempsey, K.V. & Sandler, H.M. (1995). Parental involvement in children's education: Why does it make a difference? *Teachers College Record, 97*(2), 310–31.

Jokhan, M. (2017). *Exploring the "barrel children" cycle: Parent-child separation due to migration*. Childhood Explorer: Childhood Education International. https://www.childhoodexplorer.org/exploring-the-barrel-children-cycle-parentchild-separation-due-to-migration

Miks, J. & McIlwaine, J. (2020). Keeping the world's children learning through COVID-19[UNICEF Article]. UNICEF. Retrieved https://www.unicef.org/coronavirus/keeping-worlds-children-learning-through-covid-19

Stewart, S. (2015). Schooling and coloniality: Conditions underlying "extra lessons" in Jamaica. *Postcolonial Directions in Education Journal, 4*(1), 25–52.

Contributors

Dr. Carmel Roofe is a Senior Lecturer in Curriculum and Instruction in the School of Education, at The University of the West Indies, Mona where she is the programme co-ordinator for masters and doctoral programmes in Curriculum Studies. She is the co-founder and current president of the Caribbean Association for the Advancement of Curriculum Studies. She has authored and co-authored several peer reviewed journal articles, special issue journals, books and book chapters. Dr. Roofe is also a research fellow at the University of Huddersfield.

Claudine Mighty has been an educator for over 17 years. She is currently a member of the academic staff (Department of Humanities) at Denbigh High School in Clarendon, Jamaica, where she teaches English Language (grades 10 and 11) and Communication Studies and serves as the Coordinator for Sixth Form. She obtained a Teaching Diploma in Secondary Education from Church Teachers College, a Bachelor of Arts in History and a Masters in Education (Educational Administration) from the University of the Wes Indies.

Danielle Campbell embarked on her journey into Early Childhood Education after completing her first degree in psychology at the University of the West Indies and volunteered for a year at Mona Heights Primary School. She completed her Post Graduate Teaching Diploma at the Shortwood Teachers College with honours. She then went on to complete her Master's degree in Leadership in Early Childhood Development at the University of the West Indies where she culminated her studies with her paper "Parental Involvement and Academic Success at the Early Childhood level" with distinction.

K. Kayon Morgan holds a B.Sc. in international relations and Spanish from the University of the West Indies, a MMIN and MDIV in leadership from Cincinnati Christian University, and a Ph.D. in educational leadership from the University of Denver. As a community-engaged scholar, her research centers on advancing spaces, systems, and policies to better serve historically marginalized populations. She grounds her work in community and organizational knowledge to co-construct and re(shape) opportunities for minoritized groups.

Kadine Haynes-Williams has been a teacher for eighteen years and considers parental involvement as a major factor in her success hence her central interest in this area.

Lois George, PhD, holds graduate degrees with specialized study in mathematics education from the University of Southampton and measurement, testing and evaluation from UWI Cavehill Campus. She has approximately twenty years of combined work experience in the field of mathematics education and in secondary school management.

Natalia Wright is a high school educator for over thirteen years. She taught for four years at Hillel Academy, an international school, and is currently teaching at Glenmuir High School in Jamaica.

Natrecia Whyte Lothian currently serves as Principal at Oracabessa High school. She is a graduate of Moneague College, University of Technology and the University of the West Indies, Mona.

Roncell A. Brooks currently serves as the principal at the Norman Manley High School. He holds a BSc (Hons.) in Psychology and Human Resource Management (UWI), a Post Graduate Diploma in Education (UTECH, Jamaica) and a MEd. in Educational Administration (UWI). He also completed the Professional Qualification for Principalship (PQP) with the National College for Educational Leadership (NCEL).

Saran Stewart is Associate Professor of Higher Education and Student Affairs and Director of Global Education, Neag School of Education, University of Connecticut, Storrs, Connecticut. She was formerly a Senior Lecturer and Deputy Dean at the University of the West Indies, Mona, Jamaica. Dr. Stewart is also the Director of Academic Affairs at the University of Connecticut, Hartford.

Sharline Cole PhD lecturer in Educational Psychology and Applied Research in the School of Education, The University of the West Indies, Mona. As a researcher Cole focuses on parenting, parental involvement, family engagement, children with special needs, psycho-social, academic and emotional wellbeing of students and educators, aggression and violence and teacher effectiveness. Dr Cole worked at the primary and high school level as a Guidance Counsellor and at the primary level as a Vice Principal.

Shenhaye Ferguson holds a PhD in higher education from the Morgridge College of Education, University of Denver. Shenhaye is also an adjunct faculty for the University of Denver Graduate School of Social Work.

Susan Anderson is a retired Senior Lecturer in the School of Education and coordinated the Educational Psychology Programme. For several years, she worked with her students to provide a structured programe for at-risk children in a behavioural summer camp.

Tashane Haynes-Brown is a Lecturer in Teacher Education and Teacher Development at the School of Education, UWI and she serves as Coordinator for the Undergraduate Programmes in the School of Education. Dr. Haynes-Brown has over 18 years of combined work experience in the field of education at the secondary and tertiary levels. She has conducted research focused on understanding how teachers' beliefs shape their use of technology, and on the use of mixed methods reserach.

Therese Ferguson is a Senior Lecturer in Education for Sustainable Development (ESD) in the School of Education at The University of the West Indies, Mona Campus, Jamaica. She is the Coordinator of the ESD Working Group within the School of Education and the Programme Leader for Change from Within, a school-based initiative in Jamaica that addresses violence and indiscipline. Her research interests include ESD, climate change education and peace education.

Yewande Lewis-Fokum holds a PhD in Language, Literacy and Culture from the University of Iowa, USA. She is a Lecturer in English language and literacy education, and teacher training at the School of Education, the University of the West Indies, Mona, Jamaica.

Zoyah Kinkead-Clark is a Senior Lecturer and researcher in early childhood education at the University of the West Indies, Mona. Dr. Kinkead-Clark currently serves as an external examiner in Early Childhood Education for the Joint Board of Teacher Education. She is a member of Jamaica's Early Childhood Development Oversight Committee, the body tasked with overseeing the development of a comprehensive strategy to revitalize the vision for Jamaican children eight years and younger.

Index

Abouchaar, A., 1, 100, 160, 161
abuse against children, 202
academic achievement, 13; parental involvement impact on, 121–123
academic outcomes, 116–117; children's gender, parental involvement and, 123–124; cognitive development, 120–121; design, 124; Epstein's Overlapping Spheres of Influence, 118–119; Hoover-Dempsey and Sandler's Parental Involvement Model, 119–120; instrument, 125–128, 127; involved and efficaciousness of parents, 132–134, 134; literature review, 117–118; parental involvement and students' academic outcomes relationship, 129–130, 130; and parental involvement between males and females, 130–132; parental involvement impact on academic achievement, 121–123; participants, 124; procedure, 124–125
academic socialization, 175, 177–178, 186; school-based involvement and, 178
academic success, at early childhood level, 80; academic support-extending school into home, 86–88; barriers to parental involvement, 83–84; of children, 116; communication and parent-teacher interaction, 88–89; cultural learning, 80–81; data analysis procedures, 85–86; data collection, 85, 86; family/community involvement, 81–83; methodology, 84–86; resources, 89–90
active parental involvement, 2
Afolabi, O.E., 100

Aina, F.F., 121
Airasian, P., 183
Al-anqoodi, Y., 39, 47
Almeida, L.S., 121
Altschul, I., 123
Alvarez-Jimenez, A., 52
Alves, A.F., 121, 134
Amatea, E.S., 66, 69
American Federation of Teachers, 219
American Psychological Association (APA), 151
Anderson, P., 4, 17
Anderson, S.R., 96, 100, 109, 206, 210–211
Anfara, V.A., Jr., 174
Angus, G.L., 202
Aries, R., 179
attendant research, 143
Avvisati, F., 161

Bailey, A., 220
Bak-Srednicka, A., 66
Balli, D., 99, 100, 109
Bandura, A., 219, 220, 229
Bantuveris, K., 209
Barnett, W.S., 90
barrel-children phenomena, 2, 172
Bates, S.C., 102
Benner, A., 178
Berk, L.E., 134
Berla, N., 61
Bernadowski, C., 39, 44, 47
Berryhill, M., 43
Besbas, B., 161
Bhargava, S., 147, 161, 164
Boonk, L., 101, 111
Bourne, P.A., 61
Bowe, F.G., 111
Bower, H., 147
Boyle, A., 178

Bronfenbrenner, U., 80, 81, 174
Brown, K.M., 99
Browne, D., 70, 178
Brubaker, E., 211
Bunijevac, M., 122, 135
Burke, T., 43, 51–53

Cabus, S., 179
Cai, J., 61, 62
Campbell, A., 117, 123
Campbell-Livingston, C., 202
Career and Technology Center, 148
Caribbeanized epistemological frameworks, 226
Caribbean Secondary Education Certificate (CSEC) mathematics examinations, 57, 170, 171; pass percentage of public schools, 57, 60
Carpenter, K., 21, 22
case study approach, 102
Castro, M., 178
CBP. *See* Coalition for Better Parenting (CBP)
cellular telephones, use of, 70
Chen, M., 84, 96, 97, 117, 147, 160
child-related barriers, 100
children: about behaviour, parents communication with, 217, *218*; abuse against, 202; academic development, 92; academic success of, 116; exposure to violence, 207; gender, parental involvement and academic outcomes, 123–124; IQ and academic performance, 84; parents role in education, 96
children with disabilities: cognitive and social development of, 100; in cognitive and social outcomes of, 103–105; parental involvement in, 99–100; parents involvement/ non-involvement in education of, 107–109
Child Trends Databank, 207, 219
Choudhuri, R., 121, 122
Chunnu, W., 12
Coalition for Better Parenting (CBP), 2, 171
co-constructors, 85
coding procedures, 16, *18–19*

cognitive development, 120–121
Cole, S.A., 38
Cole, S.M., 82, 83, 95, 101, 102, 210, 211
Coleman, P., 23
collaborating with community, 37, 65, 146
communicating, 36–37, 64, 145–146, 161; students' academic performance, 155
communication, 119; cellular telephones, use of, 70; between home and school, 45–47; official language for, 67, *67*; parents with children about behaviour, 217, *218*; parent-teacher face-to-face contact, 122; and parent-teacher interaction, 88–89; school-to-home and home-to-school, 38; in school violence, 208–209; between teacher and school, 228; between teachers and parents, 40, 229; two-way channels of, 162; WhatsApp, 69, 70
communication gap, 39
community, 81–82; partnership and collaboration between, 98; relevance of, 228–229; socio-economic activity of, 172
community-based schooling, 228
Compton, M., 122
COMVOL PI framework, for non-traditional high schools, 49, *49*
Connors-Tadros, L., 148
Conway, K., 123, 146
Cook, L.D., 21–23, 25, 181, 189
Cooper, H., 180
Cortina, K.S., 70
Costa, M.P., 181
Cousins, L.H., 122–123
Covid-19 pandemic, 1, 231
Cozby, P.C., 102
Creole language, 67, 68, 228
Creswell, J.W., 213
Cronbach Alpha (C-Alpha), 126, 127, 183, 213
cross-sectional descriptive research design, 212
crosstab analysis, 131
cultural-capital approach, 38, 228

cultural learning, 80–81
culture of poverty approach, 37

Darnell, A.J., 52
data analysis procedures, 85–86
data collection, 85, 86, 212
Dauber, S.L., 66, 180
Daubner, S., 81, 83, 84, 90, 91
Davies, D., 47
Davis, D., 149, 179, 209
decision-making process, 37, 65, 98, 146, 161, 165; students' academic performance, 157–158
Denessen, E., 177
Denzin, N.K., 85
Descartes, C., 178
Desforges, C., 1, 100, 160, 161
Devonish, J., 17
Dollahite, D.C., 101, 109
Dowker, A., 68
Down, L., 207
Driessen, G., 147
Droop, M., 177
Dubis, S., 39, 44, 47
Dunkley A., 202
Đurišić, M., 122, 135

Eccles, J.S., 48
Ecological Systems Theory, 80, 81
education: family-school partnerships in, 17; outcomes of children, 21; parental involvement in, 33–36; transformative power of, 21
educational barriers, 83, 84
educators, 2
Edwards-Kerr, D., 211
effective communication, 39, 50, 98, 209; between home and school, 49, 68
effective parent-school communication, non-traditional high schools, 38–41
electronic communication technologies, 40
"elp di pikni a yaad" category, 70–71
El Shourbagi, S., 101, 111
empowerment, 110; parental and family, 106
English language, 67, 67

Englund, M.M., 84
Epstein, J.L., 3, 4, 6, 20, 36–38, 41, 44, 47, 64, 66, 81, 83, 84, 90, 91, 97, 99, 110, 117, 122, 135, 136, 144–146, 148–150, 163, 174, 176, 177, 180, 183, 185, 188, 190, 191, 208–210, 219, 229; factors that influence parental involvement, 145–146; model of parental involvement, 64–65; Overlapping Spheres of Influence, 118–119, 226; rural high school framework, 174–175; theory of overlapping spheres of influence, 143–144
Erchul, W.P., 120
Erikson, Erik, 170
Evans, H., 49
Ezenne, A., 23

familial socio-economic status, influence of, 227–228
family: collaboration between school and, 99; outcomes for, 26; partnership and collaboration between, 98
family/community involvement, 81–83
family empowerment, 106
family engagement, 1–3, 7, 226; co-construction of, 25–26; debate between parent involvement and, 11–12; forms of, 25; parents role in, 229–231
family engagement in postsecondary and workforce readiness (FEPWR) framework, 23–24, 24, 26
family learning, 82
family-school construct, 16
family-school partnerships, 11; in education, 17
family structure, 83; affects level of parental involvement, 101
Fan, X., 41, 48, 84, 96, 97, 117, 145, 147, 160
Faria, L., 181
Fernald, L.C., 206
Fernández-Alonso, R., 121, 147
fighting, 207–208; percentages of students involved in, 218–219, 219

Index | 239

financial barriers, 83, 84
Finn, A.S., 121
Fongkong-Mungal, C., 70, 178
formal learning, 87
Fox, K., 13
Frankfort-Nachmias, C., 159

Garvey, Marcus, 69
Gay, L.R., 183
gender, 123–124
Gentle-Genitty, C., 206
GFNT. *See* Grade Four Numeracy Test (GFNT)
Gleaner, 48, 202
GOILP. *See* Grade One Individual Learning Profile (GOILP)
Gomes, C.M., 121
Gonida, E.N., 70
Goodall, J., 80, 83, 90, 143, 147, 161–164
good communication, 40, 50, 51, 88
government-built secondary schools, 3n1
Grade Four Literacy Test, 13, 117, 125–127, 129–130, 136
Grade Four Numeracy Test (GFNT), 56, 58, 117, 125–127, 129, 130, 133, 136
Grade One Individual Learning Profile (GOILP), 117, 125–127
Grade Six Achievement Test (GSAT), 56–57, 59, 117, 125–127, 133
Green, C.L., 135
Griffin, D., 36, 50, 147
Griffith, S., 171
Grover, S., 210
GSAT. *See* Grade Six Achievement Test (GSAT)
guardians, influence of, 227–228
Guo, X., 122, 135
Gurbuzturk, O., 45, 52
Guyon, N., 161

Hackman, D.A., 79
Hagiwara, S., 179
Harden, K.P., 79, 91
Harris, A.L., 80, 83, 90, 143, 147, 161–164, 169

Hawes, C., 143
Hayakawa, M., 116
Hayes, D., 40, 41, 43, 46, 51, 52
Headstart Programme, 90
Henderson, A.T., 61
Hill, N.E., 33, 175, 177, 180
Hofferth, S.L., 123
Holloway, S.D., 120, 122, 136, 180
Holness, Andrew, 171
home: academic support-extending school into, 86–88; collaboration between school and, 111; communication between school and, 45–47; effective communication between school and, 68; formal learning in, 87; relevance of, 228–229; social bond between school and, 48
home-based involvement, 190
home-school leadership groups, 21
home-school partnership, 22, 221
home-school relationship, 23
homework, parental involvement in, 179–180, 186
Hong Kong, special school in, 41–42
Hoover-Dempsey, K.V., 3, 6, 20, 63, 65–66, 98–101, 110, 111, 117, 125, 135, 136, 174, 180, 183, 189, 226; Parental Involvement Model, 119–120; rural high school framework, 175–176
Hornby, G., 100, 110
Ho Sui-Chu, E., 34, 37–38, 40, 41, 43, 46, 50–52
Houtenville, A., 123, 146
Huang, G.H.C., 1
Hungi, N., 177
Hustedt, J.T., 90

Ice, C.L., 20
IDEA. *See* Individuals with Disabilities Education Act (IDEA)
IEP. *See* Individual Educational Plan (IEP)
Individual Educational Plan (IEP), 96, 99, 106, 110, 112
Individuals with Disabilities Education Act (IDEA), 96, 99
institutional approach, 37

instrumentation, students' academic performance, 149; reliability, 149, 150; validity, 149–150; variables, 150, 150
integrated family engagement, 26
internet, 71
interval/ratio measures, 127

Jack, A., 122
Jafarov, J., 123, 135
Jaiswal, K.S., 121, 122
Jamaica Association for the Deaf (JAD), 106, 111
Jamaica Disabilities Act (2014), 96, 99
Jamaica Information Service (JIS), 202
Jamaican social workers, 230n2
Jamaica Partners for Educational Progress (2011), 34, 35, 44, 45
jam dung style model, 4, 65–68, 67
Jennings, Z., 21, 22, 25, 181, 189
Jethro, O.O., 121
Jeynes, W.H., 97, 117, 145, 147, 161, 163
JIS. *See* Jamaica Information Service (JIS)
Johnson, E.J., 178
Johnson, J., 21, 22

Kalimullin, A.M., 211
Kimaro, A.R., 121, 122
King, R., 206
Klevan, T., 169
Krane, V., 169
Kuperminc, G.P., 52
Kuttner, P.J., 25

LaBahn, J., 208
Lafaele, R., 100, 110
Lamb, S., 177
language, 120
Lareau, A., 37, 42, 49, 50
learning at home, 37, 65, 146, 162; students' academic performance, 156–157, 157
Least Restrictive Environment (LRE), 96
Lee, T., 41, 48
Leedy, P.D., 184
Leon-Guerrero, A., 159

Levin, Diane, 209, 219
Lightfoot, 37
Lincoln, Y.S., 85
Lindsay, J.J., 180
Link, M., 211
Looi, C.Y., 68
Lopez, A., 42, 50
LRE. *See* Least Restrictive Environment (LRE)

Machumu, H.J., 121, 122
Mahuro, M.G., 177
Mann Whitney U test, 130
Mapp, K.L., 25
Marissa, O., 95–96
Marshall, I.A., 70, 178
Martins, A., 121
Mason, K.L., 1
mastery, 56
mathematics, 71–72; academic performance and behaviour, 61; "elp di pikni a yaad" category, 70–71; Epstein model of parental involvement, 64–65; improvement strategies, 59–60; issue of underachievement in, 59; jam dung style, 65–68, 67; link between achievement and parental involvement, 60–64; negative experiences in learning, 63; performance in, 62; "taak tu di tiicha" category, 68–70
Mattingly, D.J., 66
Mayo, A., 43
McDowell, K., 122
McWayne, C., 95–96
Meador, D., 207
Meeks-Gardner, J., 206
Mertens, S.B., 174
Mickelson, R.A., 122–123
middle-class parents, 42
Mills, G.E., 183
mixed-methods doctoral thesis, 95
model of parental involvement, 97–99, 119–120
Molnar, B.E., 49
Moon, U.J., 123
Morrisette, D.L., 111
Morrisette, P.J., 111

Morsy, L., 79
mothers, role in parental involvement and family engagement, 229–231
multiple linear regression, 150, 151
multiple regression analysis, 132
Munroe, G., 171, 191
Munroe, G.-C., 62
Murphy, S., 41, 42, 178, 180
Murray, N., 211

National Centre for Learning Disabilities, 96
National Children's Registry (NCR), 202
National Parenting Commission Act (2012), 1
National Parenting Support Commission (CNPSC), 2
National Parenting Support Commission Act, 13
National Parent-Teacher Association of Jamaica (NPTAJ), 171
National Parent Teachers' Association (NPTA), 35
National Quality Framework for Early Childhood Education, 99
NCR. See National Children's Registry (NCR)
Nelson, J., 172, 191
Ng, S., 41, 48
Njoroge, P.M., 61
non-traditional high schools, 34, 227n1; COMVOL PI framework for, 49, 49; effective parent-school communication, 38–41; human and non-human resources for, 44; implications for practice in, 51–52; improving communication between home and school, 45–47; parental involvement framework for Jamaican context, 48–51, 49; parental volunteering and students' success, 41–42, 47–48; participating in association for principals, 35; socioeconomic status and parental involvement, 42–44; theoretical framework, 36–38
NPTA. See National Parent Teachers' Association (NPTA)

Nyabuto, A.N., 61
Nye, B., 180

Okpala, A.O., 148, 163
Okpala, C.O., 148, 163
Olmstead, C., 40, 45
online library databases, 15
open communication, 88
Ormod, J.E., 184
Orr, A.J., 43
O'Shea, D.J., 111
O'Shea, L.J., 111

Palardy, G.J., 33
parental academic socialization, 177
parental effort, 146
parental empowerment, 106
parental involvement, 17; on academic outcomes. See academic outcomes; barriers to, 83–84; in children with disabilities, 99–100; coding procedures, 16, 18–19; debate between family engagement and, 11–12; Epstein model of, 64–65; and family engagement, 1–3, 7, 226; form of social capital, 33; at high school level, 170; in homework, 179–180, 186; impact on academic achievement, 121–123; inclusion and exclusion criteria, 14–15; link between mathematics achievement and, 60–64; models of, 1; and parent efficaciousness, 128; parents role in, 229–231; positive relationship between, 81; and quality of assistance, 84; research questions, 14; sample articles, 20–23; school violence, 203–204, 208; search procedures, 15–16; selection of articles, 15; socioeconomic status and, 42–44; in special education, 96; systematic review, 13–14; types of, 36–37, 47
Parental Involvement Questionnaire, 125
parental participation, 96; in special education, 96; through training sessions, 110

parental volunteering and students' success, 41–42, 47–48
parenting, 36, 64, 145, 162; school violence, 209–212; students' academic performance, 155
parenting assistance, 20
Parenting Partners Caribbean (PPC), 171
parent-initiated involvement, 118
parent-related barriers, 100
parent-related factors, 181
parents: attitudes towards school-parent partnerships, 215–216, 216, 217; cognitive functioning, 79; communication with children about behaviour, 217, 218; educational level of, 101; influence of, 227–228; low efficacy beliefs, 180; positive relationship between students' academic performance and, 147; role in parental involvement and family engagement, 229–231; sense of efficacy, 134
parent-school engagement, 34–35
parents efficaciousness, 120, 125, 126, 128, 132–136
Parent's Place project, 171
parents' questionnaires, demographic data for, 215
Parent Survey instrument, 183, 184
parent teacher association (PTA), 2, 34, 35, 43, 46, 47, 91, 119, 143, 171, 192
parent-teacher conferences, 175
parent-teacher face-to-face contact, 122
parent-teacher interactions, 170; communication and, 88–89
parent/teacher-related barriers, 100
Park, E., 33
Park, S., 122
Patall, E.A., 62
PATH. *See* Programme of Advancement Through Health and Education (PATH)
Patois, 67
Patterson, C., 202
Pearson Product Moment Correlation, 150

Pennsylvania Parent Teacher's Association, 208
PEP. *See* Primary Exit Profile (PEP)
Perrucci, R., 40, 42
personal barriers, 83
physical presence, at libraries, 15
Piaget, J., 120
Pires, H.S., 123, 135
Plourde, L., 143
positive parent-teacher partnership, 209
postsecondary and workforce readiness (PWR), 26–27; FEPWR framework, 23, 24
Potter, D., 163
Pottinger, A., 207, 220
poverty, 21, 227
Poyser, A., 206
Primary Exit Profile (PEP), 56, 57, 59, 125n1
Programme of Advancement Through Health and Education (PATH), 172
PTA. *See* parent teacher association (PTA)
public school system, achievement gaps in, 116

qualitative survey study, 22–23
quantitative survey study, 22

Rafiq, H.M.W., 208
Rasheed, S., 146
Razalli, A.R., 96, 99, 110
reference searches, 15–16
regression model, 161
reliability: school violence, 213, 213; students' academic performance, 149, 150
research questions, 14
resources: academic success, 89–90; for non-traditional high schools, 44
Rickett, H., 4
Robinson, K., 169
Roksa, J., 163
Rothstein, R., 79
rural high school: background study, 170–172; data analysis procedures, 185; data collection and analysis, 183, 184; Epstein's

framework, 174–175; factors affecting parental involvement, 180–181; factors affecting parents' level of involvement, 187–188, *188*; Hoover-Dempsey and Sandler's framework, 175–176; involvement in academic life of children, 187; literature review, 176–182; parental involvement in homework, 179–180, 186; parents' satisfaction with parental involvement, 181–182; purpose and research questions, 173–174; recruitment procedures, 184–185; research design, 183; sampling, 183–184; theoretical perspective, 174–176; types of parental involvement, 177–179; ways in which parents involved, 185–186
rural school for deaf, 109
Rutherford, M.D., 134

Sad, S., 40, 45, 52
Sadler, S., 178
Salinas, K.C., 209, 219
Samms-Vaughan, M., 116
Sanders, M.G., 144–146, 148, 150
Sandler, H.M., 3, 6, 63, 65–66, 98–101, 110, 111, 117, 125, 174, 180, 183, 189, 226; Parental Involvement Model, 119–120; rural high school framework, 175–176
Sarkar, A., 68
SBA. *See* School-based assessment (SBA)
scaffolding, 80, 84
school barriers, 83, 84
school-based activities, 192–193; parents engaging in, 175
School-based assessment (SBA), 170–171, 192
school-parent partnerships: parents attitudes towards, 215–216, *216*, *217*; responses to, 215, *216*
School Resource Officers (SROs), 220, 221
schools: for blind, 107; collaboration between family and, 99; collaboration between home and, 111; communication between home and, 45–47; effective communication between home and, 68; home-school leadership groups in, 21; optimum students' successes, 143; outcomes for, 26; partnership and collaboration between, 98; positive relationships with, 96; social bond between home and, 48; structures and systems of, 82; violence among youths in, 205–207
school-to-home communication, 50
school violence, 201–203, 221; data analysis procedures, 213–214; defined as, 206; demographic data for parents' questionnaires, 215; direct and indirect costs of, 201; ethical considerations, 214; fighting, 207–208; importance of communication in parent involvement, 208–209; instrumentation, 212–213; limitations, 214; parental involvement, 203–204, 208; parenting, 209–210; parenting and violence, 210–212; parents' attitudes towards school-parent partnerships, 215–216, *216*, *217*; parents' communication with children about behaviour, 217, *218*; percentages of students involved in fights, 218–219, *219*; population and sample, 212; reliability, 213, *213*; research design, 212; Social Learning Theory, 204–205; theoretical framework, 203; violence among youths in schools, 205–207; volunteering, 209
search procedures, 15–16
Seginer, R., 180
self-concept, 210
SES schools. *See* socioeconomic status (SES) schools
Shajith, B.I., 120
Shaw, C., 148, 149, 162
Sheldon, S.B., 64, 122
Shen, J., 80
Shoaga, O.O.M., 146

Shute, V.J., 161
single-parent households, 79
single parenting, 79
single-stage sampling design, 148
Siraj, I., 43
6-point Likert-scale response, 125, 126
Sleegers, P., 147
Smar, B., 41, 47
Smit, F., 147
Smith, F.E., 123, 148, 163
Smith-Adcock, S., 66, 69
Social Learning Theory, 204–205, 229
Sociocultural Theory, 80
socioeconomic reality, 111–112
socioeconomic status (SES), 40, 42, 46, 50–52, 146; and parental involvement, 42–44
socioeconomic status (SES) schools, 34, 36
socio-emotional development, 100
special education: cost of, 97; factors impacting parental involvement, 100–101; model of parental involvement, 97–99; overlapping spheres of influence, 97–98; parental involvement in, 96; parental involvement in children with disabilities, 99–100; research method, 101–103; school personnel perspectives on parental involvement, 105–107
special-needs schools, 112
special school, in Hong Kong, 41–42
SPSS. *See* Statistical Package for the Social Sciences (SPSS)
Stacer, M.J., 40, 42
Statistical Package for the Social Sciences (SPSS), 184, 185, 214
Steen, S., 36, 50
Steinberg, L., 210, 211
students: cognitive development of, 96; involved in fights, percentages of, 218–219, 219; number of incidents declined as, 208; success of, 41–42, 47–48
students' academic performance, 144; communicating, 155; data analysis, 150–151; decision making, 157–158; defined as, 144;
descriptive statistics, 152–154, 152–158, 156, 157; empirical results for inferential statistics, 158; ethical considerations, 151; learning at home, 156–157, 157; limitations, 151, 160; parental involvement and impact on, 146–148; parenting, 154; parents' data, 158–160, 159; positive relationship between parents and, 147; profile of parent participants, 152–153, 153; profile of student participants, 152, 152; rate of parental involvement, 153–154, 154; research design, 148–150, 150; research hypothesis, 144; volunteering, 155–156, 156
Survey System Online Sample Size Calculator, 184
Suzuki, S., 120, 136
systematic review, 13–14

"taak tu di tiicha" category, 68–70
Taylor, L.C., 33, 175, 180
Technical and Vocational Education and Training (TVET), 172
technological communication, 40
traditional high schools, 34
triangulation, 103
Troupe, K., 181
Tucker-Drob, E.M., 79, 91
TVET. *See* Technical and Vocational Education and Training (TVET)
two-way communications, 38–39

underemployment, 227
unemployment, 91
United Nations Development Programme (UNDP), 201, 205
United Nations Office of Drugs and Crime (UNODC), 201
unsatisfactory mathematics achievement, 56
urban school for deaf, 105, 107–109

Valeeva, R.A., 211
Valley High School, 189, 190
Valley High School of Jamaica, 172–173
Van Voorhis, F., 99

Vennum, A., 43
Villares, E., 66, 69
volunteering, 37, 41, 47, 48, 51, 52, 64, 91, 146, 163; school violence, 209; students' academic performance, 155–156, 156
volunteerism, 6, 34, 49, 98, 110, 119, 208, 215
Vygotsky, L.S., 80, 120

Walker, C., 179, 182
Walker, J.M.T., 65, 99
Walsh, P., 42
Watson-Williams, C., 13, 21, 82, 91, 171, 178, 182, 191
WhatsApp, 50, 69–71, 193
Whitaker, M.C., 20
Wigfield, A., 48
Wilder, S., 177, 181

Willms, J., 34, 37–38, 40, 41, 43, 46, 50–52
Witherspoon, D., 147, 161, 164
working-class parents, 42, 49
World Health Organization (WHO), 205
Wright, N.K., 66, 183, 212, 213

Xu, M., 179

yaad, relevance of, 228–229
Yamamoto, Y., 120, 136, 180
Yoder, J., 42, 50
youth population, violence among, 202
Yulianti, K., 177

Zafar, A.R., 39
Zone of Proximal Development (ZPD), 80